W9-BGQ-769

THE WORKS

Sketches From the Premier
Christian Comedy Group

DAN RUPPLE
and DAVE TOOLE

MERIWETHER PUBLISHING LTD.
Colorado Springs, Colorado

Meriwether Publishing Ltd., Publisher
P.O. Box 7710
Colorado Springs, CO 80933-7710

Editor: Rhonda Wray
Typesetting: Sharon E. Garlock
Cover design: Tom Myers

© Copyright MCMXCVII Foolish Guys
Printed in the United States of America
First Edition

All rights reserved. No part of this publication, except where specifically noted, may be reproduced, stored in a retrieval system, or transmitted in any form or by any means, electronic, mechanical, photocopying, recording or otherwise, without permission of the publishers. Permission to reproduce copies and perform any of the drama sketches included in this text is granted to amateur groups with the purchase of this book. Copies of these sketches and performance rights are for the purchaser and the purchasing organization only. These rights are not transferable to any other group or third party. These drama sketches may be produced by amateur groups without payment of a royalty fee. Permission for non-amateur presentation (professional stage, radio or television performances) must be obtained in writing from the publisher.

Unless otherwise specified, all Scripture is taken from the King James Version.

Library of Congress Cataloging-in-Publication Data

Isaac Air Freight (Comedy troupe)
    Isaac Air Freight : the works : sketches from the premier
Christian comedy group / [compiled by] Dan Rupple & Dave Toole.
        p.   c.m.
    Originally published: Costa Mesa, Calif. : Maranatha! Music,
1982-1984. In 2 v.
    ISBN 1-56608-034-7 (pbk.)
    1. Christian life--Wit and humor. 2. American wit and humor.
I. Rupple, Dan, 1955-   II. Toole, Dave, 1953-   III. Title.
BV4517.I73   1997
277.3'0825'0207--dc21   96-19906
                                                                          CIP

2   3   4   5   01   02   03   04

*To all the talented buffoons out there
with a Bible in one hand and a
nose and glasses in the other.*

CONTENTS

*These sketches were performed on the *Isaac Air Show*.

Publisher's Note

"Why don't you carry any Isaac Air Freight scripts?" We'd grown accustomed to this frequent query and began to wonder ourselves. A bit of detective work uncovered Dan Rupple and Dave Toole, alive and well in Southern California. Though involved in other responsibilities and no longer touring or recording as Isaac Air Freight, the two graciously consented to release thirty-four of their most popular original scripts from their performing years.

Isaac Air Freight pioneered the use of sketch comedy from a Christian perspective. These hilarious sketches were written in the late seventies/early eighties — at the peak of Isaac Air Freight's performing days. Although the truths they represent are unchanging, please feel free to update the language and situations to reflect our current times as you wish.

We have tried to supply production information whenever possible. Some of these sketches were only performed in a recording studio and never live, so you'll have to use extra staging ingenuity when presenting them. We feel confident that all the scripts can be effectively performed in front of a live audience. They may be used singly as sermon illustrations or grouped together for a night of comedy.

Although the setting is given for each sketch, this is merely to set the context. There's no need to recreate Jerusalem, a baseball field, the Wild West, etc. In most cases, the dialog, costumes and props establish the setting. When originally performed by Isaac Air Freight, many of these sketches were taken "on the road," where it was impractical to tote along elaborate backdrops or set pieces.

When Scripture is quoted in the scripts, it has frequently been paraphrased by the author(s). You may substitute the Bible version of your choice. The Scripture references included are for informational purposes only and are not to be read aloud when performing.

The numerals running vertically down the left margin of each script page are for the convenience of the director. With these, he/she may easily direct attention to a specific passage.

Performance of these scripts requires purchase of the book. Only the buyer of the book and his/her group may use it. Please — no photocopies for friends! Because Isaac Air Freight has been so generous with their original material, we want to ensure that they are fairly repaid for their efforts. In order to legally photocopy any script from the book, we must have your name (or someone from your group) on record as a purchaser of the book.

For maximum fun, encourage audience participation whenever possible, e.g., in the sketches with a game show theme. Applause and other appropriate audience responses will help set the scene.

Whether you're an established fan of Isaac Air Freight's material or a fan-to-be, it is our hope that these sketches will inspire and entertain *your* audiences, just as they did when originally performed by America's first Christian comedy group.

Introduction

Even before the days of a foolish jester using the opportunity to communicate harsh realities to an otherwise unhearing king, comedy has been an effective tool in communicating imperative truths to needy hearts.

Through fourteen years of concert tours, eight best-selling comedy albums and numerous radio and television appearances, *Isaac Air Freight* pioneered a fresh approach to comedy from a Christian perspective. Laced with satire and colorful characters, their hilarious sketches convey deep spiritual truths that are guaranteed to find responsive ears whenever they are performed.

Available for your amusement and use is this collection of classic *Isasac Air Freight* sketches from their following albums:

Fun in the Son

In the Air/On the Air

Foolish Guys...to Confound the Wise

Snooze Ya Looze

My Kingdom Come/Thy Kingdom Come

and scripts from the radio feature *The Isaac Air Show.*

God has chosen the foolish things of the world to confound the wise...

LET'S TRADE YOUR SALVATION

By Dan Rupple

1   **CAST:** Jay — Announcer; Monty — Host; Buck — Contestant.

2   **SETTING:** A game show. *A1*

3   **PROPS:** A small paper bag for ~~BUCK~~ with a Bible inside. A

4   tray with a Crock Pot on it, covered by an upside-down

5   flashy box (perhaps covered with metallic gift wrap). *5 bills*

6   **COSTUMES:** JAY and MONTY wear suits. BUCK should wear

7   any outlandish costume.

8

9   *(Optional intro theme music. JAY is On-stage. He speaks*

10   *into a microphone.)*

11 **JAY:** **Good evening, ladies and gentlemen, and welcome to**

12   **the marketplace of America, *Let's Trade Your***

13   ***Salvation,* where hundreds of people have come**

14   **dressed in ridiculous costumes, hoping for the**

15   **chance to trade their salvation for unknown riches.**

16   **And now, here's that old wheeler-dealer himself,**

17   **seeing whom he may devour, Monty Lucifer!**

18 **MONTY:** *(Entering)* **Thank you, Jay. Hi, everybody, welcome**

19   **to *Let's Trade Your Salvation.* Well, you all know how**

20   **the game is played, so right off I'm gonna need a**

21   **contestant. You, sir, you want to come out here?**

22 **BUCK:** *(In audience)* **Me?**

23 **MONTY:** **Let's hear it for him, come on!** *(BUCK runs up.)*

24   **What's your name, sir?**

25 **BUCK:** **Uh, Buck, Buck Wheezer.**

26 **MONTY:** **Where are you from, Buck?**

27 **BUCK:** **Chula Vista, California!**

28 **MONTY:** **You're not nervous being on television for the**

Let's Trade Your Salvation

1   first time, are you?

2   BUCK: Naw, I just didn't think I'd get chosen.

3   MONTY: Yes, well, Buck, what do you have there in the
4   bag?

5   BUCK: Oh, it's my salvation.

6   MONTY: That's right, your bag of salvation, and to start
7   the game going, I'm going to offer him one hundred
8   dollars for that little bag. What do you say, Buck?

9   BUCK: No way!

10   MONTY: I'm going to up it two hundred dollars more. I'm
11   going to go to three hundred dollars cash for that
12   little bag of salvation. What do you say now?

13   BUCK: Is that your final offer?...He's so tricky!...The bag,
14   the bag, I'm going to keep the bag.

15   MONTY: He's going to trade away the money and keep the
16   bag.... OK, Buck, I'm going to go up to my final offer –
17   two hundred dollars more. I'm going up to five
18   hundred dollars cash for that little bag of salvation.
19   What do you say now?

20   BUCK: Ahhh...I'm sticking with the bag.

21   MONTY: He's going to keep the bag and trade away all that
22   money. OK, Buck, you passed up a great deal there,
23   but don't worry, there're bigger deals yet to come.
24   *(Enter JAY with tray with flashy box on it.)* **OK, Buck,**
25   **Jay's coming out here with a tray. How would you like**
26   **to know what's on that tray?**

27   BUCK: I sure would!

28   MONTY: I bet you would, but I'm not gonna tell you. But I
29   will tell you that what's on that tray can be yours for
30   that little bag of salvation. What do you say?

31   BUCK: Do I get any clues?

32   MONTY: No, it's totally up to you.

33   BUCK: Oh, ahhh, I don't know.

34   MONTY: Five seconds...

1   BUCK: OK, I'll take the...

2   MONTY: Two seconds...

3   BUCK: The bag! I'm gonna keep the bag.

4   MONTY: He's going to keep the bag and trade away the
5   tray. Bad news, Buck. Jay, show him what was on the
6   tray. *(Lifts box.)*

7   BUCK: Oh, no!

8   MONTY: A Crock Pot. And now here's Jay to tell you about
9   it. *(Optional prize music)*

10 JAY: That's right, Monty, a Spiegel Crock Pot. The cooker
11   that really cooks. Cooks chicken to a tender, tasty
12   morsel in only four hours. That's Spiegel Crock Pot.
13   When you say Spiegel, you mean quality. When you
14   say Crock Pot, you mean Crock Pot. Monty? *(JAY covers
15   tray and exits.)*

16 MONTY: Thank you, Jay. Well, Buck, you passed up a great
17   deal there.

18 BUCK: Boy, my wife in going to kill me! We just had crock
19   the other night, you know....

20 MONTY: Well, don't worry, Buck, there're bigger deals yet
21   to come. OK, Buck, I want you to look back there to
22   the curtain that Carol Barrel is pointing to.

23 BUCK: *(Looks behind audience.)* Is she the one in blue?

24 MONTY: Yes, siree, Buck. And what's behind that curtain
25   can be yours if you want to trade that little bag. What
26   do you say?

27 BUCK: It's not another Crock Pot, is it?

28 MONTY: No, Buck, but I'll tell you what. How would you
29   like to see part of what's behind that curtain?

30 BUCK: Could I?

31 MONTY: Pull the curtain, Jay.

32 BUCK: Wow!

33 MONTY: A color television, and here's Jay to tell you about
34   it. *(Optional prize music)*

1   JAY: **Right, Monty. A Spiegel twenty-four-inch, digit-**
2   **controlled color television, stylishly decorated in**
3   **hand-carved wood. And when you say Spiegel, you**
4   **mean quality. And when you say television, you mean**
5   **TV. Monty?** *(Fade out optional music)*
6   MONTY: **Thank you, Jay. And that's not all, Buck. You said**
7   **you're married?**
8   BUCK: **Yes, my wife's sitting back there on the trading**
9   **floor.**
10   MONTY: **Then she'll love you forever when you give her**
11   **what Carol Barrel is wearing – a beautiful mink coat!**
12   *(Optional prize music)*
13   JAY: **That's not just any mink coat, Monty. That's a Spiegel**
14   **mink coat. The coat is so real you'll have to hang it in**
15   **a cage. Be the envy of everyone, get a Spiegel mink**
16   **coat. Spiegel, Chicago 666, Illinois. Monty?** *(Fade out*
17   *optional music)*
18   MONTY: **Well, Buck, what do you say?**
19   BUCK: **I'm not sure.**
20   MONTY: **Well, Buck, you know that bag probably won't**
21   **last very long, but you can watch that TV forever, and**
22   **your wife will love that mink coat. And all for that**
23   **little bag. What do you say, Buck?**
24   BUCK: **It *is* tempting.**
25   MONTY: **I know it is, and I'll tell you what – I'll include**
26   **the five hundred dollars cash, the Crock Pot and**
27   **Carol Barrel.**
28   BUCK: **The one in blue?**
29   MONTY: **Yes, siree, Buck! It can all be yours for that little**
30   **bag of salvation. What do you say now, Buck?**
31   BUCK: **Ahhh...all right, all right, I'm gonna take the bag.**
32   MONTY: **OK, Buck, you ol' horse trader you. Go ahead,**
33   **open it up and see what's inside that stupid bag.**
34   BUCK: **Now?**

1   **MONTY: Sure, go ahead, you traded for it.**

2   **BUCK: Let's see: Holly, Bibble.** (Holy Bible)

3   **MONTY: That's the instruction book.**

4   **BUCK: Instructions for what? There's nothing else in this bag.**

5   **MONTY: That's right, Buck, just God's promise of salva-**
6   **tion, and even that's no good unless you believe it. But**
7   **I'll tell you what, Buck. How'd you like a chance to**
8   **win something you can put your hands on right now?**
9   **That's right, Buck, the big Deal of the Day, and here's**
10 **Jay to tell you about it.** *(Optional prize music)*

11 **JAY: That's right, Monty. We start off with Spiegel asbestos**
12 **water skis and a new sixteen-foot Spiegel water**
13 **cruiser. When you say Spiegel, you mean quality.**
14 **When you say water cruiser, you mean boat. And you'll**
15 **need that boat when you arrive at your eternal vaca-**
16 **tion at the Lake of Fire. Yes, Buck, you'll look like a**
17 **million skimming across the coals amid the wailing**
18 **and gnashing of teeth. Monty?** *(Fade out optional music)*

19 **MONTY: Thank you, Jay. Sounds great, doesn't it, Buck?**
20 **Buck? What do you say?**

21 **BUCK:** *(Looking in open Bible)* **Yeah, I was just looking at**
22 **this book here.**

23 **MONTY: Oh, don't look at that.**

24 **BUCK: Why? I traded a Crock Pot for it. Look, it says**
25 **here, "What shall it profit a man if he shall gain the**
26 **whole world, and lose his own soul?"** (Mt. 16:26,
27 author's paraphrase)

28 **MONTY: We're not asking for your soul, just your salva-**
29 **tion. Come on, Buck, the price is right.**

30 **BUCK: But it says here, "The wages of sin is death, but the**
31 **gift of God is eternal life through Jesus Christ our**
32 **Lord."** (Rom. 6:23, KJV)

33 **MONTY: Gifts?** *(Sweeping arm to indicate room)* **These are**
34 **gifts, Buck. Those are lies.**

1   **BUCK: Well, it says here, "He that believeth and is baptized**

2   **shall be saved; but he that believeth not shall be**

3   **damned."** (Mark 16:16) **That means they're going to hell!**

4   **MONTY: Oh, no it doesn't. They just wrote that to confuse**

5   **you, to make you feel guilty.**

6   **BUCK: But it says, "These things are written, that ye might**

7   **believe that Jesus is the Christ, the Son of God; and**

8   **that believing ye might have life through his name."**

9   (John 20:31, author's paraphrase)

10   **MONTY: I know, I know. I'll tell you what, Buck, you seem**

11   **to have your heart set on this stuff. But why don't you**

12   **put it off until tomorrow? These gifts are right here**

13   **waiting for you tonight. You can put them in your**

14   **Winnebago.**

15   **BUCK: It says, "Behold, now is the accepted time; behold,**

16   **now is the day of salvation."** (2 Cor. 6:2, KJV)

17   **MONTY: OK, Buck, we're good sports here, so go ahead**

18   **and keep the bag, but anytime you want to trade it,**

19   **just come on back.**

20   **BUCK: Anytime?**

21   **MONTY: Sure, just come on down.**

22   **BUCK: That's funny, my wife took me to church the other**

23   **day, and they said Jesus was coming back soon and**

24   **your show was gonna be canceled.**

25   **MONTY: Rapture, uh, rumor, Buck, rumor.** *(Running off)*

26   **Jay, grab the tray.** *(JAY grabs tray and runs off. Optional*

27   *prize music)* **Carol, pull the curtain!** *(BUCK follows.*

28   *Fade out music.)*

29

30

31

32

33

34

Religion Store

RELIGION STORE

By Dave Toole

1   **CAST:** Salesman, Man, Bill, Cowboy, Astro Freak.
2   **SETTING:** A small shop.
3   **PROPS:** Red pen and magazines for SALESMAN. Twenty-
4   dollar bill for MAN. Play gun for COWBOY.
5   **COSTUMES:** A suit for the SALESMAN. A cowboy hat, big belt
6   buckle, western shirt, jeans and boots for the COWBOY. A
7   headband, sunglasses, beads, and bell-bottom jeans for
8   the ASTRO FREAK.
9
10 *(SALESMAN is behind counter. Enter a MAN.)*
11 **MAN: Excuse me.**
12 **SALESMAN: Yes, can I help you?**
13 **MAN: I saw your sign out front. My wife's birthday is**
14 **coming up in a few weeks and I thought she might**
15 **like something religious.**
16 **SALESMAN: Oh, well, I'm very sorry, but we don't sell reli-**
17 **gious *items*, we sell religions.** *(Smug smile)*
18 **MAN: Oh, yeah? How do you do that?**
19 **SALESMAN: Well, we...** *(Enter BILL.)* **Excuse me one**
20 **moment.** *(Turns.)* **Yes, sir?**
21 **BILL: Yes, I'm here to see about starting my own religion.**
22 **SALESMAN: Fine, fine. Did you have anything specific in**
23 **mind?**
24 **BILL: No, not really. I just don't want no hell, that's all. It's**
25 **getting so a guy can't even fall asleep in church**
26 **without hearin' "lake of fire" this and "hellfire and**
27 **brimstone" that. I want a church where a guy like me**
28 **can feel comfortable.**

1   **SALESMAN: Yes, I see. Well, I can certainly do away with**
2   **hell. Was there anything else you wanted?**
3   **BILL: Ah, no, not really – anything I *should* want?**
4   **SALESMAN: Well, let's see...what about heaven? Do you**
5   **have any stipulations about entrance?**
6   **BILL: Any what?**
7   **SALESMAN: Stipulations, rules. How will you decide who**
8   **gets into heaven? Do you want everyone to go or what?**
9   **BILL: Oh, uh, let's see. No, no, there's definitely some**
10   **people I don't want in heaven. How do you keep 'em**
11   **out?**
12   **SALESMAN: Well, you make a rule that keeps them out.**
13   **Personally, I prefer a rule that says one must earn his**
14   **salvation by working for the church. Painting the**
15   **sanctuary, gardening, going door-to-door selling**
16   **church literature. This also provides you with free**
17   **labor.**
18   **BILL: Sounds good to me. Go ahead and write it in. Hey,**
19   **wait a minute, I ain't got no church to paint or**
20   **garden to weed. What do I do?**
21   **SALESMAN:** *(Hands him a stack of magazines.)* **Why don't**
22   **you send your followers door-to-door with these?**
23   **BILL: *Wishtower*, huh? Not much of a name, is it?**
24   **SALESMAN: I admit, sir, they may not be much to look at,**
25   **but if you send your followers door-to-door asking**
26   **money for them, it won't take long for your church to**
27   **develop *quite* a reputation.**
28   **BILL: Sounds good to me.**
29   **SALESMAN: All right, now, what do we do with those who**
30   **don't make it into heaven?**
31   **BILL: Send them to.... Oh, wait a minute, we got rid of that,**
32   **didn't we?**
33   **SALESMAN: Yes, we did.**
34   **BILL: Well, I don't know. What do you do with them?**

1   SALESMAN: Might I suggest annihilation?

2   BILL: Annia what?

3   SALESMAN: Annihilation. Simple, quick, painless. It's

4   really the best way.

5   BILL: Whatever you say.

6   SALESMAN: Now, what do you plan to call your church?

7   BILL: Was hopin' to call it Bill 'n Fran's Church of Fun.

8   Fran's my wife's name.

9   SALESMAN: Yes, well, sir, if I may be so blunt, you really

10   need a flashier name than that. I mean, Bill 'n Fran's

11   Church of Fun would be fine for a restaurant, but it's

12   hardly a religious title. Don't you agree?

13   BILL: Well, I guess you're right. What would you suggest?

14   SALESMAN: How about the New Christ Church or the

15   Jesus Workers?

16   BILL: No, no, I want to keep "Jesus" and "Christ" out of

17   this as much as I can.

18   SALESMAN: Excellent idea when one makes up his own

19   religion. How about the Jehovah Watchers?

20   BILL: I don't know. This is kind of a big decision. Do I have

21   to come up with something right now? I kinda think

22   Fran will want to have a say.

23   SALESMAN: No problem. However, when you do finally

24   decide on an official name, you need to have the form

25   signed by a notary. Oh, and a witness.

26   BILL: Hey! That's it! That's the name! The Jehovah Notaries.

27   What do you think?

28   SALESMAN: Maybe Fran will have some ideas. In the mean-

29   time, just sign here, and we'll bill you later. Ah, the

30   red pen, sir. It's customary.

31   BILL: OK, swell. *(He signs.)* Boy, this is great. Wait till I tell

32   Fran. *(Exiting)* She'll die.

33   SALESMAN: Yes, she will. *(Turns.)* Now, sorry to keep you

34   waiting. Is there anything I can help you with?

1   **MAN: Well, I'll be! You really do sell religions here. Holy**
2   **moly!**
3   **SALESMAN: Precisely.**
4   **MAN: Business any good?**
5   **SALESMAN: I should say so! And getting better all the**
6   **time. *All the time*.**
7   **MAN: It's amazing what people will believe!**
8   **SALESMAN: Always get a kick out of these people.**
9   **MAN: I'll bet you hear a lot of different things.**
10   **SALESMAN: Not really. You know, most of them think**
11   **they're onto something new and different. Not really.**
12   **Oh, sure, you get an occasional new twist, but for the**
13   **most part, Ol' Solomon was right – there is nothing**
14   **new under the sun.** *(Enter COWBOY. To MAN)* **Excuse**
15   **me.** *(Turning to COWBOY)* **Yes?**
16   **COWBOY: Howdy. You the dude givin' out the religions?**
17   **SALESMAN: Yes, I am.**
18   **COWBOY: Good! I want a religion that worships cows and**
19   **horses.**
20   **SALESMAN: I'm sorry, but that's already taken.**
21   **COWBOY:** *(Slams SALESMAN into wall.)* **What's that?**
22   **SALESMAN: I said that's been taken. A gentleman. This**
23   **morning. The Hindus. They believe *all* animals are**
24   **sacred.**
25   **COWBOY: Well, I'll be a skunk's armpit. I come all this way**
26   **with my heart set on a religion that worships cows**
27   **and horses, and you tell me some varmint beat me to**
28   **it. What am I gonna do?** *(Cocks pistol.)* **I mean, what**
29   **are *you* gonna do?**
30   **SALESMAN: Well, you could start a *reformed* Hindu**
31   **movement.**
32   **COWBOY: Come again?**
33   **SALESMAN: Your own brand of Hinduism. You might like**
34   **it, you know. They don't believe that sinning is**

1   *always* **bad.**

2   **COWBOY: Oh, yeah. Heh-heh. I like that. Where do I put**

3   **my mark?**

4   **SALESMAN: Right here. We'll bill you later.**

5   **COWBOY: Kinda thick ink, isn't it?**

6   **SALESMAN: Thicker than water, you might say.**

7   **COWBOY: You ain't seen the water I drink.**

8   **SALESMAN:** *(Handing him some papers)* **Yes, well, these are**

9   **your official church documents. Just read them over**

10   **and fill in the blanks.**

11   **COWBOY: I don't know how to read.**

12   **SALESMAN: Wonderful. Perhaps someone could read**

13   **them to you.**

14   **COWBOY: Well...**

15   **SALESMAN: Sir, do you like bedtime stories? Fairy tales?**

16   **COWBOY: Yeah.**

17   **SALESMAN: These are quite a bit like that. I'm sure you'll**

18   **enjoy them.**

19   **COWBOY: OK, thank you kindly, partner. Look out**

20   **Tombstone, here I come.** *(COWBOY exits.)*

21   **MAN: That's amazing!**

22   **SALESMAN: What is?**

23   **MAN: How you make this stuff up like that.**

24   **SALESMAN: I beg your pardon. I don't make anything up.**

25   **I'm like any other salesman. I merely ask the**

26   **customer what he wants, and then I give it to him.**

27   **MAN: Well, I've been around a long time, and I've never**

28   **seen anything like this! Is this all legal?**

29   **SALESMAN: But of course! My good man, it's everybody's**

30   **constitutional right to worship *anything, any way* he**

31   **chooses.**

32   **MAN: But what about God?**

33   **SALESMAN: Who?**

34   **MAN: God.**

1　SALESMAN: Oh, him. Well, God is really just a relative
2　　　　term. You know – it means different things to
3　　　　different people. *(Enter ASTRO FREAK.)* You'll excuse
4　　　　me.... Yes – were you looking for something?
5　ASTRO FREAK: Oh, yeah, is this where you come to get
6　　　　your own religion, man?
7　SALESMAN: Yes, it is. What is it you're interested in?
8　ASTRO FREAK: Who, me? Oh, well, I'm into the space bag,
9　　　　you know, man? Stars, cosmos, planets, all that stuff.
10　SALESMAN: And were you interested in starting a religion
11　　　　based on these things?
12　ASTRO FREAK: Wow, could I? Far out!
13　SALESMAN: I'm sure something can be arranged. Did you
14　　　　want something in just space, or perhaps something
15　　　　a little broader, say science fiction in general?
16　ASTRO FREAK: Oh, yeah! Science fiction is where it's at.
17　　　　Might say I'm kind of a sci-fi high man. The other
18　　　　night I had a close encounter of the fourth kind. I
19　　　　thought I was a UFO. I was flying around the room,
20　　　　ricocheting off the walls...you had to be there.
21　SALESMAN: Yes, I can see where that might make your
22　　　　evening. Well, we do offer a special mystic package
23　　　　which incudes UFOs, ESP, the stars, numerology and
24　　　　a lifetime subscription to the *National Gossiper.*
25　ASTRO FREAK: Far out! That's it, that's it. That's what God
26　　　　is all about.
27　SALESMAN: Very good. By the way, did you have a name
28　　　　for this church?
29　ASTRO FREAK: Oh, yeah, man, dig this. My friend Clem
30　　　　and I thought of this one. How about the Knights in
31　　　　White Satin? Can you dig it? Can you get the feel, man?
32　SALESMAN: Yes, and so can about a million others. I'm
33　　　　afraid it was the name of a hit song some years back.
34　ASTRO FREAK: Bummer, man.

1   SALESMAN: Yes, I can see where that could bring you
2   down. Might I suggest the Unitarian Church?
3   ASTRO FREAK: That's copacetic. OK, go for it.
4   SALESMAN: Fine. Sign here, and we'll bill you later.
5   ASTRO FREAK: Far out, red ink. Kind of like my eyes. Hey,
6   man, I'm into kind of a Unitarial bag. Wanna buy
7   some flowers and send a dope fiend to camp?
8   MAN: Well, all I have is this twenty dollars for my wife's
9   birthday....
10   ASTRO FREAK: That's cool. *(Takes the twenty, leaves.)*
11   MAN: Hey! Come back here, you crook! He took my last
12   twenty dollars! Look, that guy just took twenty dollars
13   from me, and he didn't even leave the flowers. Aren't
14   you gonna call the cops or something?
15   SALESMAN: Why? It's all part of his religion. Look here –
16   under fund raising – it's all there in black and white.
17   Read it for yourself.
18   MAN: Look, I don't like this place, and I don't think I like
19   you, either. Now if stealing people's money is part of
20   his religion and *you* helped him with it, then you
21   should pay back the twenty bucks.
22   SALESMAN: Now, hold on a minute! Just one minute! I
23   merely sell religions. I fill in the documents and file
24   the forms. After the customer signs on the dotted
25   line, he's on his own. I don't guarantee these things.
26   MAN: No guarantee?
27   SALESMAN: Of course not. Sir, do you think I would've
28   sold a religion to Mary Maker Beddy if I had to guar-
29   antee it? The poor woman was falling apart. No, no,
30   my boy. Besides, everyone in this business knows
31   there's only one *guaranteed* religion, and that one's
32   free.... Fortunately, none of my customers know
33   about it!
34   MAN: What – Christianity?

1   SALESMAN: Please – don't say that!

2   MAN: Christianity? What's wrong with Christianity?

3   SALESMAN: Sir, sir – control yourself. You're going to

4   ruin a perfectly good sales area. Let me give you a

5   little pointer, strictly off the record. Christianity and

6   the products that I sell do not mix. It's like oil and

7   water, black and white, light and darkness.

8   Christianity is just too simple! All you have to do is

9   believe in Jesus Christ, and the only thing to read is

10   the Bible! Now how could that confuse anyone?

11   MAN: Who wants to confuse anyone?

12   SALESMAN: I do! I do! Young man, aren't you paying atten-

13   tion?! For thousands of years I've been trying to

14   clutter men's minds with false doctrines, earning

15   salvation, worshiping idols – anything to bury them

16   in confusion, to keep them from seeing the Light.

17   MAN: The Light?

18   SALESMAN: Young man, I really don't have time to stand

19   here and dilly-dally with you. We're going out of busi-

20   ness soon.... Here's my card. If you ever want anything

21   in the spiritual realm, don't hesitate to look me up. In

22   fact, next week we're having a sale.

23   MAN: What kind of sale?

24   SALESMAN: A fire sale.

25

26

27

28

29

30

31

32

33

34

777
PEARLY GATES

By Dan Rupple

1   ***CAST:*** Jesus Christ, Claude Grover, Devil.

2   ***SETTING:*** Heaven.

3   ***PROPS:*** Scroll or book for JESUS.

4   ***COSTUMES:*** JESUS should wear a biblical robe and beard.

5   CLAUDE should be dressed as the overbearing tourist

6   that he is, with several cameras hanging from his neck,

7   sunglasses, hat, Hawaiian shirt, shorts, black socks, dress

8   shoes, and a suitcase with travel stickers plastered all

9   over it. DEVIL should be dressed all in black.

10

11   *(Start optional background music. JESUS is On-stage,*

12   *standing at the podium. CLAUDE enters.)*

13   **JESUS: Can I help you?**

14   **CLAUDE: Yeah, I'm looking for 777 Pearly Gates.**

15   **JESUS: This is 777 Pearly Gates.**

16   **CLAUDE: Great! Is there a door or driveway or somewhere**

17   **I can get in?**

18   **JESUS: Wait. What's your name?**

19   **CLAUDE: Suppose you want to see if I've got a reservation,**

20   **huh?**

21   **JESUS: Something like that.**

22   **CLAUDE: No problem. The name's Grover. Claude Grover.**

23   **JESUS: Let's see. Gibson, Grant, Green, Gunderson. I'm**

24   **sorry, no Grover.**

25   **CLAUDE: What do ya mean, no Grover? There must be a**

26   **mistake.**

27   **JESUS: No mistake. Your name's not in the book.**

28   **CLAUDE: That's ridiculous. After all the things I've done.**

777 Pearly Gates

1   JESUS: I know what you've done.

2   CLAUDE: Well, I know you're supposed to know, but what
3   about the time I donated twenty-five bucks to that
4   telethon? See! Saved the receipt...tax deductible, you
5   know. And what about when I was chief of my kid's
6   Trail Blazer's Club and they wanted that weird new
7   kid to join? I didn't complain. I even gave him his own
8   little tent on camp outs.

9   JESUS: I'm sorry, Claude. That doesn't make it.

10   CLAUDE: Oh! I get it. You probably want something
11   religious, huh? Let's be honest for a minute. Well, I
12   admit I didn't go to church every Sunday. But I went
13   every Easter and a couple of Christmases, too. And
14   remember that time a couple years ago when my wife
15   kept nagging me and I went two Sundays in a row?
16   Two in a row! Even missed a Ram's game. I heard it,
17   though. Had a little earplug in my transistor. I didn't
18   think anyone could hear those things, but after the
19   sermon the preacher wanted to know who won the
20   game. He was quite a fan.

21   JESUS: Well, Claude, there still isn't a place for you.

22   CLAUDE: Well, what did you want me to do, go door to
23   door with Bibles? Put an "I Found It" bumper sticker
24   on the Pinto?

25   JESUS: Claude, you didn't have to do anything. I did all the
26   work for you, if only you would've accepted it.

27   CLAUDE: Come on. You act like I'm some kind of bad guy
28   or something. Look, I never killed anyone or robbed a
29   bank. I can see you keeping those guys out, but come
30   on, this is me, Claude Grover! You know, life-of-the-
31   party, lamp shades Grover, good ol' law-abiding
32   American citizen. I never did anything *really* bad.

33   JESUS: Claude, "All have sinned and come short of the
34   glory of God." (Rom. 3:23, KJV)

1   **CLAUDE: Oh, yeah, if all have sinned, then none of us has**
2   **a chance. That's not fair. You're supposed to be fair.**
3   **How do you fix that?**
4   **JESUS: I died for you, so that by my grace you could be**
5   **redeemed.**
6   **CLAUDE: What do you mean, you died for me? Who are**
7   **you, anyway?**
8   **JESUS: You don't even know me. I'm Jesus Christ.**
9   **CLAUDE: Come on. Who are you, really? Where's St. Peter?**
10   **JESUS: I've told you. Now go.**
11   **CLAUDE: Hang on. Is there a back door or something? I**
12   **could wash dishes. I love to wash dishes.**
13   **JESUS: I am the Way, the Truth and the Life.** (John 14:6, KJV)
14   **CLAUDE: Well, is there someone else I can talk to? The**
15   **manager or the owner? Let me talk to the owner right**
16   **now!**
17   **JESUS: No man comes unto the Father but by me.** (John 4:6,
18   author's paraphrase)
19   **CLAUDE: Hardy, hardy, har. How many times have I heard**
20   **that before?**
21   **JESUS: It doesn't matter how many times you heard it, it**
22   **only matters if you believe it.** *(Fade optional music)*
23   **CLAUDE: Well, that's just great. Where do I go now?**
24   **DEVIL:** *(Entering)* **Mr. Grover?**
25   **CLAUDE: Yeah?**
26   **DEVIL: We have a place for you over here.** *(Exits.)*
27   **CLAUDE: Well, all right, that's what I call service. There's**
28   **a voice I recognize. Is it just me, or is it getting hot in**
29   **here?** *(Follows DEVIL off.)*
30
31
32
33
34

THE LAST WORLD SERIES REPORT

By Dave Toole

1   **CAST:** Robbie Robenowitz, Apostle Peter.

2   **SETTING:** A baseball field.

3   **PROPS:** A microphone for ROBBIE. A bat for PETER.

4   **COSTUMES:** ROBBIE wears a suit. PETER wears a wild

5   combination of biblical costume and baseball uniform,

6   such as a long robe, baseball cleats, and a baseball cap

7   with a long cloth head drape under it.

8

9   *(Optional intro music. ROBBIE and PETER are at Center*

10   *Stage.)*

11   **ROBBIE: Hello, sports fans. Robbie Robenowitz here with**

12   **the Last World Series report. An exciting preview of**

13   **this season's biggest showdown between the Heavenly**

14   **Saints and the Demons of Darkness. Down here on the**

15   **field with us is that zealous shortstop for the Saints,**

16   **the Apostle Peter. Pete, you and the Saints seem to be**

17   **having quite a surge here in the final days of the**

18   **season. What do you feel are some of the reasons?**

19   **PETER: Well, Robbie, we owe a lot of credit to our team**

20   **trainer, the Holy Spirit. He's given this team the**

21   **strength and courage to really come through in the**

22   **clutch. As you know, the Demons are highly depen-**

23   **dent on all kinds of drugs to keep their guys going,**

24   **which we feel is wrong and very dangerous. In fact,**

25   **that's how they've lost many of their key players lately.**

26   **ROBBIE: Good point, Pete, but tell us a little about some**

27   **of the individual testimonies. Paul of Tarsus, for**

28   **example. How's he working out?**

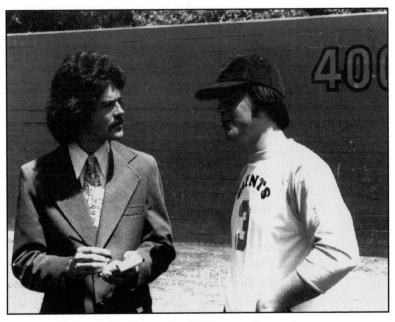

The Last World Series Report

1   PETER: Well, Robbie, as you know, we got Paul in the
2   trade with the Demons for Judas Iscariot, and we're
3   very happy with the way things have worked out. We
4   originally intended to have Judas play second base,
5   but he was always wandering around out in left field,
6   doing his own thing. I don't think he ever wanted to
7   be a team player. As it turned out, he didn't play much
8   for the Demons, either. Paul, on the other hand, has
9   had a real turn-around year here with the Saints. As I
10   was saying, he started the season with the Demons
11   and was quite a slugger, as many of our players can
12   tell you. But since coming to the Saints, he's not only
13   shown himself to be a man who can swing a bat, but
14   someone who can field even the hardest questions in
15   life and turn them into real victories.
16   ROBBIE: Well, Peter, how about the coaching staff? How
17   are they holding up this late in the season?
18   PETER: Oh, just great, Robbie. You know, the Demons rely
19   on fear and intimidation to motivate their players,
20   but we believe in positive reinforcement. Coach
21   Isaiah, Coach Daniel, Coach Zechariah, all the
22   coaching staff are prophesying a mighty victory. In
23   fact, Daniel was saying in the clubhouse yesterday
24   that the victory is already ours, all we have to do is
25   claim it and go out and play the game.
26   ROBBIE: And Daniel ought to know. I still remember that
27   great game he played some years back against the
28   Lions. Shut 'em out, as I recall. But Peter, I'd like to
29   ask you about Jesus Christ, undoubtedly the most
30   talented and powerful player in the league. Now the
31   Demons claim they put him out for the season, but
32   you guys claim he's coming back. What's the scoop?
33   PETER: Well, that's right, Robbie. Jesus promised to come
34   back in the final days, and we hope he'll return soon.

1   We give him all the credit for the team, both as indi-
2   viduals and as a group. He's changed our lives. As you
3   know, he took this team literally from a handful of
4   sandlot fishermen and changed us into a precision
5   team of miracle workers. Obviously, we're anxious
6   about his return.
7   **ROBBIE:** Then he *is* coming back?
8   **PETER:** Robbie! Jesus promised, didn't he? And that's one
9   thing Jesus is famous for: He always keeps his
10   promises.
11   **ROBBIE:** Well, OK, Pete, our time is just about up. I'd like
12   to thank you for being with us today, and we'll have a
13   Spiegel gift certificate for you a little later. Best of
14   luck to you and your team in the rest of the series.
15   **PETER:** Thank you very much, Robbie, but on our team,
16   luck has nothing to do with it. Praise the Lord!
17   *(PETER exits.)*
18   **ROBBIE:** Thanks again, Peter. Now back to you in the
19   booth, Joe.
20
21
22
23
24
25
26
27
28
29
30
31
32
33
34

BIBLE JUNKIE

By Dan Rupple

1 **CAST:** Bible Junkie.
2 **SETTING:** Anywhere.
3 **PROPS:** Assorted Bibles, including a pocket-sized New
4   Testament and a large King James Version.
5 **COSTUMES:** Regular dress.
6
7 **BIBLE JUNKIE: I have a confession to make: I'm a junkie.**
8   **A Bible junkie. It all began one day when I was sitting**
9   **on a park bench eating my lunch, and I started**
10   **looking around and I saw this little black book under**
11   **the bench. So I picked it up and thumbed through it.**
12   **It was a pocket-sized New Testament. And I thumbed**
13   **through some more, then I did it. I *read* a *verse*! Now**
14   **don't ask me why. Lord knows I didn't want to. I just**
15   **did. It was in Matthew, and within a couple of days, I**
16   **was through Mark and Luke and heading toward**
17   **John. I tried to stop, but I just couldn't. Well, that was**
18   **just the start. Then I went on to a bigger Bible. I read**
19   **a full King James Version with concordance. I just**
20   **couldn't put it down. I bought about eight different**
21   **Bibles and I stashed them everywhere. In my drawer,**
22   **in my car, by the drinking fountain at work. I just**
23   **couldn't get through the day without the "Word." Oh,**
24   **that's addict slang for the Bible. I was getting by until**
25   **one weekend I went to the mountains and I did it, I**
26   **forgot my Bible. It's hard to talk about it now. I got the**
27   **shakes, I broke out in a cold sweat. I might not be**
28   **here today if a Boy Scout hadn't recited John 3:16 to**

1   me for four hours straight.

2   Well, of course, then my so-called friends found
3 out. I mean, I might've been reading a lot, but I wasn't
4 blind. All of a sudden I didn't get invited to "those
5 kinds of parties" anymore. They voted me "most
6 likely to become a nun" in the college newspaper. But
7 it still didn't bother me until last month. The father
8 of this girl I liked said he wouldn't let his daughter go
9 out with "that kind of guy!" Like I had some kind of
10 disease or something. I really don't know how he
11 found out. I guess he saw my tracts.

12   Well, that just got me deeper into it, and pretty
13 soon I became a pusher. I started getting other people
14 hooked. Oh, I know what you're thinking. I'm a sicko,
15 a real scum. Well, I've been to doctors. They couldn't
16 help. They tried putting me on dosages of *Reader's*
17 *Digest*, but that just put me to sleep.

18   I didn't know where to turn. The doctors couldn't
19 help me, and my friends deserted me.... Then one day
20 I slowed down, and instead of just reading the Bible,
21 I started to believe it. Can you imagine that? Believing
22 it! And as if believing wasn't enough, I started living
23 it! And all of a sudden I looked around and found I
24 didn't have a problem anymore. It no longer
25 mattered what my friends or a girl's father thought of
26 me, but what mattered was that Jesus loves me. And
27 that right there is so neat that now I'm proud to be
28 not just a Bible Junkie, but a Jesus Junkie. I'm
29 hooked, *but* I'm hooked on the real thing. Thank you.

30

31

32

33

34

JERUSALEM DRAGNET I

By Dan Rupple, Dave Toole, and Larry Watt

1 **CAST:** Sergeant Good Friday (Goodie), Officer Frank Gannon,
2 Thomas, Peter, Judas, Narrator (may be On-stage or off),
3 Farmer, Host.
4 **SETTING:** Jerusalem. THOMAS and PETER's homes may be
5 pantomimed at different locations On-stage.
6 **PROPS:** A fast-food bucket of fish and a stick pony for
7 GOODIE and FRANK.
8 **COSTUMES:** GOODIE and FRANK may wear police uniforms
9 and tall, centurion-type hats. GOODIE also wears a
10 whistle around his neck and carries a badge — either a
11 toy or one made of cardboard. THOMAS, PETER and
12 JUDAS may wear biblical robes, headpieces and sandals.
13 The FARMER may wear a flannel shirt, overalls, work
14 boots and a straw hat.
15 **SOUND EFFECTS:** Rooster crowing (optional).
16
17 *(Optional music. Enter GOODIE.)*
18 **GOODIE: This is the city Jerusalem. It's righteous. Lots of**
19 **people live here. Most of 'em good, but when they fall**
20 **from grace, that's where I come in. My name's Friday**
21 **— Good Friday. I carry a badge.**
22 **NARRATOR: The story you are about to hear is true. None**
23 **of the names have been changed, because only one**
24 **was innocent.** *(Optional music)*
25 **GOODIE: Thursday, April sixth, 11:07 a.m. My partner,**
26 **Frank, and I had just completed the Barabbas case.**
27 **Booked him on a 314. Call came in on a 432 — city**
28 **ordinance fourteen — walking on water. Sent Malloy**

Jerusalem Dragnet I

1   **and Reed out to investigate. They came back empty-**
2   **handed. The suspect had outrun the patrol boat.**
3   *(Optional music)* **12:07 – Member of the Jewish**
4   **persuasion subpoenaed a man from Nazareth named**
5   **Jesus Christ – the charge, blasphemy. Frank saddled**
6   **the donkey. I got the light. We headed out the door.**
7   *(Optional music)* **12:42 – We arrived at the home of a**
8   **follower of mentioned suspect and approached with**
9   **caution.** *(Enter FRANK.)*
10   **FRANK: Gee, Goodie, mind if I knock this time?**
11   **GOODIE: Sure, Frank, live it up!** *(FRANK knocks. The door*
12   *opens.)*
13   **THOMAS: Oh, hello, officers. What can I do for you?**
14   **GOODIE: Your name Thomas?**
15   **THOMAS: Uh, yeah. Did I do something wrong?**
16   **GOODIE: We just want the facts, that's all, just the facts.**
17   **Do you know a man named Jesus?**
18   **THOMAS: Uh, yeah, I know him. What's this all about?**
19   **FRANK: Says he's the Son of God.**
20   **GOODIE: What do you think?**
21   **THOMAS: Oh, well, he's a great guy. You should see the**
22   **miracles he does....**
23   **GOODIE: We just want the facts.**
24   **THOMAS: Well, the Son of God? I doubt it.**
25   **GOODIE: Reports say he's in the Garden of Gethsemane.**
26   **What do you say?**
27   **THOMAS: Gethsemane? I doubt it.**
28   **GOODIE:** *(Aside to FRANK)* **I guess that makes him a**
29   **doubting Thomas.**
30   **THOMAS: You write your own material?**
31   **FRANK:** *(Awkward pause)* **They say this Jesus is the King of**
32   **the Jews?**
33   **GOODIE: What do you say?**
34   **THOMAS: Well, I doubt it.**

1   **FRANK: Calls himself the Light of the World.**

2   **GOODIE: What do you think?**

3   **THOMAS: I doubt it.**

4   **FRANK: They claim he's mankind's salvation.**

5   **GOODIE: How about you?**

6   **THOMAS: Well...**

7   **GOODIE and FRANK:** *(Together)* **I doubt it!**

8   **GOODIE: Right. Look, you gonna be available for any**

9   **further questioning?**

10 **THOMAS: I doubt it.** *(Exit THOMAS and FRANK, opposite*

11   *ways. Optional music)*

12 **GOODIE: 2:18 – Frank and I stopped at a fish stand for**

13   **lunch. Ate, got back on the donkey and headed to the**

14   **house of yet another Jesus follower.** *(Exit GOODIE.*

15   *Optional music. Enter GOODIE and FRANK, eating fish*

16   *out of a fast-food bucket.)*

17 **FRANK: Gee, Goodie, this is great fish, and only $1.50 a**

18   **bucket. What a deal!**

19 **GOODIE: Must've had a good catch.** *(He knocks on the door.)*

20   **You've got some cole slaw on your nose, Frank.** *(Door*

21   *opens.)*

22 **PETER: Yes?**

23 **GOODIE: Your name Simon, also called Peter?**

24 **PETER: Yes.**

25 **FRANK and GOODIE: Which is it?**

26 **PETER: It's both.** *(FRANK and GOODIE simultaneously)*

27 **FRANK: Listen, Peter...   GOODIE: Listen, Simon...**

28 **GOODIE: What do your friends call you?**

29 **PETER: The Rock.** *(FRANK and GOODIE do a double-take.)*

30 **FRANK: How are you listed in the phone book?**

31 **PETER: I don't have a phone.**

32 **GOODIE: What's it say on your driver's license?**

33 **PETER: I haven't got a donkey.**

34 **FRANK: What's it say on your fishing license?**

1 **PETER: Retired.** *(FRANK and GOODIE look frustratedly at*
2   *each other and try again.)*
3 **GOODIE: Look, you know a guy named Jesus?**
4 **PETER: Jesus? No, I never heard of him.**
5 **GOODIE: We've got over a dozen witnesses who say they**
6   **saw you with him.**
7 **PETER: Naw, maybe it was just someone who looked like**
8   **me. I told you I don't know him.**
9 **FRANK:** *(Trying to remove some fish from between his teeth)*
10   **Hey, Rocky, you got a toothpick?**
11 **PETER: Look, I don't know him!** *(Optional rooster crowing.*
12   *All exit. Optional music. Enter GOODIE.)*
13 **GOODIE: 3:43 – When we arrived back at headquarters, a**
14   **farmer was waiting with a 402 complaint – willful**
15   **destruction of private property. Frank went to call his**
16   **wife. I went to question the farmer.** *(Enter FARMER*
17   *singing.)* **You the farmer?**
18 **FARMER: Sure am. You the officer?** *(Blows GOODIE's*
19   *whistle.)* **Love whistles. Think you could get me one**
20   **of those?**
21 **GOODIE:** *(Grabs whistle and wipes it off.)* **I'll get you a whole**
22   **box if it'll keep you from singing. What's your**
23   **problem?**
24 **FARMER: It's this Jesus fella.**
25 **GOODIE:** *(Aside)* **Jesus again.** *(To FARMER)* **What happened?**
26 **FARMER: He killed one of my fig trees.**
27 **GOODIE: What'd he do? Tear it out or something?**
28 **FARMER: No, he never even touched it. He just cursed it.**
29 **GOODIE: He what?**
30 **FARMER: He cursed it.**
31 **GOODIE: Look, just give me the facts.**
32 **FARMER: Well, I've got these five fig trees out by the fence,**
33   **and this Jesus fella comes sashaying along, figuring**
34   **he's gonna mooch one of my figs. Well, sir, when he**

1   **seen there were none to be had, he cursed it.**

2   **GOODIE: I see. We'll get right on it. Let you know if**

3   **anything comes up.**

4   **FARMER: Listen here, bullethead, now I'm a taxpayer and**

5   **twenty percent of my crop is gone. What am I gonna do?**

6   **I got a wife, I got a kid, I just bought a dishwasher....**

7   **GOODIE: OK! What was he driving?**

8   **FARMER: A donkey.**

9   **GOODIE: What color?**

10   **FARMER: Light brown. Galilee plates.**

11   **GOODIE: Get the number?**

12   **FARMER: Nope.**

13   **GOODIE: Why not?**

14   **FARMER: Taillight was out.** *(Exit FARMER. Optional music)*

15   **GOODIE: 4:45 – Frank and I headed back to the fish**

16   **stand. The donkey made a wrong turn, and we**

17   **proceeded down an alleyway by the temple. Ran into**

18   **yet another Jesus follower.** *(Exit GOODIE. Optional*

19   *music for riding donkey. Enter FRANK and GOODIE on*

20   *stick pony. Cross stage twice. Enter JUDAS, looking*

21   *tough.)* **Hey, buddy. You know the way back to**

22   **Goldstein's Fish Stand?**

23   **JUDAS: Yeah.**

24   **FRANK: Wanna tell us?**

25   **JUDAS: OK, go down to the end of the alley, hang a right,**

26   **down two blocks, can't miss it. There's a big fish going**

27   **around in the sky.**

28   **GOODIE: Thanks. By the way, what are you doin' back**

29   **here?**

30   **JUDAS: Oh, I have a meeting with the Pharisees a little**

31   **later on.**

32   **GOODIE: Who are you?**

33   **JUDAS: Name's Iscariot. Judas Iscariot.** *(FRANK and GOODIE*

34   *react.)*

1   **GOODIE: You one of the Twelve?**

2   **JUDAS: What's it to you, gum-sandal?**

3   **GOODIE: We're looking for Jesus. You know where he is?**

4   **JUDAS: Maybe yes, maybe no. What's in it for me?**

5   **FRANK: I've got some more fish back on the donkey.**

6   **JUDAS: No, I just ate. Spare change?** *(FRANK and GOODIE*

7   *huddle.)*

8   **FRANK: Let's see, that's my bowling money.**

9   **GOODIE: I've got some change from the coffee machine.**

10   **FRANK: Here's twenty silver pieces.**

11   **GOODIE: I've got ten.** *(To JUDAS)* **Thirty pieces of silver**

12   **do you?**

13   **JUDAS: That'll do. OK, you've gotta promise me one thing.**

14   **GOODIE: What's that?**

15   **JUDAS: Don't tell Jesus I ratted on him, OK?**

16   **GOODIE: Ten-four. No one will ever know it was you. How**

17   **do you want to set it up?**

18   **JUDAS: Well, let's see, it's gonna be the Passover. We're**

19   **gonna eat around eight o'clock. You pick him up in**

20   **the garden about ten-thirty.**

21   **GOODIE: Fine. How will we know this Mr. Jesus?**

22   **JUDAS: I'll point him out to ya.** *(FRANK and GOODIE shake*

23   *their heads.)*

24   **GOODIE: Not good enough.**

25   **JUDAS: Why not?**

26   **FRANK: We need something more definite. What if we get**

27   **the wrong guy?**

28   **JUDAS: OK. I'll go up to him and shake his hand.**

29   **GOODIE: Not good enough.**

30   **JUDAS: Why?**

31   **FRANK: What if someone shakes your hand first?**

32   **JUDAS: Well, what do you want me to do? Kiss him?**

33   **FRANK and GOODIE:** *(FRANK and GOODIE do a double-*

34   *take.)* **Sounds good.**

1   **GOODIE: OK, we'll see you tonight. Where we gonna meet**
2   **you?**
3   **JUDAS: Don't worry. I'll be hanging around.** *(Exit JUDAS*
4   *and FRANK, opposite. Optional music)*
5   **GOODIE: That night Frank and I broke the "Son of God"**
6   **ring and arrested Jesus Christ. Friday, 6:00 a.m. We**
7   **turned him over to Pontius Pilate.** *(Optional music.*
8   *Enter FRANK.)*
9   **FRANK: I don't know, Goodie. I've been a cop a long time,**
10   **but this time I really think we did the wrong thing. I**
11   **mean, this Jesus guy didn't look like a criminal to me.**
12   **GOODIE: Yeah, even Pilate and Herod couldn't find**
13   **anything wrong with him. I wonder what the**
14   **Pharisees have against him.**
15   **FRANK: He was so nice and gentle. Ya know, I even think**
16   **he smiled at me.**
17   **GOODIE: Yeah, well that's how it goes in this business. We**
18   **don't make the laws, we just enforce them. Well, I**
19   **guess I'll take the rest of the day off. See ya Monday.**
20   **FRANK: Aren't you working Sunday?**
21   **GOODIE: No, Frank. Sunday's Easter!** *(Both exit. Optional*
22   *music)*
23   **NARRATOR:** *(Over music)* **Friday, April seventh, in depart-**
24   **ment six of the Jewish Supreme Court, Jesus Christ**
25   **was tried and convicted of blasphemy. Later that**
26   **same day, he was crucified for the sins of the world.**
27   **In a moment, the results of the Crucifixion.**
28   **HOST:** *(Enters.)* **The result of the Crucifixion is that when**
29   **each one of us were dead in our sins, Jesus Christ,**
30   **who is perfect in every way, was made to be sin for us.**
31   **He was nailed to the cross, and his blood was shed.**
32   **But then three days later, he arose again, so that we,**
33   **by receiving him as our Lord and Savior, have eternal**
34   **life and a day-to-day relationship with God. We'd like**

1   to thank you, and we pray that through our words, the
2   Lord has revealed his truths to your heart so that you,
3   too, would receive this gift of life through Jesus
4   Christ. God bless you.
5
6
7
8
9
10
11
12
13
14
15
16
17
18
19
20
21
22
23
24
25
26
27
28
29
30
31
32
33
34

CELEBRITY CORNERED

By Dan Rupple

1　**CAST:** Wally Wickenshield — reporter; Rod Bentley — superstar.

2　**SETTING:** TV show on location outside a luxury hotel.

3　**PROPS:** Microphone for WALLY.

4　**COSTUMES:** WALLY wears a suit; ROD is dressed in flashy

5　　garb and wears sunglasses.

6

7　**WALLY: Hi there! Wally Wickenshield here again with**

8　　***Celebrity Cornered.* We're standing outside the luxu-**

9　　**rious Fittey Hotel with thousands of celebrity**

10　　**seekers, waiting for the momentary arrival of famous**

11　　**millionaire actor, singer and business tycoon Rod**

12　　**Bentley, who should arrive momentarily, at any**

13　　**moment. Fans of all ages have lined the streets since**

14　　**early this morning, hoping for just a glimpse of Rod,**

15　　**let alone an autograph. The excitement is building**

16　　**with each second, and...wait...** *(Sound of sirens. WALLY*

17　　*looks behind audience.)* **I think...yes, the motorcade is**

18　　**coming around the corner now and pulling up in**

19　　**front of the hotel. Of course, fans are swarming**

20　　**around the flamingo pink metal-flaked limo. Ladies**

21　　**and gentlemen, pandemonium is breaking out**

22　　**throughout the grandstands and out onto the side-**

23　　**walks. So far the limo door has not been opened and**

24　　**because of the curtains, we are unable to see if Rod**

25　　**Bentley is actually inside the vehicle. Of course, in**

26　　**case you didn't know, Rod is in town for the premiere**

27　　**of his new film, *Banjo Fever.* As of yet, I have...wait...I**

28　　**believe the...yes, the door has opened...two of Rod**

1	Bentley's bodyguards have exited the vehicle and are
2	attempting to clear the sidewalk for Rod. Now local
3	security police have joined in. They're having quite a
4	battle trying to control the frenzy of...
5	It's Rod Bentley! There he is, ladies and gentlemen...
6	Rod Bentley. The fans are bombarding him with papers
7	and pencils, hoping for a rare autograph. Rod is
8	making his way up the sidewalk. I'm going to try for a
9	quick interview. *(Enter ROD.)* **Rod! Rod Bentley! Over**
10	here! Wally Wickenshield, *Celebrity Cornered.* Just a
11	quick word if we could, please? Move the camera
12	around, Fred. Clear the way, please...ladies and gentle-
13	men, I'm talking with superstar Rod Bentley. Rod,
14	you're causing a lot of excitement here. How does it feel?
15	**ROD:** Just great, Wally. It's good to be here, and I'm
16	pleased that so many of my fans have shown up.
17	**WALLY:** You know, some people in this town have said that
18	you're fading fast in popularity, that you're washed
19	up and over the hill. Are you surprised at this kind of
20	a turnout?
21	**ROD:** No, not at all. As you know, my new movie with Lydia
22	Hearn...
23	**WALLY:** *Banjo Fever?*
24	**ROD:** Yes, it's opening tomorrow night, and I'm sure it'll
25	be a blockbuster.
26	**WALLY:** You produced it yourself, didn't you?
27	**ROD:** Yes, I did. It's all my money that went into the
28	picture, and I stand to make quite a bit on the film.
29	Heh-heh!
30	**WALLY:** So, on the lighter side, how's life going for you?
31	**ROD:** Just great, couldn't be better. I've got everything I
32	could ever want, and just last week I was named
33	International Celebrity of the Year. Couldn't be
34	better.

1　WALLY: Well, OK. Thanks so much, Rod. Great to have you
2　　　　here, and great to hear things are going so well. Of
3　　　　course, you do know the Bible says, "What shall it
4　　　　profit a man if he gains the whole world and loses his
5　　　　soul?" (Matt. 16:26, author's paraphrase) **But anyway,**
6　　　　**this is Wally Wickenshield...**
7　ROD: Say what?
8　WALLY: Well, everyone knows Jesus said it is easier for a
9　　　　camel to go through the eye of a needle than for a rich
10　　　　man to enter the kingdom of God. This is *Celebrity*
11　　　　*Cornered,* saying...
12　ROD: Uh, Wally, I'm a star. I've sold billions of records, my
13　　　　movies...
14　WALLY: No, no, Rod. The Bible says treasures of wicked-
15　　　　ness profit nothing, but righteousness delivers from
16　　　　death. (Prov. 10:2, author's paraphrase)
17　ROD: No kidding?
18　WALLY: You have to set your affections on things above,
19　　　　not on the things of earth. (Col. 3:2, author's paraphrase)
20　ROD: Wow, man...what do I do?
21　WALLY: Ah, Rod, it's awful you haven't heard any of this.
22　　　　Maybe we should step inside. You've got to get some-
23　　　　thing eternal going here. *(They start to exit.)*
24　ROD: Bad news!
25　WALLY: No, no, this is the *Good News.* You have to look to
26　　　　the Lord, Rod.
27　ROD: I thought I was cool.
28　WALLY: Oh, no, not unless you've got it eternally, pal. All
29　　　　that stuff will fizzle out. The money, the girls... *(Fade*
30　　　　*away)*
31
32
33
34

Front Desk Angel

FRONT DESK ANGEL

By Dan Rupple and Dave Toole

1   **CAST:** Chief — the Front Desk Angel; Welford — Angel assis-
2   tant; Barlow — Angel assistant; Off-stage voice (may also
3   read the Lord's line).
4   **SETTING:** The FRONT DESK ANGEL's office. There is a desk
5   with a chair.
6   **PROPS:** Assorted papers and a telephone for CHIEF. A
7   trumpet for BARLOW.
8   **COSTUMES:** Long, flowing robes (such as choir robes) for all
9   three characters. CHIEF needs a hat or some other acces-
10   sory to set him apart from the other two angels.
11   **SOUND EFFECTS:** Ringing phone, trumpet sound.
12
13   *(CHIEF is seated at the desk, shuffling papers.)*
14   **OFF-STAGE VOICE: Far beyond the physical realm of this**
15   **world, there is a realm of great power and signifi-**
16   **cance. Two divisions of light and dark compose the**
17   **realm of the spirit. Many people don't believe in it.**
18   **Few truly understand it, but the spiritual realm plays**
19   **a mighty role in our every decision, our every move,**
20   **and even our every word. Join us now as we take a trip**
21   **into the other world on our weekly adventure**
22   **of...*Battle of the Invisible Empires!***
23   **CHIEF:** *(Phone rings — CHIEF answers.)* **Hello, Front Desk**
24   **Angel, yeah, uh, Rev. Prophecy, chapter thirteen,**
25   **Belgium division? Great, yeah, I left a message**
26   **earlier. How's the computer that we ordered coming?**
27   **Great, all ready to go. Now are you guys sure it can**
28   **handle every single financial transaction in the**

1   world? Because it's got to be set up "that no man
2   might buy or sell, save he that had the mark, or the
3   name of the beast, or the number of his name." (Rev.
4   13:17) **OK, that's great, now the Bible says the number**
5   **is 666. Now how we gonna do that? We can't give**
6   **everyone the same number. What? You say you've got**
7   **three sets of six digits? Perfect. Well, keep up the good**
8   **work. I'll get back to you....** *(Hangs up and redials.)*
9   **Mark of the Beast department? Front Desk Angel**
10   **here. Yeah, just talked with Belgium. The computer's**
11   **all set, now we've got to have that mark. What's going**
12   **on? No, no, a card won't do. The Bible specifically**
13   **states a mark on the right hand or forehead. Oh, yeah,**
14   **I see, so you can't lose your card, people will want the**
15   **mark on their hand or forehead. Now have you guys**
16   **decided how we're gonna put it on? A tattoo or what?**
17   **A laser beam or ultraviolet ray? OK, as soon as you**
18   **decide, get back to me. Catch you later. God bless you.**
19   *(Hangs up. WELFORD enters.)*
20   **WELFORD: Hi, Chief.**
21   **CHIEF: Oh, Welford. What are are you doing here? It's**
22   **your day off, isn't it?**
23   **WELFORD: I know. I just dropped in because I've got a**
24   **flight lesson today. I get to go solo.**
25   **CHIEF: Great, great.**
26   **WELFORD: Say, how're things going up here, anyway?**
27   **CHIEF: Just great, Welford. Just perfect.**
28   **WELFORD: You gonna get all the last day's prophecies**
29   **finished?**
30   **CHIEF: We finished all the other ones, didn't we?**
31   **WELFORD: Yeah, so what's left?**
32   **CHIEF: Well, let's see. We got Israel back together as a**
33   **nation in 1948, we made sure they got Jerusalem in**
34   **'67. Russia is a world power, we got pollution, earth-**

1   quakes. The Lord's allowed famines, droughts, pesti-

2   lence, population explosion... *(Trumpet sound)*

3   CHIEF: Welford, do you know what that means?

4   WELFORD: Oh, boy, I sure do! Sure, it's the wedding feast.

5   *(Trumpet sound)*

6   CHIEF: Come on, Welford, let's get over to the banquet

7   hall. *(Enter BARLOW laughing and carrying a trumpet.)*

8   BARLOW: Hi, guys. Boy, did I ever fool you two. Pretty

9   funny joke, huh?

10   CHIEF: Barlow!

11   BARLOW: Yes, Chief?

12   CHIEF: Barlow, you know the rules. No trumpets in the

13   office!

14   BARLOW: But, Chief, Michael's always walking around

15   with his trumpet.

16   CHIEF: That's different, Barlow. And besides, he hasn't

17   played it yet, has he?

18   BARLOW: Well, no. But he's gonna!

19   CHIEF: Well, that's different. OK, now what do you have

20   for me?

21   BARLOW: Well, Chief, I just came down from wars and

22   rumors of wars. As you know, there are wars all over

23   the world: the Middle East, the Far East, Africa,

24   Europe, South America, everywhere. So anyway, they

25   felt we needed a few more rumors of war. And we've

26   got a great one! How about a rumor of a war between

27   Rhode Island and Samoa?

28   CHIEF: *(Shocked)* Boy, Barlow, that would be *quite* a

29   rumor!

30   BARLOW: I'll say! So, do I get the go-ahead?

31   CHIEF: Sounds good to me, but the Lord is in charge here,

32   so I'll take it before the throne. *(Phone rings.)*

33   CHIEF: Front Desk Angel. Really, Scott Kincade! Praise

34   the Lord! *(Hangs up.)* Guys, Scott Kincade just accepted

1   **Jesus!** *(Optional celebration sounds, cheering and*
2   *dancing)* **OK, back to work.**
3   **WELFORD: Chief, whatever happened to my suggestion of**
4   **Puerto Rico joining the world confederacy?**
5   **CHIEF: Well, Welford, the Bible calls for a ten-nation**
6   **confederacy that needs to come together as a world**
7   **power. At the time, we had nine nations in the**
8   **European Common Market, so we needed one more.**
9   **Angel Henderson suggested Greece, and it's working**
10   **out perfectly. Being in Europe and bordering Italy, it**
11   **just sets the stage for a world government centered in**
12   **Rome. We appreciate the idea of Puerto Rico, but it**
13   **just wasn't what the Lord had in mind.** *(Phone rings.*
14   *CHIEF answers.)* **Front Desk Angel. Woo, boy, that's a**
15   **toughie. I hadn't thought of that. OK, I'll get a couple**
16   **of angels on it right away.** *(Hangs up. In deep thought)*
17   **Let's see. I'm gonna need a couple of angels I can**
18   **really depend on. Two of my best. Who am I gonna**
19   **get?** *(Notices WELFORD and BARLOW.)* **No. Not you two.**
20   *(They sadly start to leave.)* **Well, OK. Here's the scoop.**
21   **Someone down in prophecy just noticed that right**
22   **after the Russian-Israeli war, the weapons have to**
23   **burn for seven years.**
24   **BARLOW: Yeah, so?**
25   **CHIEF: Barlow, have you ever tried to set a tank on fire?**
26   **BARLOW: No, Chief, that's silly. That would be impossible.**
27   **You could flick your Bic under that baby all day and**
28   **never light it up.**
29   **CHIEF: That's right, Barlow. Get the picture? We gotta**
30   **find a way to burn those weapons.**
31   **WELFORD: Gee, Chief, why don't we make the tanks out**
32   **of wood?**
33   **BARLOW: Wood! Boy, that's really silly. Wood'll never**
34   **work. You can't make tanks and trucks out of two by**

1   **fours...could you, Chief?**

2   **CHIEF: I don't know. What do you mean, Welford?**

3   **WELFORD: Well, in Norway they're making compressed**

4   **wood now that's as strong as metal, and we could**

5   **make them out of that.**

6   **CHIEF: Great idea, Welford. Then the weapons would**

7   **burn.**

8   **WELFORD: Yeah.**

9   **CHIEF: Come on, let's get over to prophecy and see about**

10   **setting this thing up.** *(FRONT DESK ANGEL and*

11   *WELFORD leave.)*

12   **BARLOW: Hey, you guys, wait up.** *(BARLOW is left alone on*

13   *the stage — he notices the phone.)* **Oh...hey, wait a**

14   **minute! What an opportunity!** *(He goes over to the*

15   *phone, picks it up and dials. He tries to imitate FRONT*

16   *DESK ANGEL.)* **Hello, personnel? This is the Front**

17   **Desk Angel. I'd like to put in for a promotion for an**

18   **Angel Barlow. Barlow, that's B-A-R-L-O-W.**

19   **LORD:** *(Off-stage voice)* **Barlow!**

20   **BARLOW:** *(Hanging up the phone)* **Just kidding, Lord, just**

21   **kidding.** *(Runs off.)*

22

23

24

25

26

27

28

29

30

31

32

33

34

Demons' Dilemma

DEMONS' DILEMMA

By Dave Toole

1 **CAST:** Demon #1, Demon #2, Demon #3 (Baylic), Off-stage
2   Voice.
3 **SETTING:** Around the time clock.
4 **PROPS:** Cut out of cardboard a pitchfork that has been cut in
5   half and is held together with wire. That goes around
6   DEMON #3's waist (like Steve Martin's arrow through the
7   head).
8 **COSTUMES:** Lab coats with black gloves, or the DEMONS
9   may wear all-black or all-red clothing.
10
11 **NARRATOR: For we wrestle not against flesh and blood,**
12   **but against principalities, against powers, against the**
13   **rulers of the darkness of this world, against spiritual**
14   **wickedness in high places.** (Eph. 6:12) **For the**
15   **weapons of our warfare are not carnal, but mighty**
16   **through God.** (2 Cor. 10:4)
17   *(Enter DEMONS #1 and #3 from opposite sides.)*
18 **DEMON #1: Morning, hot stuff. How's business?**
19 **DEMON #3: Great, great. How're things with you?**
20 **DEMON #1: Just fine. Whatcha got for lunch?**
21 **DEMON #3: Deviled ham. How about you?**
22 **DEMON #1: Deviled eggs. You see the schedule?**
23 **DEMON #3: Yeah, I saw it. Who did you get?**
24 **DEMON #1: Norman Weltz.**
25 **DEMON #3: Norman Weltz! That's like a day off! Whatcha**
26   **gonna do?**
27 **DEMON #1: I'll probably knock his coffee in his lap or nick**
28   **him shaving. Something to put him in the mood to**

1   **fight with his wife. I can usually get a good grip on**

2   **him like that. Hee-hee! Maybe I'll give him another**

3   **flat on the freeway! Ha-ha!**

4   **DEMON #3: Sounds like you've got a great day ahead. I**

5   **wish we could trade.**

6   **DEMON #1: Why? Who did you get?**

7   **DEMON #3: Joe Parker.**

8   **DEMON #1: *The* Joe Parker? Oh, boy! I had him one day**

9   **last week. He spent the whole day talking about Jesus!**

10   *(They shiver.)*

11 **DEMON #3: He's even worse now! He's starting his own**

12   **home Bible study.**

13 **DEMON #1: You're kidding! How much damage has that**

14   **done?**

15 **DEMON #3: Plenty! He's been talking with his boss, and**

16   **now his boss just accepted Jesus.** *(They shiver.)* **As you**

17   **can imagine, that smashed the hold we had on him**

18   **with alcohol! Not only that, but now his boss is**

19   **sharing with his daughter, and she's thinking about**

20   **giving up dope! Think you can give me a hand?**

21 **DEMON #1: No way. One day with him was enough.**

22   **Besides, I've got a special project I'm working on for**

23   **next week.**

24 **DEMON #3: Maybe I can get our supervisor to assign**

25   **another demon to help out.**

26 **DEMON #1: Speak of the devil, here he is now.** *(Enter*

27   *DEMON #2.)*

28 **DEMON #2: Baylic, Beelzebub wants to see you in his**

29   **office – right away!**

30 **DEMON #3: Uh-oh!** *(BAYLIC exits.)*

31 **DEMON #1:** *(Practicing seance voices)* **I'm your Uncle**

32   **Ralph...** *(Etc.)*

33 **DEMON #2: What are you doing?**

34 **DEMON #1: Oh, I got that seance scheduled next week.**

1   Just workin' on some voices. How's this? "Hello,
2   Jimmy, I'm your Uncle Ralph. Things are just *great*
3   over here."
4   **DEMON #2:** Try a little lower.
5   **DEMON #1:** "Hello, Jimmy. I'm your Uncle Ralph."
6   **DEMON #2:** Yeah, that's pretty close.
7   **DEMON #1:** What if he says I don't sound like him?
8   **DEMON #2:** Tell him you have a cold.
9   **DEMON #1:** What if he starts asking a lot of questions?
10 **DEMON #2:** Ah, just tell him you gotta go somewhere.
11   Anything!
12 **DEMON #1:** OK, I'll keep working on it.
13 **DEMON #2:** By the way, I never got your report on Betty
14   Swetzer. What happened?
15 **DEMON #1:** I got her dating some non-Christian guy. She
16   thinks she's gonna lead him to the Lord.
17 **DEMON #2:** What makes you so sure she won't?
18 **DEMON #1:** They never do! You taught me that! *(They*
19   *laugh.)* Yeah.
20 **DEMON #2:** Who's the guy?
21 **DEMON #1:** Lance Stocker.
22 **DEMON #2:** Oh, good! He's been doing business with us for
23   a long time.
24 **DEMON #1:** On top of that, I hid her Bible about two weeks
25   ago, and she hasn't even bothered to look for it.
26 **DEMON #2:** Great! Can't do any damage without a sword.
27   *(BAYLIC howls in pain Off-stage. Enter DEMON #3 with a*
28   *pitchfork stuck in him.)*
29 **DEMON #2:** What happened to you?
30 **DEMON #3:** I was supposed to watch Rod Bentley.
31 **DEMON #2:** Uh-oh. I told you to keep him away from
32   Wickenshield! How's Beelzebub?
33 **DEMON #3:** He's still pretty sore. *(Indicates pitchfork.)* But
34   not as sore as I am! He put me on U.F.O. duty.

1   **DEMON #1:** U.F.O. duty?

2   **DEMON #3:** Yeah. I've got to paint myself with light and fly

3   around the world until Armageddon.

4   **DEMON #2:** Well, look on the bright side. That won't be too

5   long now.

6   **DEMON #3:** Yeah, I guess so.

7   **DEMON #1:** Things sure are getting tough lately.

8   **DEMON #3:** I'll say!

9   **DEMON #1:** You know, it seems like you work your tail off

10   night and day just to drag someone down. And how

11   does he reward you? He goes and get saved!

12   **DEMON #3:** And we get shafted! *(Indicates pitchfork again.)*

13   **DEMON #1:** I sure do miss the good old days when you

14   could find an astrologer or palm reader and take it

15   easy.

16   **DEMON #2:** Yeah. Remember that old gypsy we used to

17   have? Now those were some high times!

18   **DEMON #1:** He was fun, wasn't he? I remember how

19   excited he used to get when we would help him with

20   his spells. I sure wish we could get us a transfer to

21   Africa or China or South America and find a witch

22   doctor or somebody we could all move into.

23   **DEMON #2:** Don't be foolish. There's plenty of things to do

24   here. Drugs, booze, sex, celebrities.

25   **DEMON #3:** I wouldn't count on celebrities. No more!

26   **DEMON #1:** I don't think we can count on anything

27   anymore! It's getting tougher and tougher every day.

28   The Holy Spirit is running wild! There's Christians

29   getting into everything. I sure hope this doesn't lead

30   to a revival. That would burn me up!

31   **DEMON #3:** Me, too.

32   **DEMON #2:** *(Disappointed)* Hey, you guys, I'm surprised at

33   you. How do you expect to do any damage with an atti-

34   tude like that? May I remind you what our fearless

1 leader once said, "Behold, I stand at the door and
2 pick the lock." Don't try to kick the door in – just pick
3 the lock! Why try to freeze someone's faith when
4 lukewarm is good enough to do them in?
5 **DEMON #3:** Yeah, but I got *Joe Parker!*
6 **DEMON #2:** Sure, Christians like Joe Parker are tough, and
7 they can do a lot of damage too, but you can't just stop
8 him cold! You've got to turn them around – *slowly.*
9 Little by little. You don't destroy them, you just
10 compromise them. Just get their eyes off Jesus *(All*
11 *shiver)* with anything!
12 **DEMON #1:** Remember where the Apostle Peter was when
13 we got him to deny... *(He catches himself)* you know
14 who. He was following from afar! Trick them into
15 sliding away, even a little, and you've got them! Ha-ha!
16 **DEMON #3:** Yeah, that makes sense. After all, that's why
17 they're called backsliders!
18 **OFF-STAGE VOICE:** Attention! Attention! All demonic
19 personnel! Altar call now in progress. All available
20 demons report to sector 042.
21 **DEMON #2:** Come on. Let's go. Maybe after work we can get
22 together for some *angel food cake. (All exit.)*
23
24
25
26
27
28
29
30
31
32
33
34

The Day After Tomorrow Show

THE DAY AFTER TOMORROW SHOW

By Dan Rupple

1   ***CAST:*** Tom, Noah, Governor Bill Watkins.

2   ***SETTING:*** A TV talk show. Three chairs are at Center Stage.

3   ***PROPS:*** Umbrella for NOAH.

4   ***COSTUMES:*** TOM and BILL wear suits. NOAH wears a sailor

5   uniform, captain's hat and long, white beard.

6   ***SOUND EFFECTS:*** Thunder and rain.

7

8   *(TOM is On-stage. Optional intro music.)*

9   **TOM: Hi, everybody. Welcome to The Day After Tomorrow**

10   **Show. I'm Tom Snooter, and tonight we have an inter-**

11   **esting show. I'm sure you won't want to miss it. My**

12   **guest this evening has been producing a lot of contro-**

13   **versy around town. I'm sure you've read about him in**

14   **the papers. He's basically a quiet, simple man. But**

15   **lately he's been receiving a lot of notoriety. Captain...**

16   **or Mister...well, to be honest, I'm not really sure at**

17   **this point...Noah.** *(NOAH enters.)* **Welcome to the show.**

18   **NOAH: Thank you, Tom.** *(TOM and NOAH sit.)*

19   **TOM: To begin, Noah, as you realize, all the people in town**

20   **have been talking about this boat-shaped thing you're**

21   **building downtown on the corner of Washington and**

22   **Fig. Can you tell us what it is you're building there? A**

23   **fancy casino? A massage parlor? What?**

24   **NOAH: No, Tom. I'm just building a boat – an ark, if you**

25   **prefer.**

26   **TOM: An ark, huh? As I remember, it's quite large, isn't it?**

27   **NOAH: Yes, Tom. It's four hundred and fifty feet long and**

28   **forty-five feet high.**

1   **TOM: Wow, that's no Tinker Toy.** *(Laughs.)*

2   **NOAH: No, it's not, Tom. And I might add, I believe it's the**

3   **finest aquatic vessel ever built. Solid gopher wood.**

4   **TOM: It is a beaut. How long have you been working on it?**

5   **NOAH: Tom, I've been working on it for one hundred**

6   **twenty years now and I'm just days away from**

7   **completion.**

8   **TOM: Now rumor has it that you're putting animals on**

9   **this thing. What's the scoop?**

10   **NOAH: Well, Tom, I'm loading the ark with a male and**

11   **female of every species of bird, reptile, and animal.**

12   **TOM: I see. Must be kind of hard to tell in some cases,**

13   **though...birds and fish and lizards and things.**

14   *(Laughs.)*

15   **NOAH: Well, as the Lord leads.**

16   **TOM: Ah! Now, Noah, let's get to the real question here, a**

17   **question that cuts right to the bone. Why are you**

18   **doing all of this?**

19   **NOAH: Well, Tom, if I may be serious for a moment. Today**

20   **we have so much criminal activity, sexual perversion**

21   **and just basic unrighteous living. I mean, man is**

22   **totally out of God's will. His whole lifestyle is an**

23   **abomination in the sight of God. Well, God has been**

24   **as patient and long-suffering as possible, and now**

25   **he's going to bring his wrath upon the whole world**

26   **for man's evil rebellion against his divine plan.**

27   **TOM: Now wait a minute. That's quite a statement. How's**

28   **he gonna do this, anyway?**

29   **NOAH: He's going to flood the entire earth by making it**

30   **rain for forty days and forty nights.**

31   **TOM: Ho-ho. Wait a minute. I think we're playing the**

32   **fool's game, and I'm the fool.**

33   **NOAH: Yes, you are, Tom. You see, only my family and I**

34   **will be saved.**

1   TOM: Well, that's not fair! Now just hold on a minute. If
2   what you say is true and this God of yours is really
3   angry, why didn't he tell someone? He could've taken
4   an ad out in the *Free Press* or come on the show. I
5   would've gladly had him on the show.
6   NOAH: God *has* been warning us about the end for quite a
7   while, but no one's been listening. You've all been
8   too busy caring about yourselves. No one's slowing
9   down long enough to seek God and his plan for us.
10   People think they can take care of themselves, but
11   they can't.
12 TOM: Well, let's not get into that again. That's all water
13   under the bridge anyway. Ha-ha. *(Laughs.)* I'd like to
14   pause here for a special surprise. Noah, you don't
15   know anything about this, but we do have a special
16   guest this evening, and I'd like to bring him out now.
17   I'm sure everyone is going to recognize him. Ladies
18   and gentlemen, our beloved governor, Mr. William
19   Watkins. Bill? *(Enter BILL.)*
20 BILL: Thank you, Tom.
21 TOM: Now, Governor, to start right off, why don't you lay it
22   right on the line? Just what's your beef with Noah?
23 BILL: Well, Tom, may I first say it's always a pleasure to be
24   on your show. It's always nice to face the nation, as
25   your show does so well. My beef, as you say, Tom, is
26   this Noah here and this big boat he's building.
27 TOM: The one downtown we've been talking about?
28 BILL: That's right, Tom. Smack-dab in the middle of
29   Bernie's Liquor and the Red Light Lounge. Quite an
30   eyesore.
31 TOM: Now, Governor, I understand this is causing quite a
32   problem with the local businesses.
33 BILL: Yes, that's right, Tom. You know with our tremen-
34   dous population increase that parking is a major

1   problem in the downtown area, and we figure that
2   that big tugboat of his is taking up approximately
3   three hundred spaces. And figuring three people per
4   vehicle, that's about nine hundred voting citizens
5   who are affected.
6   TOM: Well, Governor, I do have to mention that Noah *does*
7   have valid parking permits for all three hundred
8   parking spaces.
9   BILL: Tom, that's just one of the problems. The other day
10 the women's club wanted to put up another idol in
11 the park, but Sweeney's Lumber Yard was plumb out
12 of gopher wood. And what about progress? That
13 thing's been there for over a century. I don't have to
14 remind you that those animals don't smell like no
15 flower shop, if you get my drift. *(Laughs.)*
16 TOM: That's right, Governor.
17 BILL: You know, Tom, as a public official, I see all kinds,
18 but this man is your basic thorn in the flesh. Thinks
19 he's holier than Swiss cheese! I don't know what this
20 world's coming to.
21 NOAH: I do.
22 TOM: Oh, yes, ah, Noah was telling us earlier that this is all
23 a plan of God's.
24 BILL: Oh, yeah? Which god?
25 NOAH: The only true God, Governor.
26 BILL: You mean the "rain" god. Did he tell you the stuff
27 about the rain?
28 TOM: Cute story.
29 BILL: Busted my britches first time I heard it. I mean,
30 come on, it hasn't rained here as long as I can
31 remember.
32 NOAH: It will now.
33 BILL: How do you know all of this?
34 NOAH: God speaks to me.

1   **BILL: Now I've heard everything. What? Ya got a CB there**
2   **in the boat or something?**
3   **NOAH: No, God just talks to me.**
4   **BILL: Come on, I've been around gods all of my life. I've**
5   **got three idols in the kitchen alone, and I've never**
6   **heard a peep out of 'em!**
7   **NOAH: That's because they're just hunks of wood. I'm**
8   **talking about the *living* God.**
9   **BILL: Tom, it's quite obvious – this Noah guy is a radical**
10   **madman. He's just trying to bring people down – you**
11   **know, put them on a bummer.**
12   **TOM: Listen, Noah, is there a good side to this story? Is**
13   **there any hope for humankind? I mean, how can we**
14   **get on this boat of yours? Buy a ticket or what?**
15   **NOAH: No, Tom, you can't buy your way onto the boat. You**
16   **must call upon the Lord, humble yourself and turn**
17   **from your wicked ways. Then the Lord will forgive**
18   **you, and you will be saved.**
19   **TOM: And if we don't, we're all pretty much in the same**
20   **boat, or out of it, as the case may be?**
21   **NOAH: Yes, Tom, you might say you're up the old prover-**
22   **bial creek without a paddle.**
23   **TOM: Ah, listen, ladies and gentlemen, we only have a few**
24   **moments here. I'd like to take them to thank our**
25   **guests for this evening. Noah, good luck with this ark**
26   **you're building and this God of yours. I hope things**
27   **work, really, but I want to encourage you to look into**
28   **making that thing into a massage parlor or a casino.**
29   **You could make yourself a pretty penny and do the**
30   **community a service. And Governor, good luck in the**
31   **upcoming election. Guess I'll just see you in the pool.**
32   *(Laughs.)*
33   **BILL: Yeah, float by the house sometime.** *(Laughs.)*
34   **TOM: Ladies and gentlemen, this is Tom Snooter saying**

1   **happy day after tomorrow. Bye-bye.** *(Optional music.*
2   *Thunder and rain sounds. NOAH puts up umbrella and*
3   *leaves. TOM and BILL panic and run off.)*
4
5
6
7
8
9
10
11
12
13
14
15
16
17
18
19
20
21
22
23
24
25
26
27
28
29
30
31
32
33
34

THE SAVING GAME

By Dan Rupple and Dave Toole

1   **CAST:** Narrator (On-stage or off); Jim — *The Saving Game*
2   host; Buck — contestant; Savior #1; Savior #2 — Jesus
3   Christ; Savior #3.

4   **SETTING:** A game show in the style of *The Dating Game*. A
5   chair for BUCK should be on one side of a partition, with
6   three chairs for the SAVIORS on the other side.

7   **PROPS:** Large cards with BUCK's questions printed on them.

8   **COSTUMES:** Suits for JIM and BUCK.

9

10   *(Optional music)*

11   **NARRATOR:** *(Over music)* **It's time for *The Saving Game*.**
12   **The game where each contestant has the opportunity**
13   **of choosing his very own savior. And now, here's your**
14   ***Saving Game* host, Jim Kennedy.** *(Music fade out.*
15   *Optional applause. Enter JIM.)*

16   **JIM: Thank you, and good evening. Welcome to *The Saving***
17   ***Game*. As you know, each week our contestant gets to**
18   **question three saviors cleverly hidden behind our**
19   ***Saving Game* partition. Through their answers, the**
20   **contestant hopes to make the right decision in**
21   **choosing the one to be his very own savior. And now**
22   **it's time to meet our contestant.** *(Optional music)*

23   **NARRATOR:** *(Over music)* **Jim, tonight's *Saving Game***
24   **contestant is a Winnebago salesman from Chula Vista,**
25   **California.** *(Enter BUCK.)* **His hobbies include minia-**
26   **ture golf, underwater cooking, and in his spare time,**
27   **he makes papier-mâché jewelry. Audience, please**
28   **welcome Buck Wheezer!** *(Music fade out. Applause)*

The Saving Game

1   JIM: Welcome to the show, Buck.

2   BUCK: Thank you, Jim. It's good to be here.

3   JIM: You're sure looking sharp. That a new suit?

4   BUCK: Yeah, I got it out of the Spiegel catalog. Spiffy, eh?

5   JIM: It is a beaut! OK, you know how the game is played,

6   don't you?

7   BUCK: Sure do! Me and the missus watch you all the time.

8   You know, it's amazing what a little makeup will do.

9   You look a lot younger in black and white.

10   JIM: Ah, thanks. Let's begin our game.

11   BUCK: Got my questions right here. *(Holds up his question*

12   cards.)*

13   JIM: Great! Have a seat, and I'll ask our three saviors to say

14   hello to Buck Wheezer...Savior #1?

15   SAVIOR #1: *(Gruffly)* Hi, Wheezer.

16   JIM: Savior #2?

17   SAVIOR #2: Hello, Buck.

18   JIM: And Savior #3?

19   SAVIOR #3: Oh, hi, Buck, ol' buddy. How are ya?

20   BUCK: Fine, fine. Little nervous.

21   JIM: OK, Buck, go ahead and start your questioning.

22   BUCK: All righty. Savior #3, if I was out in the ocean and I

23   started sinking, what would you do to save me?

24   SAVIOR #3: Gee, I don't know. I get seasick just thinking

25   about it. I'm sure someone would be there to help

26   you. I wouldn't worry about it.

27   BUCK: Mmmm. Savior #2, what would you do if I started

28   sinking?

29   SAVIOR #2: If you have faith in me, you will not sink.

30   BUCK: What if I don't have much faith and I sink anyway?

31   SAVIOR #2: Oh, ye of little faith. Then I will stretch forth

32   my hand and catch you.

33   BUCK: Wow! You must have long arms!

34   JIM: Your next question, Buck?

1 **BUCK: OK.** *(Aside to JIM)* **I got kind of a trick question here.**
2   **Savior #1, knock, knock.**
3 **SAVIOR #1: Who's there?**
4 **BUCK: Ha-ha. Savior #3, knock, knock.**
5 **SAVIOR #3: Who is it?**
6 **JIM: Buck, why are you asking that question?**
7 **BUCK:** *(Aside to JIM)* **If any of these saviors is for real, he'll**
8   **know who's knocking! Savior #2, knock, knock.**
9 **SAVIOR #2: What is it, Buck?** *(BUCK smiles and the audience*
10   *applauds.)*
11 **BUCK: See?**
12 **JIM: Wahoo, that was a question, Buck. Did you think of**
13   **that yourself?**
14 **BUCK: Well, yeah, I...**
15 **SAVIOR #2:** *(Chiding)* **Buck...**
16 **BUCK: What I mean to say is, my wife thought of it.**
17 **JIM: Mrs. Wheezer?**
18 **BUCK: Her friends call her Wilma.**
19 **JIM: Oh, is she here tonight?**
20 **BUCK: No, Jim, she couldn't make it tonight. Had a**
21   **meeting of the International Button Collectors, you**
22   **know. She's sergeant at arms.**
23 **JIM: I see. Ah, shall we move on?**
24 **BUCK: All right, Savior #3. Why do I need a Savior? To keep**
25   **me out of hell or what?**
26 **SAVIOR #3: Oh, I don't know. Maybe you don't. Besides,**
27   **there really ain't a hell anyway. People just made that**
28   **up to keep you in line. You seem to be a nice guy. I**
29   **guess only real criminals need a savior.**
30 **BUCK: Yeah, I guess you've got a point there, thanks.**
31   **Savior #2?**
32 **SAVIOR #2: Because "all have sinned and come short of**
33   **the glory of God."** (Rom. 3:23) **All, like sheep, have**
34   **gone astray.** (Isa. 53:6, author's paraphrase)

1   BUCK: Mmmm.
2   JIM: OK, Buck, time's runnin' out. This is your last ques-
3   tion before the big decision.
4   BUCK: Oh, wow! My last question. Let's see...OK! Savior #3,
5   what do you like best with meat – stuffing or potatoes?
6   JIM: Buck, this is your last question. Don't you have some-
7   thing a little more important to ask?
8   BUCK: Oh...all right, here's one. Savior #2, different ques-
9   tion. What must I do to be saved?
10   SAVIOR #3: Potatoes!
11   BUCK: Huh? Oh, well, Savior #1, what must I do to be
12   saved?
13   SAVIOR #1: You gotta earn it doing religious things. First
14   off, I want you never to sleep past five-thirty, eat only
15   vegetables and Twinkies, cut your hair and only wear
16   blue. If you're diligent, you *might* make it.
17   BUCK: Well, I don't have much blue on, but I do have
18   Twinkies, and I put in a lot of time at the Save the
19   Concrete Foundation. Savior #2, what must I do to be
20   saved?
21   SAVIOR #2: If you will confess me with your mouth
22   and believe in your heart that God has raised me
23   from the dead, you shall be saved. (Rom. 10:9, author's
24   paraphrase)
25   BUCK: That's it? Don't I have to do anything?
26   SAVIOR #2: No. By grace you are saved, not by works, lest
27   any man should boast. (Eph. 2:8, 9, author's paraphrase)
28   JIM: There you have it, Buck. Quite a choice. But before we
29   hear your decision, we're going to break for a short
30   message, and then it's time for you to choose your
31   very own savior. We'll be right back. *(Optional music)*
32   NARRATOR; *(Over music)* Say, Mom, kids thirsty after a
33   hard day at play? They want something cold and
34   quick, but you know that commercial soda isn't good

1   **for a growing child. Well, why not try new "Living**
2   **Water"? That's right, Living Water in the bottomless**
3   **cans. You've tried other drinks, but soon you're**
4   **spittin' cotton. But when you drink Living Water,**
5   **you'll never thirst again! What? Never thirst again?**
6   **No! Never thirst again! So get your family some today.**
7   **Living Water. It'll quench the thirst, but it won't**
8   **quench the spirit.** *(Music fade out)*
9   **JIM: OK, Buck, this is it. You've heard the answers, and**
10   **now it's up to you. Will it be savior #1, Savior #2, or**
11   **savior #3?**
12   **BUCK: Gee, it gets kind of confusing. They all sound right,**
13   **but I'm gonna go with Savior #2.** *(Optional applause;)*
14   **JIM: OK, Savior #2 it is! Any particular reason?**
15   **BUCK: His words just seem to make sense. Besides, I think**
16   **he likes me.**
17   **JIM: Well, Buck, I'll bet you'd like to meet your Savior in**
18   **person now, wouldn't you?**
19   **BUCK: I sure would!**
20   **JIM: You can't actually see him physically right this**
21   **moment. You see, he's gone to prepare a place for you,**
22   **but he's coming back soon, and then you will be**
23   **present with the Lord.**
24   **BUCK: That's neat, but what about now? I need something**
25   **for now. I've got lots of problems and questions.**
26   **JIM: Don't worry, Buck. He's left you a Comforter.**
27   **BUCK: You mean one of those bedspread things?**
28   **JIM: No, no, Buck, not that kind. I mean the Holy Spirit.**
29   **He will abide with you forever, and he will teach you**
30   **all things.**
31   **BUCK: All right, but what if I have problems? You know, I**
32   **make a lot of mistakes, I'm not very good on my own.**
33   **JIM: Don't worry, Buck. He said as many as receive him, to**
34   **them he gives power to become the sons of God.** (John

1   1:12, author's paraphrase)

2   **BUCK: I guess I don't have anything to worry about.**

3   **Thanks a lot.**

4   **JIM: Don't thank me.**

5   **BUCK: Wait till I tell Wilma!** *(Exits. Optional music and*

6   *applause)*

7   **JIM: OK, Buck. Well, that's our show for tonight. And**

8   **remember, you don't have to be on the show to choose**

9   **your Savior. You can play the home version of *The***

10   **Saving Game* right in the privacy of your own heart.**

11   **But remember, if you're playing to win, you must**

12   **choose the winner! Thank you, and see you next week**

13   **on *The Saving Game*.** *(Fade out)*

14

15

16

17

18

19

20

21

22

23

24

25

26

27

28

29

30

31

32

33

34

Prodigal Joe

PRODIGAL JOE

By Dan Rupple

1   ***CAST:*** Little Joe-Joe, Papa, Horse, Old Man, Phineas Clamby.

2   ***SETTING:*** The Old West.

3   ***PROPS:*** Three stick ponies for HORSE, LITTLE JOE-JOE and

4   PAPA. A "customized" stick pony for LITTLE JOE-JOE. It

5   should be painted a bright color and be embellished with

6   details such as bike handlebars, bells, fuzzy dice and a

7   mirror. Also needed is money for PAPA, a map with a

8   large hole burned into the center, and a can of Alpo.

9   ***COSTUMES:*** "Old West" attire for everyone: cowboy hats,

10   boots, jeans, vests, Western shirts, etc. PHINEAS

11   CLAMBY's clothing may be all black.

12

13   *(LITTLE JOE-JOE enters.)*

14   **LITTLE JOE-JOE: Howdy. I'd like to tell you all a story that**

15   **happened once upon a time. How do I know it really**

16   **happened? Because it happened to me. You see, I live**

17   **out here in the West with my wise and rich father and**

18   **my fat but lovable brother. We have a huge ranch and**

19   **plenty of farm hands. I had everything I could ever**

20   **want, but there comes a time in a man's life when he**

21   **has to make a choice as to which trail he's gonna**

22   **follow. Well, this story is about when I made that**

23   **choice. Oh, I didn't introduce myself. My name's**

24   **Little Joe-Joe, and this here's the Ponderosa.** *(Exit*

25   *LITTLE JOE-JOE. Optional music. PAPA, HORSE, and*

26   *LITTLE JOE-JOE ride out on stick ponies, wave and ride*

27   *off. PAPA enters.)*

28   **PAPA: Horse! Little Joe-Joe! Time for supper. Get in here**

1   before it gets cold. *(Enter HORSE.)*

2 HORSE: Hot dog! Supper time! You know, Papa, other
3   than lunch and breakfast, this is my favorite time of
4   the day. What're we having?

5 PAPA: Pork and beans.

6 HORSE: Pork and beans? Pork and beans? Gee, Papa, we
7   had pork and beans last night. Doesn't Hop Sting
8   know how to cook anything else? You know, I was out
9   in the pasture today and saw that big fat heifer. It
10   would be great with a little gravy, maybe a side of
11   potatoes. How about it, Papa?

12 PAPA: Well, Horse, I'm saving that heifer for a special
13   occasion.

14 HORSE: Today is a special occasion. My horse made it
15   halfway to the field today.

16 LITTLE JOE-JOE: Papa, I gotta talk with you.

17 PAPA: What about, Little Joe-Joe?

18 LITTLE JOE-JOE: Papa, there comes a time in a man's life
19   when he has to make a choice as to which trail he's
20   gonna follow.

21 PAPA: I know, son. I heard you tell the audience earlier.

22 LITTLE JOE-JOE: Well, I'm tired of this old ranch. I want
23   to be my own boss. I want thrills, excitement
24   and...and...well, a chance to be funky and free. So I
25   want you to give me my part of the Ponderosa, and
26   I'm heading for the bright lights and big city.

27 PAPA: Won't you settle for a little house on the prairie?

28 LITTLE JOE-JOE: What?

29 PAPA: Doesn't matter. Well, son, if that's the way you want
30   it. I wish you'd stay here with me, but I'm not gonna
31   stop you. I've always let you make your own decisions.
32   So, here you are. *(Gives him money.)* Good luck, son.

33 LITTLE JOE-JOE: Don't worry about me, Papa. I've got it all
34   planned out. *(PAPA and LITTLE JOE-JOE start to exit.)*

1   **HORSE: Little Joe-Joe?**

2   **LITTLE JOE-JOE: Yeah?**

3   **HORSE: Can I have your pork and beans?** *(All exit. Optional*

4   *music. Enter LITTLE JOE-JOE on a stick pony.)*

5   **LITTLE JOE-JOE: I packed up my belongings, got my horse**

6   **and headed out. I was finally on my own. No more**

7   **bothering with Papa's advice. I was headed for the big**

8   **city. The land of fun, glamour and disco saloons. But**

9   **on the way there, I ran into an old man. Now I didn't**

10   **know it then, but he would teach me a lesson that**

11   **would change my whole life.** *(Enter OLD MAN.)* **Hi,**

12   **Gramps.**

13   **OLD MAN: Hi, Sonny. You're new in these parts, aren't cha?**

14   **LITTLE JOE-JOE: Yeah. I just left my father's ranch. I'm**

15   **headed for the big city.**

16   **OLD MAN: What fer?**

17   **LITTLE JOE-JOE: I want thrills, excitement and...and a**

18   **chance...**

19   **LITTLE JOE-JOE and OLD MAN:** *(In unison)* **To be funky**

20   **and free.**

21   **LITTLE JOE-JOE: Yeah. How'd you know?**

22   **OLD MAN: I see hundreds like you every week. Let me give**

23   **you a little advice. Go on back to your Papa's. It's the**

24   **only place you'll ever really be happy.**

25   **LITTLE JOE-JOE: Are you kiddin'? I'm happy now. I'm**

26   **young, healthy, rich and extremely good-looking.**

27   **OLD MAN: Well, you may not be no teenage werewolf, but**

28   **kids like you are a dime a dozen.** *(Optional villain*

29   *music. Enter PHINEAS)*

30   **LITTLE JOE-JOE: Who's that?**

31   **OLD MAN: That's Phineas Clamby. Stay away from him.**

32   **LITTLE JOE-JOE: Why?**

33   **OLD MAN: He's always looking for someone to con. He'll**

34   **fill your head with lies, lead you down a dead-end**

1   road and laugh at you when you crash into the wall.

2   **LITTLE JOE-JOE:** He looks OK to me.

3   **OLD MAN:** I'm warning you. *(Exit OLD MAN.)*

4   **LITTLE JOE-JOE:** Hi.

5   **PHINEAS CLAMBY:** Hello there! Headed for the big city, eh?

6   **LITTLE JOE-JOE:** I sure am.

7   **PHINEAS CLAMBY:** Bet you're looking for thrills, excite-

8   ment and...

9   **LITTLE JOE-JOE:** A chance to be funky and free.

10 **PHINEAS CLAMBY:** Of course you are, and why shouldn't

11   you? After all, you're young, healthy, rich and

12   extremely good-looking.

13 **LITTLE JOE-JOE:** Right on.

14 **PHINEAS CLAMBY:** Well, I'm just the man you want to talk

15   to. I can give you everything you'll ever need for true

16   happiness. First off, I bet you'd like to have a girl, eh?

17 **LITTLE JOE-JOE:** You betcha.

18 **PHINEAS CLAMBY:** Yes, and have I got a girl for you! Her

19   name's Mona. She's beautiful.

20 **LITTLE JOE-JOE:** Really? What's she like?

21 **PHINEAS CLAMBY:** Blonde hair, blue eyes, lips like roses...

22 **LITTLE JOE-JOE:** She intelligent? Good personality?

23 **PHINEAS CLAMBY:** Like I said, blonde hair, blue eyes, lips

24   like roses.

25 **LITTLE JOE-JOE:** Sounds great! How much?

26 **PHINEAS CLAMBY:** Two hundred dollars. But for an extra

27   twenty-five, I'll throw in a case of Phineas Clamby's

28   Brew 42. The finest liquor this side of the Pecos. Stirs

29   the passions.

30 **LITTLE JOE-JOE:** It's a deal! Thanks a lot!

31 **PHINEAS CLAMBY:** Not so fast. If you're gonna take her on

32   a date, you're gonna need some transportation.

33 **LITTLE JOE-JOE:** Well, I got my horse here. *(Indicates stick*

34   *pony.)*

1   **PHINEAS CLAMBY:** You call that creature a horse? My
2   friend, if you're gonna date a woman with class like
3   Mona, you've got to impress her.
4   **LITTLE JOE-JOE:** You're right. What do I do?
5   **PHINEAS CLAMBY:** Well, I just happen to have a brand-
6   new luxury horse. Automatic transmission, mag
7   hooves, racing stripes and an in-saddle tape deck.
8   **LITTLE JOE-JOE:** How much?
9   **PHINEAS CLAMBY:** Seven hundred dollars. But for an
10   extra fifty, I'll include an angora bridle and a set of
11   fuzzy dice to hang around the mirror.
12   **LITTLE JOE-JOE:** Wow, what a deal! I'll take it!
13   **PHINEAS CLAMBY:** Good man. Oh, there's one more thing.
14   **LITTLE JOE-JOE:** What?
15   **PHINEAS CLAMBY:** Where are you gonna take her?
16   **LITTLE JOE-JOE:** Oh, yeah. How about Miss Kitty's Saloon?
17   **PHINEAS CLAMBY:** No, no, that will *never* do. Everyone
18   goes there. Besides, that's another show.
19   **LITTLE JOE-JOE:** Got any ideas?
20   **PHINEAS CLAMBY:** I just happen to have a beautiful bach-
21   elor ranch for only two thousand dollars with
22   wall-to-wall carpet, a fireplace and it's freeway close.
23   **LITTLE JOE-JOE:** That sounds great! *(Thinks.)* Two thou-
24   sand dollars. That's everything my papa gave me. I'd
25   be broke.
26   **PHINEAS CLAMBY:** Who needs that stuff your *father* gave
27   you when you've got all the things *I've* given you?
28   **LITTLE JOE-JOE:** *(Pause)* **OK, it's a deal.** *(Gives him the money.)*
29   **PHINEAS CLAMBY:** You know, you remind me very much
30   of another young man a few years back. He gave me
31   everything he had for a little piece of fruit.
32   **LITTLE JOE-JOE:** Well, I did have a brother who left the
33   ranch some years back.
34   **PHINEAS CLAMBY:** What was his name?

1   **LITTLE JOE-JOE:** Adam.

2   **PHINEAS CLAMBY:** *(Aside)* **Well, that's a long way to stretch**

3   **for a joke, but it makes a point.**

4   **LITTLE JOE-JOE:** **I was all set. I had everything I needed to**

5   **conquer the big city.** *(LITTLE JOE-JOE exits.)*

6   *(Optional disco music. Enter LITTLE JOE-JOE, disco-danc-*

7   *ing with a "customized" pony. Dances off as music ends.)*

8   *(Enter LITTLE JOE-JOE.)*

9   **LITTLE JOE-JOE: Everything that Phineas sold me was**

10   **fun for a while, but pretty soon it all started falling**

11   **apart, and I was left with nothing. I didn't know what**

12   **to do. Then I met up with that old man again.** *(Enter*

13   *OLD MAN.)*

14   **OLD MAN: What happened to you?**

15   **LITTLE JOE-JOE: I sure wish I had taken your advice.**

16   **OLD MAN: Hit the dead end, huh?**

17   **LITTLE JOE-JOE: Yep.**

18   **OLD MAN: Lost everything?**

19   **LITTLE JOE-JOE: Uh-huh. You were right about that**

20   **Phineas. He lied to me about everything. That horse**

21   **he sold me tripped over the fuzzy dice and broke his**

22   **leg, so I shot him and sold him to the glue factory.**

23   **OLD MAN: Well, at least you got some money for him.**

24   **LITTLE JOE-JOE: Yeah, but that just paid for the hospital**

25   **bills. That cheap booze he sold me gave me liver**

26   **poisoning. I was sick for a month.**

27   **OLD MAN: What about Mona?**

28   **LITTLE JOE-JOE: Well, you know, looks aren't everything.**

29   **She had about as much personality as Hop Sting. And**

30   **all she did was nag. Do this. Do that.**

31   **OLD MAN: What about the house?**

32   **LITTLE JOE-JOE: Indian raid! Burned to the ground.**

33   **OLD MAN: Too bad.**

34   **LITTLE JOE-JOE: No, that was kind of lucky. Mona ran off**

1 **with the chief. She always did like those Mohawk**
2 **haircuts.** *(Optional villain music)* **Wait a minute,**
3 **there's Phineas! I'm gonna get a refund. Phineas,**
4 **everything you sold me was a fake. I didn't get happi-**
5 **ness out of any of them. They were a bunch of**
6 **headaches.**
7 **PHINEAS CLAMBY: Of course they were!**
8 **LITTLE JOE-JOE: You mean you knew they were?**
9 **PHINEAS CLAMBY: Of course I knew! That's the way of**
10 **the world!** *(Aside)* **It's surprising how many people fall**
11 **for it, really.**
12 **LITTLE JOE-JOE: I want back what my father gave me.**
13 **PHINEAS CLAMBY: You came to the wrong man for that.**
14 **I've already invested all the cash you gave me.**
15 **LITTLE JOE-JOE: What am I gonna do? I'm broke. I'm**
16 **starving. I don't have anywhere to go.**
17 **PHINEAS CLAMBY: Well, you could work for me. I need**
18 **someone to sweep my stables.** *(Villainous laugh)* **I'll give**
19 **you one meal a day, and you can sleep with the pigs.**
20 **LITTLE JOE-JOE: All right. I guess I have no choice. OK,**
21 **what's for dinner? I'm starved.**
22 **PHINEAS CLAMBY: Here!** *(Hands him a can.)*
23 **LITTLE JOE-JOE: A can of Alpo?**
24 **PHINEAS CLAMBY: What'd you want? A frozen pizza?**
25 **LITTLE JOE-JOE: The Ponderosa animals eat better than**
26 **that.**
27 **PHINEAS CLAMBY: Take it or leave it.**
28 **LITTLE JOE-JOE: Forget it!** *(Gives back can.)* **I don't want**
29 **your crummy job. I'm going back to my Papa's.**
30 **PHINEAS CLAMBY: Don't be foolish. He'll never take you**
31 **back. He probably can't even stand the sight of you if**
32 **he remembers you at all.**
33 **LITTLE JOE-JOE: Well...I'll see.** *(PHINEAS exits in anger.)*
34 **OLD MAN: Let me tell you something, son. I know your**

1   **Papa really wants you to come home.**
2   **LITTLE JOE-JOE: Really? How do you know?**
3   **OLD MAN: Well, let's just say that your Papa and I, we have**
4   **the same spirit.**
5   **LITTLE JOE-JOE: Boy, if that's true, it'd sure be good news.**
6   **I'll tell you what I'm gonna do. I'm gonna head home**
7   **and ask his forgiveness and see if he'll let me be one**
8   **of the hired hands. I'd even do Horse's chores.**
9   **OLD MAN: What's Horse do?**
10 **LITTLE JOE-JOE: He's one of the sides of the barn.**
11 **OLD MAN: Oh.** *(OLD MAN shakes his head and exits.)*
12 **LITTLE JOE-JOE: Well, I turned my back on my Papa for**
13   **the big city and now the big city turned its back on**
14   **me, so I headed for home. I didn't think Papa would**
15   **let me come back, but I didn't have anywhere else to**
16   **go. I was at the end of the trail.** *(Exit LITTLE JOE-JOE.*
17   *Enter PAPA with can.)*
18 **PAPA: Alpo time!** *(To audience)* **Look at that old dog come**
19   **walkin'! You know, he's sixty-four. That's three thou-**
20   **sand years for you and me. But you know that old dog,**
21   **he'd come running, if he didn't miss Little Joe-Joe as**
22   **much as I miss Little Joe-Joe.** *(Enter LITTLE JOE-JOE.)*
23 **LITTLE JOE-JOE: Papa, Papa! I'm back.**
24 **PAPA: Little Joe-Joe! You've returned.** *(Optional happy*
25   *organ music. They run together to embrace, but knock*
26   *each other down — all in slow motion.)*
27 **LITTLE JOE-JOE:** *(Getting up)* **Papa, I really blew it. I'm not**
28   **even worthy to be called your son. But if you'll forgive**
29   **me, Papa, would you take me back as one of your**
30   **farm hands?**
31 **PAPA: You're my son. I want to give you rings for your**
32   **fingers, brand-new boots, a nice double-knit leisure**
33   **suit...Anything else you want?**
34 **LITTLE JOE-JOE: Well, I could fly the Galactica tonight.**

1   **PAPA: The what?**

2   **LITTLE JOE-JOE: Oh, never mind. I sure am hungry!**

3   **PAPA: Bring on that big heifer.** *(HORSE enters.)* **Not you,**

4   **Horse.** *(HORSE leaves.)* **Don't worry, I'll have Hop Sting**

5   **get it. You go wash up, Little Joe-Joe.** *(Exit LITTLE JOE-*

6   *JOE. HORSE enters.)*

7   **HORSE: Papa, what's happening? Hop Sting's in the**

8   **kitchen trying to wrestle that big heifer into the stove!**

9   **PAPA: Little Joe-Joe's returned!**

10   **HORSE: Is that all? Papa, that don't seem fair. Golly, Papa,**

11   **I've been here working with you day and night, and**

12   **all I got was pork and beans. Little Joe-Joe goes off**

13   **lolly-gagging around, and you give him the big heifer.**

14   **Is it cuz I'm fat?**

15   **PAPA: No, Horse. You're always with me, and the whole**

16   **Ponderosa's yours for the asking. But today Little Joe-**

17   **Joe's returned.**

18   **HORSE: That just don't seem fair, Papa. No, sir, he should**

19   **at least take over some of my chores at the barn. I'm**

20   **tired of all those birds nesting on my nose.**

21   **PAPA: No, Horse. I've forgiven him completely. Things will**

22   **be just as if he never left.**

23   **HORSE: Dag nab it. Well, I don't want to have nothin' to do**

24   **with him. I'm going to go find my horse and drag her**

25   **back to the barn, if I can find her.**

26   **PAPA: Why don't you use the Ponderosa map?**

27   **HORSE:** *(Takes out map with a huge hole in the center.)* **I**

28   **would, Papa, but someone burned a hole in it.** *(Both*

29   *exit. Optional music.)*

30

31

32

33

34

Editorial Reply

EDITORIAL REPLY

By Dave Toole

1   **CAST:** Dave, Daryl, Hooto Crunk, Announcer (On-stage or off).

2   **SETTING:** TV station. A podium is needed for HOOTO.

3   **PROPS:** Headphones for DARYL. Typed pages for HOOTO's

4   speech. Microphone for HOOTO.

5   **COSTUMES:** A suit and tie and glasses for HOOTO. Casual

6   clothes for DAVE and DARYL. A suit for the ANNOUNCER,

7   if On-stage.

8

9   *(DAVE and DARYL are On-stage doing producer/director*

10   *busy work.)*

11   **DAVE: Daryl, are we about ready to do this thing?**

12   **DARYL: We sure are.**

13   **DAVE: Great. Is Mr. Crunk around?**

14   **DARYL: Let's get him up here and get going.** *(DARYL exits.)*

15   **DAVE: Boy, it'd be great to get this done before...** *(Enter*

16   *DARYL with HOOTO, who is carrying his speech.)*

17   **DARYL: Right over here, Mr. Crunk. Here he is, Dave.**

18   **DAVE: Hello, Mr. Crunk.**

19   **HOOTO: Call me Hooto.**

20   **DAVE: Hooto, huh? That's an interesting name. Is it**

21   **Hungarian?**

22   **HOOTO: No, it's...**

23   **DAVE: Oh, well, great. Ah, let me give you a rundown on**

24   **what we're doing here. I see you've got your speech**

25   **typed up all neatly, double-spaced...**

26   **HOOTO: Double-spaced, pica.**

27   **DAVE: I'm sorry, I don't understand.**

28   **HOOTO: *Pica!* It's a technical term. Only the *elite* use it.**

1   **DAVE: Oh, I see. Well, it's too bad you don't have an IBM**

2   **machine, then you'd really have a ball. Ha-ha. Well,**

3   **anyway, there's your camera,** *(Points behind audience)*

4   **and this is your mic, and over here...**

5   **HOOTO:** *(Yells directly into microphone.)* **Testing, one, two,**

6   **three, four.** *(DARYL throws off headset and winces.)*

7   **DAVE: No, no. Mr. Crunk, don't ever...** *(DARYL holds his*

8   *hands over his ears.)* **Daryl?**

9   **DARYL: Huh? Oh, yeah, it's four-thirty.**

10   **DAVE: Ah, yeah. Listen, Daryl, maybe you should sit down**

11   **for a while. Mr. Crunk, please don't touch the equip-**

12   **ment, OK?**

13   **HOOTO: Oh, yeah. Sorry, no harm, no foul.**

14   **DAVE: No, that's all right. Now, let me give you some tips**

15   **on stage presence.**

16   **HOOTO: Oh, do I get some gifts?**

17   **DAVE: No, no. Mr. Crunk, please. Now, when you give your**

18   **speech, try not to read it into the camera. "Talk" it,**

19   **like you were talking to a neighbor over a hedge.**

20   **HOOTO: Kinda casual, huh?**

21   **DAVE: Casual, right.**

22   **DARYL: Ten seconds, Dave.**

23   **DAVE: OK. Now, Hooto, stand straight and remember to**

24   **smile. You'll hear a short taped introduction, then after**

25   **that I'll cue you. That will be your turn to talk. Ready?**

26   **HOOTO: Roger, Wilco.**

27   **DARYL: Five seconds, four, three, two, one...**

28   **ANNOUNCER: And now speaking in reply to an editorial**

29   **broadcast last week on this station is Mr. Hooto**

30   **Crunk. Mr. Crunk?** *(During HOOTO's broadcast, DAVE*

31   *and DARYL unobtrusively slip out.)*

32   **HOOTO: Thank you. Last week this station had the unmit-**

33   **igated gall to broadcast its belief in Jesus Christ and**

34   **his soon return. Now, I was born in the United States**

1 and I've been to church, so I like to think of myself as
2 a Christian, but I find it hard to believe that these are,
3 as this station put it, "the final days."
4   In fact, I find a lot of what the Christians are saying
5 today hard to believe. Take, for instance, evolution.
6 Christians are saying that God made man out of dirt!
7 I find it hard to believe I'm nothing more than a big
8 mud pie. On the other hand, I have no trouble
9 believing that many of my relatives are monkeys, and
10 I'm sure most of you would agree with me.
11   And what about astrology? They say you can't even
12 rely on your horoscope anymore. I don't see anything
13 wrong with it. Of course I don't believe in astrology,
14 but then again I'm a Sagittarius, and we're naturally
15 skeptical anyway.
16   But what really gets me upset is this thing they're
17 calling the Rapture, or Rap-tur-a, where Jesus calls
18 the Christians to fly to heaven. And what's more, they
19 say it could happen at any time! Any time! Ha! Can
20 you imagine that? Thousands of Christians flying
21 around in the sky! Ridiculous! And how would he
22 know which ones to take?
23   With Christians saying things like this, it's no wonder
24 most of the folks in our community don't even go to
25 church. Now look, we all know if you want someone to
26 agree with you, you have to tell them something they can
27 believe. So let's stop all this science fiction jazz and get
28 back to preaching the Golden Rule and church potlucks.
29 And the next time you hear someone talking about Jesus
30 coming back soon or this Rapture, you tell them you
31 won't believe it until you see it! Thank you! *(Pauses as he*
32 *looks around.)* Ah, guys. Hey, I'm done...you know, el fini.
33 Hey, guys...hey, where'd everybody go? Come on...uh-
34 ohh!

Foolish guys ... ISAAC Air Freight

to confound the wise

BODY SCHISMS

By Dave Toole

1   **CAST:** Brain, Funny Bone, Nose, Armpit, Foot, Stomach, Mouth,
2   Teeth, Heart, Eye 1, Eye 2, Fingers (five).
3   **SETTING:** A meeting hall. A long table is at Center Stage with
4   sixteen chairs around it.
5   **PROPS:** A gavel for BRAIN.
6   **COSTUMES:** The simplest way to costume this sketch is for all
7   the characters to wear signs indicating who they are.
8   **SOUND EFFECT:** Ringing bell.
9
10   *(All characters are on On-stage, milling around and talking.)*
11   **BRAIN:** *(Bangs gavel.)* **Order! Order! Will everyone please**
12   **sit down? Please, would you all be seated?** *(Commotion)*
13   **Nose, would you take your place so we can get started?**
14   *(Characters are seated in cast order above except for*
15   *NOSE, who continues to stand.)*
16   **NOSE: How come I got to sit next to Armpit? He stinks.**
17   **FUNNY BONE: Ha-ha-ha-ha....**
18   **NOSE: It's not funny! Why doesn't he wear deodorant?**
19   **ARMPIT: I don't like deodorants. They're all so sticky and**
20   **gooey.**
21   **FUNNY BONE: Come on, Nose, just sit down and stop**
22   **getting all out of joint. Ha-ha...ha-ha-ha....**
23   **NOSE: Funny Bone, if you don't behave yourself, I'll...**
24   **FUNNY BONE: Easy, Nose, you're gonna blow it. Ha-ha-ha-ha.**
25   **ARMPIT: Now *that* stinks.**
26   **NOSE: Chairman Brain, why can't one of the fingers sit**
27   **over here?**
28   **FINGERS:** *(Together)* **We want to sit together.**

1   **NOSE: That's not fair. Why can't one of you guys sit over**
2   **here just once?**
3   **FUNNY BONE: Come on, if you sat over there, you'd stick**
4   **out like a sore thumb, knucklehead. Ha-ha-ha-ha....**
5   **FINGERS: Hey, watch it! He doesn't even have what it**
6   **takes to be one.**
7   **NOSE: Mister Chairman, they're picking on me again.**
8   **FUNNY BONE: Just pokin' a little fun, Chief.**
9   **FINGERS: Shut up, Funny Bone, or we'll take a poke at**
10   **you!**
11   **FUNNY BONE: That's about all you can do is poke.**
12   **BRAIN: Funny Bone, you're out of order.**
13   **FUNNY BONE: From the looks of things, you're fresh out,**
14   **too!**
15   **BRAIN: That's enough! Funny Bone, shut up! You guys**
16   **settle down, and Nose, you sit down. We got business.**
17   *(NOSE grumbles and sits down.)* **Now, if everyone will**
18   **sit still for a moment, we can get started. I've called**
19   **this meeting to see if we can stop all this petty bickering**
20   **between ourselves. It simply won't do. It's ridiculous.**
21   **FOOT: That's real easy for you to say. Flowery talk comes**
22   **cheap way up there on the shoulders. Givin' all the**
23   **orders and gettin' all the credit. Why don't you come**
24   **down and spend a little time in those leather saunas**
25   **you call shoes and let me run things a while?**
26   **FUNNY BONES: The way you run, you'd be a real "lame-**
27   **brain." Ha-ha....**
28   **FOOT: Pretty cute, Funny Bone. You get a big kick out of**
29   **your stupid jokes. Wait till I get ahold of you.**
30   *(Commotion)*
31   **BRAIN: People! People, we're not getting anywhere this**
32   **way.**
33   **STOMACH: What do ya mean? I think Foot's doin' a pretty**
34   **good job of getting things said.**

1   **BRAIN: Stomach, you're out of order.**

2   **STOMACH: I've been telling you that for weeks. What's**
3   **goin' on in that head of yours? The eyes are bigger**
4   **than I am. Just how many chocolate malts are**
5   **enough? Three? Four? Last week it was six.**

6   **BRAIN: Well, don't come to me with your bellyaching.**
7   **That's the mouth's problem.**

8   **MOUTH: I've got a sweet tooth.**

9   **STOMACH: You mean we still have some teeth up there?**
10   **Just what are they doing? You wouldn't believe some**
11   **of the stuff that makes its way down here. After**
12   **yesterday's lunch, we got a whole plum, pit and all!**

13   **TEETH: Haven't you heard? We're on strike. The condi-**
14   **tions up here are awful. The gums are rotting, decay**
15   **is on the rampage, and we're under heavy canker**
16   **attack. We need help!** *(Assorted voices: "So do we," etc.)*

17   **BRAIN: Quiet! Quiet! Everyone sit down and shut up! This**
18   **kind of arguing and squabbling is the very problem**
19   **we're here trying to solve.**

20   **HEART: May I say something?**

21   **BRAIN: Go ahead, Heart.**

22   **HEART: Thank you. All of us know we have our share of**
23   **problems, but this kind of arguing isn't going to**
24   **accomplish anything. Now God has given us all special**
25   **abilities to do different things. Look around – we have**
26   **many parts, but we all make up one body. If the foot**
27   **says, "I am not a part of the body because I am not the**
28   **hand," that does not make it any less a part of the**
29   **body. And what if the whole body were an eye?** (1 Cor.
30   12:15, 17, author's paraphrase) **How would we blink?**
31   *(General laughter)*

32   **HEART: It all sounds kind of silly, doesn't it? Because we are**
33   **many parts in one body, and because we're all the same**
34   **body, we must work together. We need each other. The**

1   head cannot say to the feet, "I don't need you." (1 Cor.
2   12:21, author's paraphrase)
3   **FOOT: Right on, pumper.**
4   **HEART: ...Nor the feet to the head.**
5   **BRAIN: Touché.**
6   **HEART: Why, some of the parts that seem weakest and**
7   **least important are really the most necessary.**
8   **Gentlemen, if one part suffers, we all suffer! Our**
9   **present situation is proof enough of that. But if one**
10   **part is honored, so are we all. Think about it. What**
11   **have we got to lose?**
12   **EYE 1 and EYE 2:** *(Together)* **Chairman Brain?**
13   **BRAIN: Eyeballs.**
14   **EYE 1: We see what Heart's getting at...**
15   **EYE 2: ...and we agree.**
16   **EYE 1 and EYE 2:** *(Together)* **How about a vote of confi-**
17   **dence? All in favor?** *(Cheers)*
18   **BRAIN: Looks like the eyes have it. This calls for a celebra-**
19   **tion! How about a candy bar?**
20   **STOMACH: Nothin' doin'.**
21   **BRAIN: Hey, hey, just kidding.**
22   **FOOT: We'll leave the jokes to Funny Bone.**
23   **FINGERS:** *(Together)* **Yeah, he never does any thinkin'.** *(All*
24   *laugh and make up.)*
25   **FUNNY BONE: Now, Foot, if I had made a pun like that, you**
26   **would've walked out.**
27   **ARMPIT: If you want, I'll try to find a deodorant.**
28   **NOSE: That's OK. I'm kind of stuffed-up anyway.** *(Alarm bell*
29   *rings.)*
30   **BRAIN: There's the signal, everyone. He's waking up. Let's**
31   **get back to our stations and see if we can't make this**
32   **the strong body we all want to be.** *(Cheers, commotion,*
33   *fade)*
34

JERUSALEM DRAGNET II

By Dan Rupple and Dave Toole

1   **CAST:** Sergeant Good Friday (Goodie), Officer Frank Gannon,
2   Apostle Peter, Local Beggar, Vendor, Mr. Oftarsus, Apostle
3   Paul, Narrator (either On-stage or off).

4   **SETTING:** Various locations within Jerusalem. Designate four
5   stage locations to be the upper room, the police station
6   (place a desk there), MR. OFTARSUS' home, and jail.

7   **PROPS:** Phone for GOODIE's desk; a crutch for the BEGGAR;
8   a painted cardboard cutout of a boat for GOODIE and
9   FRANK; programs, rocks and pennants for the VENDOR
10   and a stack of papers for PAUL's manuscript.

11   **COSTUMES:** GOODIE and FRANK may wear police uniforms
12   and tall, centurion-type hats. GOODIE also carries a
13   badge. PETER, PAUL, MR. OFTARSUS and VENDOR may
14   wear biblical robes, headpieces and sandals. The
15   BEGGAR should also wear biblical garb, though his
16   should be somewhat tattered-looking.

17   **SOUND EFFECTS:** Ringing doorbell.

18

19   *(Optional intro music. Enter GOODIE.)*

20   **GOODIE: This is the city Jerusalem. It's righteous. Lots of**
21   **people live here, lots of people die here. But when**
22   **they die here and live, that's where I come in. My**
23   **name's Friday, Good Friday. I carry a badge.** *(Exit*
24   *GOODIE. Optional music)*

25   **NARRATOR: The story you are about to hear is true. None**
26   **of the names have been changed because only one**
27   **was innocent.** *(Enter GOODIE.)*

28   **GOODIE: It was Tuesday, April 10, 9:05 a.m. My partner,**

Jerusalem Dragnet II

1   **Frank Gannon, and I were working the day watch out**
2   **of the station house when the boys in rent control**
3   **brought in forty-three rabbis in their BVDs for**
4   **processing. Frank and I had just finished sweeping**
5   **up the dust when the chief first told us about the**
6   **resurrection of Jesus Christ. We sprang into action.**
7   *(Optional music)* **At 10:45, we began our lengthy inves-**
8   **tigation at the scene of the crime, the empty tomb. We**
9   **figured for a stone that big to be rolled away, it had to**
10   **be a conspiracy. As we were collecting clues, we**
11   **spotted a couple of gardeners. We tried to question**
12   **them, but they flew away.** *(Optional music)*
13   **May 21, 12:14 p.m. Frank and I had spent six weeks**
14   **trying to find Jesus. After many close calls, we finally**
15   **caught up to him in the hills just outside Jerusalem,**
16   **but before we could question him, he rose on a cloud**
17   **into the heavens. Frank and I weren't discouraged,**
18   **though. He said he'd be back. We decided to continue**
19   **our investigation by questioning a previous suspect,**
20   **Simon Peter.** *(Optional music. Enter FRANK.)*
21   **FRANK: Gee, Goodie, that was really something the way**
22   **Jesus went up in the clouds like that.**
23   **GOODIE: Ah, Frank, come on. It was no big deal.**
24   **FRANK: Oh, really? How'd he do it?**
25   **GOODIE: Well, he...ummm, knock on the door, Frank.**
26   **FRANK:** *(Knocking)* **Do you think he used ropes?**
27   **GOODIE: Maybe not ropes, but...**
28   **PETER:** *(As PETER approaches, he can be heard leading praise.*
29   *Door opens.)* **Oh, hello, officers. Long time no see.**
30   **GOODIE: Yes, ah...what are folks calling you these days?**
31   **PETER: Peter's fine.**
32   **GOODIE: Well, Peter, we're looking for Jesus again. Have**
33   **you seen him?**
34   **PETER: Sure, I was just talking with him.**

1   **GOODIE: You see, Frank, I told you that cloud thing was a**
2   **hoax. Where is he?**
3   **PETER: He's in my heart.**
4   **FRANK: Where? In with the arteries and capillaries?**
5   **PETER: No, I mean spiritually.**
6   **GOODIE: Listen, don't try to change the subject. We under-**
7   **stand you and your friends have been spending a lot**
8   **of time in an upper room. That true?**
9   **PETER: Yes.**
10   **FRANK: The owner said he couldn't understand a word**
11   **you guys said. What was it – a translator's convention?**
12   **GOODIE: Or maybe you were speaking in code.**
13   **PETER: No, no, it was tongues of fire.**
14   **GOODIE:** *(Puzzled)* **You guys have some spicy food or some-**
15   **thing?**
16   **PETER: No, this is a whole different thing.**
17   **GOODIE: Well, stay on the subject. Now, what were you**
18   **doing up there?**
19   **PETER: Waiting.**
20   **GOODIE: Waiting for what?**
21   **PETER: The baptism of the Holy Spirit.**
22   **GOODIE: What's that – a radio show like *The Treasure of***
23   ***Sierra Madre*?**
24   **FRANK: Or *The Shadow*?**
25   **PETER: Officers, there's nothing make-believe about this.**
26   **GOODIE: Listen, stop trying to change the subject. We're**
27   **not interested in the Holy Spirit, we're looking for**
28   **Jesus!**
29   **PETER: They're both one.**
30   **GOODIE: Wait a second – you trying to tell us that two are**
31   **one?**
32   **PETER: No.**
33   **GOODIE: Good.**
34   **FRANK: Two are one – that would be ridiculous!**

1   **PETER: Everybody knows it's three.**

2   **GOODIE: What? Three are two? Two are three?**

3   **PETER: No, three are one.**

4   **GOODIE: You into new math?**

5   **PETER: No, the New Covenant.** *(PETER exits. FRANK and*
6   *GOODIE shrug and FRANK exits. Optional music.)*

7   **GOODIE: Frank and I returned to the station. It was 12:45**
8   **when we arrived. Frank went out for coffee and**
9   **donuts, and I took over at the desk. Between phone**
10   **calls, a local beggar came in to register a complaint.**
11   *(Sits at desk and picks up phone.)* **...so Mr. DiMilo, you're**
12   **sure you saw both arms on the statue last night when**
13   **you fed the cat, but this morning they were gone,**
14   **right?** *(Pause)* **OK, sir, this sounds like another case of**
15   **vandalism, sir. There's not much we can do now**
16   **except check the local pawn shops and see what turns**
17   **up.... We'll let you know if we find anything.** *(GOODIE*
18   *hangs up phone. Enter LOCAL BEGGAR.)*

19   **LOCAL BEGGAR: You in charge here?**

20   **GOODIE: I'm watching the desk, sir. What's your**
21   **problem?**

22   **LOCAL BEGGAR: What do you mean by that, buddy? You**
23   **sayin' I look like I got a problem?**

24   **GOODIE: No, sir, I didn't say that, but most people who**
25   **come in here want to talk about something.**

26   **LOCAL BEGGAR: Well, I do, but it's not me – it's blind**
27   **Alex.**

28   **GOODIE: I see. What'd he do?**

29   **LOCAL BEGGAR: Nothing! He didn't do nothing, that's**
30   **just the point. He was sitting there by the gate beauti-**
31   **fully, business as usual, you know, hockin' pencils. He**
32   **was doing real good, too. You ought to see him go. He**
33   **always has been one of the best, you know. He can**
34   **turn two or three denarii before lunch. Talk a**

1   leopard out of his spots!

2   **GOODIE: Just the facts, sir, just the facts.**

3   **LOCAL BEGGAR: Yeah, yeah, OK. Anyway, there's old Alex**
4   **going about his own business when these two Jesus**
5   **freaks walk up. Well, Al, he don't know who they are,**
6   **can't see and all, so he goes over and asks them for a**
7   **couple of farthings. Well, sir, out of the blue, the one**
8   **with the beard says, "In Jesus' name, be healed!" And**
9   **just like that, Al's eyeballs almost pop out of their**
10   **sockets!**

11   **GOODIE: So what's the problem? It sounds like your**
12   **friend got a break.**

13   **LOCAL BEGGAR: *Got a break? Got a break?* Listen here,**
14   **Domehead, how's Alex supposed to support his**
15   **family? The man's forty years old and blind from**
16   **birth. He's been begging all his life. What's he**
17   **supposed to do now? Who's gonna hire him? Would you**
18   **give a man like that a job? No way! Ain't no one gonna**
19   **give him a job! And he can't even go back to the gate**
20   **and pretend – everybody in town is talking about it.**

21   **GOODIE: Well, I don't see what I can do. It doesn't sound**
22   **like they've broken any laws.**

23   **LOCAL BEGGAR: Well, can't you get 'em for interfering**
24   **with a private business or practicing medicine**
25   **without a license?**

26   **GOODIE: No, sir. Technically, they're not even respon-**
27   **sible. Sounds like Jesus is.**

28   **LOCAL BEGGAR: Oh, I see. So you're not gonna do nothin',**
29   **huh?** *(LOCAL BEGGAR strikes GOODIE with crutch.)* **No**
30   **one ever thinks about the small businessman**
31   **anymore.**

32   **GOODIE: Sir, there's nothing we can do. We don't handle**
33   **religious matters.** *(LOCAL BEGGAR threatens GOODIE*
34   *with his crutch again.)* **But if you like, we'll notify the**

1   Pharisees about it.

2   LOCAL BEGGAR: Pharisees, eh? Well, I suppose that will

3   help.

4   GOODIE: Good, good. We'll drop by the temple later and

5   report it.

6   LOCAL BEGGAR: Oh, there ain't nobody over there today.

7   They're all over at the rock festival.

8   GOODIE: We got a musical group in town?

9   LOCAL BEGGAR: *No! (LOCAL BEGGAR sticks GOODIE.)*

10   They're stonin' some Christians. I better get over

11   there, too. It's a double-header. *(LOCAL BEGGAR exits.*

12   *Optional music)*

13   GOODIE: After spending an hour in the infirmary, Frank

14   and I went upstairs to check the file on stoning

15   permits. The event in question was scheduled for

16   2:30. We had just enough time to hobble across town.

17   *(FRANK enters.)*

18   FRANK: Boy, I didn't know these things were so popular.

19   GOODIE: At least we got a handicapped parking space.

20   FRANK: Where do we get some tickets?

21   GOODIE: You'd think as police officials we'd get a free

22   box.

23   VENDOR: *(Entering)* Programs, souvenirs. Get your pro-

24   grams. Get your rocks. Stone a Christian, please a

25   Pharisee.

26   GOODIE: Excuse me. This is where we get our tickets?

27   VENDOR: Sure is, officer. What'll it be? You can sit on

28   either side. Pharisees or Christians?

29   GOODIE: What do you suggest?

30   VENDOR: Well, there's plenty of room on the Christian

31   side, but the hot tip is if you ain't wearin' your flack

32   vest, you'd best squeeze in with the Pharisees.

33   GOODIE: OK, gimme a couple of seats behind the

34   Pharisee dugout.

1   **VENDOR: Ha! Are you kiddin'? You show up on game day**
2   **and expect to sit with the scribes? Ha-ha. You're lucky**
3   **we got some bleacher seats left.**
4   **GOODIE: Can we talk to the Pharisees from out there?**
5   **VENDOR: You could chat with the guys in the bullpen.**
6   **FRANK: Maybe we'll meet Lenny Kofax.**
7   **VENDOR: Not today, he's startin'. He's got a great fast ball.**
8   **Hasn't had a no-hitter all year. When he throws a**
9   **strike, they're out! Of course, he ain't as good as Saul**
10   **of Tarsus, but he's the best they got since Saul went**
11   **free agent.**
12   **FRANK: When did that happen?**
13   **VENDOR: Oh, that was a couple of years ago. Saul was on**
14   **his way out to Damascus for spring training when he**
15   **claims he met this Jesus of Nazareth.**
16   **GOODIE: In Damascus?**
17   **VENDOR: No, just outside.**
18   **GOODIE: This Saul know where to find Jesus?**
19   **VENDOR: He didn't say where, but he did say he knew**
20   **how. That the same thing?**
21   **GOODIE: That's good enough. Where can we get ahold of**
22   **this Saul?**
23   **VENDOR: Well, I ain't seen him lately, but you might try**
24   **his dad's place.**
25   **GOODIE: Thanks. Let's go, Frank.**
26   **VENDOR: Just a minute, officer. That'll be three sheckles.**
27   **GOODIE: Oh, we decided not to go to the game.**
28   **VENDOR: Not for the game, for the information.**
29   **GOODIE: Well...that's kind of steep, isn't it?**
30   **VENDOR: All right, I'll throw in a pennant.**
31   **GOODIE: Oh, OK.**
32   **FRANK: Gee, Goodie, mind if I pick the pennant?**
33   **GOODIE: Sure, Frank, live it up.**
34   **FRANK: You got any Christian ones?**

1　VENDOR: No way! The Pharisees own all the concessions.
2　　　In fact, that's what's wrong with the Christians, they
3　　　never make any concessions. *(VENDOR and FRANK*
4　　　*exit opposite. Optional music)*
5　GOODIE: Being an accomplished law enforcement officer,
6　　　I always follow up a solid lead. At 7:45 that evening,
7　　　Frank and I began our search for Saul of Tarsus, alias
8　　　Paul the Apostle, at the house of his father.
9　FRANK: Gee, Goodie, I just don't understand why they
10　　　were stoning all those Christians. I didn't see
11　　　anything wrong with them. They seemed nice enough
12　　　to me – 'course, I didn't see anything wrong with
13　　　Jesus, either. I hope this is the place. All these tents
14　　　look alike.
15　GOODIE: That's the trouble with tract homes. How do you
16　　　knock on these things?
17　FRANK: Why don't you use the bell?
18　GOODIE: Thanks, Frank. *(Rings bell.)*
19　MR. OFTARSUS: Yes, what do you want?
20　GOODIE: Good evening, sir. Are you Mr. Oftarsus?
21　MR. OFTARSUS: Yeah, what's it to you?
22　GOODIE: You got a son named Saul?
23　MR. OFTARSUS: Yes, but whatever he's done, I'm not
24　　　responsible.
25　GOODIE: It's all right, sir. We're just here to ask some
26　　　questions.
27　FRANK: When was the last time you saw your son?
28　MR. OFTARSUS: Quite a while ago. It was right before he
29　　　left for Damascus. He hasn't been the same since. I
30　　　don't know what hit him.
31　GOODIE: You say you've noticed erratic behavior?
32　MR. OFTARSUS: Let me tell you something. My Saulie, he
33　　　was a good kid. He had a lucrative tent business, and
34　　　he was a Pharisee, too, just like his papa. You

1　　　should've seen him. He could get out in the middle of
2　　　town and recite prayers better than anyone. He had a
3　　　better delivery than that Rabbi Youngman's boy,
4　　　Henny. But then he takes off for Damascus and light-
5　　　ning strikes. He claims this Jesus fellow talked to
6　　　him, and his whole life changes. All of a sudden, it's
7　　　bon voyage. He starts traveling around from town to
8　　　town preaching, forming churches and darn near
9　　　getting himself killed.
10　**GOODIE:** Have you heard from him?
11　**MR. OFTARSUS:** You kiddin'? Not a word. He writes the
12　　　Ephesians, the Galatians, the Corinthians, but did
13　　　you ever hear of his Epistle to Dad? Ungrateful kid!
14　**GOODIE:** You know where he is now?
15　**MR. OFTARSUS:** Yeah, he's in Rome.
16　**FRANK:** What's he doing there?
17　**MR. OFTARSUS:** I think he works for a savings and loan
18　　　company.
19　**GOODIE:** What makes you say that?
20　**MR. OFTARSUS:** He said he was in bonds. *(MR. OFTARSUS*
21　　　*and FRANK exit opposite. Optional music)*
22　**GOODIE:** July 29, 3:14 p.m. Frank and I started our voyage
23　　　for Rome in search of Paul the apostle, and then
24　　　perhaps the root of this Jesus conspiracy.
25　　　*(Optional sailing music. FRANK and GOODIE cross stage*
26　　　*twice in prop boat, exit and return seasick.)*
27　**GOODIE:** Oh, Frank, what a rough trip! The way that boat
28　　　kept rockin' back and forth, back and forth, back and
29　　　forth, back and...
30　**FRANK:** *(Gags.)* I remember, I remember.
31　**GOODIE:** Well, this must be the place. Doesn't look like a
32　　　savings and loan to me.
33　**FRANK:** Looks like jail.
34　**GOODIE:** Maybe they locked Paul up with the money.

1	*(PAUL enters.)* **Here he comes now. Excuse me, I'm**
2	**Sergeant Friday and this is my partner, Frank**
3	**Gannon. We're officers from Jerusalem P.D.**
4	PAUL: **Hello, I'm Paul, a bondservant and apostle of Jesus**
5	**Christ through the will of God. Grace be unto you, and**
6	**peace, from God our Father, and from the Lord Jesus**
7	**Christ.** (I Cor. 1:1, 3)
8	GOODIE: **Yeah, well, we want to ask some questions about**
9	**this Jesus Movement. We understand that you're the**
10	**leader.**
11	PAUL: **Oh, no, Jesus is the leader, I'm just a believer. But**
12	**I'll gladly share anything you'd like to hear about**
13	**Jesus.**
14	FRANK: **What're you writing?**
15	PAUL: **A letter to the Philippians.**
16	GOODIE and FRANK: *(Together)* **Which one?**
17	PAUL: **All of them.**
18	GOODIE: **What do you mean? That's like sending a letter**
19	**to California.**
20	PAUL: **Well, I send it to the Christians there and they pass**
21	**it around. You know, back and forth, back and forth,**
22	**back and forth.**
23	FRANK: *(Gets woozy.)* **All right, all right.**
24	GOODIE: **Mind if I have a look at what you're writing?**
25	*(PAUL gives manuscript to GOODIE. GOODIE reads.)* **"I**
26	**beseech you therefore, brethren, by the mercies of**
27	**God, that you present your bodies a living sacrifice..."**
28	(Rom. 12:1) **This stuff's kind of weird, isn't it? Where's**
29	**the stuff like having a great time, wish you were here?**
30	**I don't understand this.**
31	PAUL: **Well, the natural man can't understand the things**
32	**of the Spirit.**
33	GOODIE: *(Gives manuscript back to PAUL.)* **It's all Greek to**
34	**me. Listen, Paul. Now we have it that you were a**

1   **Pharisee before all this. That's a position of wealth**
2   **and prominence with a future. Why did you give all**
3   **that up to follow Jesus?**
4   **PAUL: Well, I was a very prideful man. Oh, sure, I was reli-**
5   **gious – I practically lived in the synagogue – but I**
6   **always tried to fit God into my plans, rather than**
7   **totally surrender to his ways. Well, I was so hard-**
8   **hearted that God had to get me flat on my back to**
9   **speak to me. And as I lay there, I heard a voice from**
10   **heaven, and do you know who it was?**
11   **GOODIE and FRANK:** *(Together)* **Cecil B. DeMille?**
12   **PAUL: No, Jesus Christ. And it was then I realized God**
13   **wanted me to have a personal relationship with him.**
14   **God doesn't care about us being religious. He looks at**
15   **our heart.**
16   **FRANK: Yeah, Peter told us something about having Jesus**
17   **in your heart.**
18   **PAUL: That's right.**
19   **GOODIE: In your heart, eh? You aware we might be able to**
20   **get you on charges of harboring a criminal?**
21   **PAUL: What're you gonna do, throw me in prison?**
22   **GOODIE: We'll see. In the meantime, don't leave here. We**
23   **may want to question you again.**
24   **PAUL: Why would I want to leave? My prison ministry is**
25   **thriving.**
26   **GOODIE: Yeah, yeah. Come on, Frank.** *(GOODIE exits.)*
27   **FRANK: Say, Paul, is following Jesus worth going to jail**
28   **for?**
29   **PAUL: Officer Gannon, I'm freer now than most people**
30   **will ever be. I've been totally pardoned.** *(FRANK and*
31   *PAUL exit opposite. Optional music)*
32   **NARRATOR:** *(Over music)* **Unlike most law-enforcement**
33   **cases, the story of Jesus Christ goes on. We see his**
34   **effect on people's lives everywhere. And now, the**

1   **results of Sergeant Friday and Officer Gannon's**
2   **investigation.** *(Enter GOODIE, disheveled, and FRANK,*
3   *police line-up style.)*
4   **Sergeant Good Friday: Sergeant Friday totally**
5   **rejected any belief in the facts of Jesus Christ. He**
6   **continued in a lifetime sentence of bondage to sin.**
7   **Currently, as a result of drunkenness and multiple**
8   **divorces, he has been demoted to a security cop at**
9   **K-Mart. Officer Frank Gannon: On November 4,**
10   **Officer Gannon gave his life to Jesus Christ. Now free**
11   **from sin, he has life, and that more abundantly.**
12   *(GOODIE and FRANK exit. Optional music)*
13
14
15
16
17
18
19
20
21
22
23
24
25
26
27
28
29
30
31
32
33
34

WOODSTOCK NOW

By Dan Rupple

1   **CAST:** Nick, Foster.

2   **SETTING:** A bar. Put two stools behind a long table.

3   **PROPS:** Drink glasses for NICK and FOSTER, a digital watch

4   and business card for NICK, and wallet with photos for

5   FOSTER.

6   **COSTUMES:** FOSTER wears Levis and a work shirt. NICK

7   wears a business suit.

8

9   *(FOSTER is sitting at the bar. NICK walks in and sits next*

10   *to him.)*

11   **NICK: I'll have a scotch and water.** *(To FOSTER)* **How ya**

12   **doing?... Foster?**

13   **FOSTER: Nick?**

14   **NICK: Foster, how ya doing?**

15   **FOSTER: OK. Wow – I haven't seen you for about...well...**

16   **NICK: About eight or nine years.**

17   **FOSTER: Has it been that long? Doesn't seem that long.**

18   **NICK: So, where ya living now?**

19   **FOSTER: I'm living here in Encino. How about you?**

20   **NICK: Oh, I have a house out in Orange County.**

21   **FOSTER: You married?**

22   **NICK: Sure, you?**

23   **FOSTER: Divorced.**

24   **NICK: Yeah. Wow, you sure look different. Last time I saw**

25   **you, your hair was way down your back.**

26   **FOSTER: Well, what about you? No beard and that head-**

27   **band you wore.**

28   **NICK: Yeah. Still got that old van?**

1   **FOSTER: No.**

2   **NICK: Remember how we used to go all over in**
3   **it...smoking and singing?**

4   **FOSTER: Yeah.**

5   **NICK and FOSTER** *(Together)* **"Everybody must get stoned.***

6   **NICK: Ah, yeah, and remember those songs you wrote.**
7   **"Chicago Seven, Meet You in Heaven." What a tune!**
8   **And that opening line: "Hey, Tom, Abbie and Jerry,**
9   **it's smellin' like a dairy." That's what it was all about.**
10   **Still writing songs, aren't you? You always were gonna**
11   **be a songwriter.**

12   **FOSTER: No, I don't write them anymore. I don't know**
13   **why. I'm a truck driver now. What about you?**

14   **NICK: I've got my own business. I sell suits. You know,**
15   **cottons, tweeds, linens. Here's my card.**

16   **FOSTER: Nick's Clothiers. Suits that suit you.**

17   **NICK: That's our slogan. I made it up myself. You know, I**
18   **could probably set you up with a $124 three-piece suit**
19   **for about ninety dollars. You'll have to give me a call**
20   **sometime.**

21   **FOSTER: Yeah, sure.**

22   **NICK: Hey, Foster, do you remember what we used to say**
23   **when we thought the cops were coming?**

24   **FOSTER: Do I remember! Pigs in a blanket.**

25   **NICK: Hog in the hamper.**

26   **FOSTER: What?**

27   **NICK: Hog in the hamper.**

28   **FOSTER: No, it was pigs in a blanket.**

29   **NICK: Nah, you're thinking of that morning we got sick at**
30   **the I-HOP. When the cops were coming, we'd say,**
31   **"Hog in the hamper."**

32   **FOSTER: Well, whatever it was.**

33   **NICK: And only you and I knew about it. When did we**

*"Rainy Day Women #12 and 35" by Bob Dylan, copyright © 1966 and 1976 by
Dwarf Music.*

1   make that up?
2 **FOSTER:** I don't know.
3 **NICK:** It was either at Kent or Woodstock. Which came
4   first?
5 **FOSTER:** I'm not sure.
6 **NICK:** Boy, Woodstock. What a trip!
7 **FOSTER:** Bad trip for you, though.
8 **NICK:** What do ya mean?
9 **FOSTER:** You almost OD'd. I had to carry you to the
10   medical tent. I thought you were dead.
11 **NICK:** Oh, yeah. I'll never forget that. After you carried me
12   all the way over to the doctor, you went, "He ain't
13   heavy, he's my brother." I know it sounds kind of
14   stupid now, but...at the time...
15 **FOSTER:** Ah...you did that kind of stuff for me, too – like
16   the time you bailed me out of jail.
17 **NICK:** Nah, that wasn't anything compared to you. You
18   were really something. We were like brothers. Like a
19   team. Whatever happened?
20 **FOSTER:** I don't know.
21 **NICK:** Boy, Foster, friendships like we had are hard to
22   come by. You know, people are changing. You got
23   many friends?
24 **FOSTER:** No, not like the old days.
25 **NICK:** Yeah, me neither. What happened? I remember you
26   and me sitting for hours, just smoking dope and
27   listening to "In-A-Gadda-Da-Vida." That was the
28   life...and that cheap wine.
29 **FOSTER:** You still drink that junk?
30 **NICK:** No, I can only have an occasional scotch. I've got
31   these ulcers, you know. I have to eat Rolaids a lot. Hey,
32   what time is it?
33 **FOSTER:** Two-twenty.
34 **NICK:** Good, my watch keeps messing up. $270 watch. It's

1   **one of those that you push the button and the time**

2   **lights up. See?**

3   **FOSTER: It just says twenty.**

4   **NICK: Shoot. It's messed up again. See, sometimes the**

5   **hour column doesn't light up.** *(Bangs watch.)* **Darn!**

6   *(Bangs again.)* **There it goes. See it?**

7   **FOSTER: Yeah, that's great.**

8   **NICK: Hey, whatever happened to that chick you used to**

9   **hang around with?**

10   **FOSTER: Zulu?**

11   **NICK: Yeah, what a funky chick.**

12   **FOSTER: I married her.**

13   **NICK: Come on.**

14   **FOSTER: We were only married for a few years. Had a**

15   **couple of kids. Then we divorced. Here's my kids.**

16   *(Pulls out wallet.)* **That's Shawn, that's Heather.**

17   **NICK: Wow, that's great. They in a school play here or**

18   **something?**

19   **FOSTER: What do you mean?**

20   **NICK: Well, those old clothes they're wearing.**

21   **FOSTER: No, that's just at the apartment.**

22   **NICK: Oh, I see.**

23   **FOSTER: Did you ever have any kids?**

24   **NICK: Nah. We tried once, but we lost it. Then I got pretty**

25   **busy with the store.**

26   **FOSTER: I guess you're doing pretty good. Financially, I**

27   **mean.**

28   **NICK: Are you kidding? You should see my house. I got a**

29   **Porsche, and next month I'm getting a motor home.**

30   **FOSTER: Wow, that's living!**

31   **NICK: Can't beat it. I got everything a guy could want. How**

32   **about you?**

33   **FOSTER: Well, I make ends meet. Things are gonna work**

34   **out.**

1   **NICK:** Hey, whatever happened to Ralph Simpson?

2   **FOSTER:** Ralph? I ran into him a few months ago. You

3   won't believe it. He's into that Christian stuff.

4   **NICK:** Come on.

5   **FOSTER:** Nope, swear to God. He was talking all about it.

6   **NICK:** Well, that figures. He never did really have it

7   together, you know.

8   **FOSTER:** Yeah, I guess. But he seems pretty together now.

9   He's really doing pretty good.

10   **NICK:** Did he try to convert ya? Ha-ha.

11   **FOSTER:** Yeah.

12   **NICK:** Figures. What did he say?

13   **FOSTER:** He was talking about God's love and that Jesus

14   could straighten out my life.

15   **NICK:** Bet he couldn't get you a Porsche.

16   **FOSTER:** No, he was talking about different kinds of

17   things. I don't know.

18   **NICK:** Well, you know old "jump on the bandwagon"

19   Ralph, so consider the source.

20   **FOSTER:** Yeah, but he's really different now. He's really

21   happy.

22   **NICK:** Well, no matter what Ralph says, I bet he's not

23   making money. And if he is, he's probably giving it all

24   to the church.

25   **FOSTER:** I don't know, Nick. You and I didn't use to

26   care about money. All we cared about was that

27   whole thing of love and peace, but we never found

28   it. Ralph kept looking, and maybe he's found it. I

29   don't know. Boy...whatever happened to us?

30   Where'd our values go?

31   **NICK:** I don't know. I guess we just grew up.

32   **FOSTER:** Or maybe we just grew into new ones.

33   **NICK:** I guess.

34   **FOSTER:** Maybe that was our problem – we were always

1   guessing. We never knew where we were going.

2   NICK: Yeah, I guess. Hey, what time is it?

3   FOSTER: Two twenty-four.

4   NICK: Shoot. Watch stopped again. I gotta go to a meeting

5   with a pants company at two-thirty. Well, it's really

6   been great seeing you again.

7   FOSTER: Yeah.

8   NICK: *(Gives FOSTER a business card.)* **Hey, give me a call,**

9   **and I'll set you up with a suit – half-price.**

10   FOSTER: We'll see.

11   NICK: Well, take care, partner.

12   FOSTER: Yeah, you too.

13   NICK: Maybe you could come out to the house for dinner

14   sometime. You could meet my wife, if I can get her out

15   of her bathrobe.

16   FOSTER: Yeah, maybe.

17   NICK: Give a call sometime, and maybe we'll set some-

18   thing up.

19   FOSTER: Sure.

20   NICK: Take care, Foster.

21   FOSTER: **You, too, Nick.** *(NICK leaves.)* **Ah, bartender,**

22   **another bourbon.** *(Crumples up business card.)*

23

24

25

26

27

28

29

30

31

32

33

34

HARDNESS OF HEART

By Dan Rupple

1 **CAST:** Hooto Crunk; Dr. Farnsworth; Joe — a Christian college
2   friend of Hooto's; The Lord — a ghost-like figure; Billie —
3   another college friend of Hooto's.
4 **OPTIONAL OFF-STAGE VOICES:** Workman, Man #1, Man #2,
5   Man #3, Man #4.
6 **SETTING:** Designate three different stage areas to serve as:
7   DOCTOR FARNSWORTH's office, HOOTO's home and
8   HOOTO's college dorm room. Put a chair in DOCTOR
9   FARNSWORTH's office, a couch (or three chairs covered
10   by a blanket) in HOOTO's house, and a bed (or table
11   made up with blankets and pillow) in HOOTO's dorm
12   room.
13 **PROPS:** Two telephones — one for HOOTO and one for DR.
14   FARNSWORTH, and a bank statement in an envelope for
15   BILLIE to give to HOOTO.
16 **COSTUMES:** Casual dress for HOOTO, BILLIE and JOE.
17   HOOTO may wear glasses. DR. FARNSWORTH wears a
18   white lab coat. THE LORD should wear a white biblical-
19   style robe and white headpiece to suggest a ghostly
20   appearance.
21 **SOUND EFFECTS:** Ringing telephone, wind (optional).
22   "Optional background" sounds: crash, siren, cars, shots,
23   thunder, rain.
24
25   *(HOOTO is seated on a chair.)*
26 **HOOTO:** **I don't know why this doctor wants to see me. I**
27   **can't understand it. I feel fine.**
28 **DR. FARNSWORTH:** *(Entering)* **Oh, hello, Hooto.**

1   HOOTO: Hi, Dr. Farnsworth.

2   DR. FARNSWORTH: And how are we doing today?

3   HOOTO: Well, I don't know how you're doing, but I'm

4   doing fine. Now let's get right to the point. Level with

5   me, Doctor. What's the problem?

6   DR. FARNSWORTH: Hooto, I'm not going to beat around

7   the bush. I've studied your tests again and again, and

8   I'm sure of the results.

9   HOOTO: What is it, Doc? I gotta quit drinking?

10   DR. FARNSWORTH: Hooto...

11   HOOTO: Smoking? I'm trying to quit...

12   DR. FARNSWORTH: Look, physically you're OK. It's your

13   spiritual life. You're in deep trouble.

14   HOOTO: Oh, come on, Doc. You mean I came all the way

15   down here to listen to you bug me about spiritual

16   junk? I hear enough of that stuff from this flipped-

17   out kid at work. He says my only problem is that I'm

18   burning off bad karma.

19   DR. FARNSWORTH: No, Hooto...

20   HOOTO: Then what? Do I have a bad moon between

21   Jupiter and Mars?

22   DR. FARNSWORTH: Hooto, it's a lot more serious than

23   those idiotic fallacies. You're suffering from hard-

24   ness of heart!

25   HOOTO: Hardness of heart? I've never even heard of it.

26   DR. FARNSWORTH: That's the problem. People don't ever

27   realize they have it, but it's one of the major causes of

28   eternal fatality. Hooto, your being stubborn to the

29   pull of God's Spirit is gonna lead you to destruction.

30   HOOTO: Nah, everything is OK. I heard that after you die

31   you just go to heaven for a couple of weeks, and then

32   you get reincarnated. I'm really looking forward to it,

33   too. I want to come back as a one-legged duck. Just

34   think of it – not a care in the world. You know, just

1   swim around and around.

2   **DR. FARNSWORTH: Hooto, see what you've done? Jesus**

3   **said that he is the Truth, and since you've rejected the**

4   **Truth, you've had to believe these lies. But Hooto, by**

5   **receiving Jesus Christ, you'll be transformed from an**

6   **eternal bout with death to everlasting life.**

7   **HOOTO: You mean as a duck?**

8   **DR. FARNSWORTH:** *No!* **As a child of God.**

9   **HOOTO: Doc, I'm a busy man. I don't have time to talk**

10   **about God, if there even is one.**

11   **DR. FARNSWORTH: Hooto, what is God going to have to do**

12   **to reveal himself to you?**

13   **HOOTO: Well, it's going to take a lot more than your**

14   **cockamamie stories. See ya later, Doc.**

15   **DR. FARNSWORTH: I'll be praying for you, Hooto.**

16   **HOOTO: Save your knees.** *(He walks home. DR. FARNS-*

17   *WORTH freezes in a praying position.)*

18   **HOOTO: Boy, imagine the** | ***Optional Background Ideas***

19   **nerve of that doctor to** | *(Off-stage)*

20   **call me all the way** | **WORKMAN: Look out below!**

21   **down to his office just** | *(Crash)*

22   **to bug me about reli-** | **MAN #1: Did you see that piano?**

23   **gion. What does he** | **MAN #2: Just missed that**

24   **want from me, any-** | **man!** *(Siren, cars, shots,*

25   **way? To shave my** | *bullets hitting all around*

26   **head and put stained-** | *HOOTO. Thunder, Rain,*

27   **glass windows in my** | *lightening.)*

28   **house? Ridiculous!** | **MAN #3: Hey, man, are you OK?**

29   **He'll probably send** | **You should've been sizzled.**

30   **me a bill, too. If I** | **Hey, did you hear me?**

31   **didn't live so close, I'd** | **MAN #4: Maybe he's deaf.**

32   **send him a bill for**

33   **wasting my time. I had a lot planned today. I was**

34   **gonna change the air in my tires.** *(At home)* **At last,**

1   **home sweet home. Think I'll take a nap.** *(Lies down on*
2   *couch and falls asleep. THE LORD enters.)*
3   **THE LORD: Hooto!**
4   **HOOTO: Huh? Who are you?**
5   **THE LORD: I'm the Spirit of the Lord, Hooto.**
6   **HOOTO: What do you want?**
7   **THE LORD: Just follow me.** *(Optional wind)*
8   **HOOTO: Where are we?**
9   **THE LORD: This is a time of witness past.**
10   **HOOTO: Wow, that's the college dorm....** *(THE LORD and*
11   *HOOTO cross the stage to a small dorm scene. A young*
12   *man [JOE] sits frozen on the end of the bed. THE LORD*
13   *sets HOOTO next to him and JOE comes to life.)*
14   **JOE: But Jesus said that in order to see the Kingdom of**
15   **God, you must be born again.**
16   **HOOTO: What? You saying I didn't do it right the first**
17   **time?**
18   **JOE: Hooto, we're all born into sin. We need to be reborn**
19   **into the righteousness of Jesus Christ.**
20   **HOOTO: Joe, if I'm born again, who's to guarantee I'll**
21   **come back as Hooto Crunk? Maybe I'll come back as**
22   **a...as a...a duck!**
23   **JOE: You've got it all wrong.**
24   **HOOTO: Look, I've got a lot more important things on my**
25   **mind. Semester break is coming up, and I don't have**
26   **any money to fly home.**
27   **JOE: I know. I've been praying for you.**
28   **BILLIE:** *(Running up)* **Mail's here.... Here's one for you,**
29   **Hooto.** *(Hands envelope to HOOTO.)*
30   **HOOTO:** *(Opens envelope and looks at statement.)* **Wow! Two**
31   **hundred dollars more than I thought I had. They**
32   **made a banking error.**
33   **JOE: Praise the Lord!**
34   **HOOTO: Are you kidding? Pure luck.** *(Optional wind. BILL*

1   *and JOE freeze. THE LORD leads HOOTO out.)* **You**
2   **mean it was you?**
3   **THE LORD: Yes, Hooto. I've been with you since you were**
4   **in your mother's womb.**
5   **HOOTO: Uh, no wonder it was so crowded in there. Ha-ha.**
6   **Oh, just a joke. Don't smite me or anything.**
7   **THE LORD: Look here. This is a time of witness present.**
8   *(As he points, a frozen DR. FARNSWORTH comes to life.)*
9   **HOOTO: Yeah, it's Dr. Farnsworth.**
10   **DR. FARNSWORTH:** *(Praying)* **And Lord, show Hooto how**
11   **much you love him. He's so confused, he wants to be**
12   **a duck!** *(Freeze and fade.)*
13   **HOOTO: You mean he really *did* mean what he was saying?**
14   **THE LORD: Yes, Hooto. I've been doing so many things to**
15   **reveal myself to you, but you have refused to see. But**
16   **beware, the Spirit will not always strive with man.**
17   (Gen. 6:3)
18   **HOOTO: Well, uh, what about a time of witness future?**
19   **THE LORD: No, you don't want to see that.**
20   **HOOTO: I do, I do, I do.**
21   **THE LORD: Very well. Behold!** *(Optional wind)*
22   **HOOTO:** *(Looking behind audience)* **Oh, no! Roasted duck!**
23   *(Optional wind, fade. THE LORD leads an anxious*
24   *HOOTO back to the couch and leaves. HOOTO awakes.)*
25   **Oh, boy! That was really something!** *(Dials telephone.*
26   *It rings.)*
27   **DR. FARNSWORTH:** *(Answering telephone)* **Hello?**
28   **HOOTO: Hello? Dr. Farnsworth?**
29   **DR. FARNSWORTH: Yes?**
30   **HOOTO: Crunk here.**
31   **DR. FARNSWORTH: Oh, Hooto, I was just praying for you.**
32   **HOOTO: I know.**
33   **DR. FARNSWORTH: You do?**
34   **HOOTO: Do you have anything for amnesia? I'm having**

1   trouble sleeping.
2   **DR. FARNSWORTH: What's wrong?**
3   **HOOTO:** *(Having second thoughts)* **Oh, nothing, just some**
4   **phony dream.**
5   **DR. FARNSWORTH: Are you OK?**
6   **HOOTO: Yeah, it's nothing important. I'll see ya later,**
7   **duck – I mean Doc.**
8
9
10
11
12
13
14
15
16
17
18
19
20
21
22
23
24
25
26
27
28
29
30
31
32
33
34

FINAL MINUTES

By Dan Rupple

1 **CAST:** Dan Rapture, Morley Savior, Mike Worship, Rick
2 Langeford, Murray, Luke Logger, Leana Logger, Lady on
3 the Street.
4 **SETTING:** Half of the playing area is the set of the *Final*
5 *Minutes* TV show. There are three chairs behind a desk or
6 table. The other side — where the RICK LANGEFORD
7 and LOGGER scenes take place, has a chair and table to
8 hold a telephone. There may be other assorted pieces of
9 furniture or knickknacks for the LOGGERS to crash into.
10 **PROPS:** Microphone for the three anchors when they go on
11 location, telephone for LEANA LOGGER.
12 **COSTUMES:** The three anchors should wear suits and ties.
13 DAN RAPTURE should wear a hat when he is on location.
14 RICK LANGEFORD and MURRAY should dress in trendy
15 clothes. The LOGGERS and the LADY ON THE STREET
16 should wear normal clothing. The logs in the LOGGERS'
17 eyes may be implied, or you may design something out of
18 cardboard — perhaps from a paper towel roll. (This
19 sketch was originally recorded, thereby avoiding the
20 literalness of this accessory!)
21 **SOUND EFFECTS:** Clock ticking and telephone ringing.
22
23 *(DAN RAPTURE, MORLEY SAVIOR and MIKE WORSHIP*
24 *are sitting behind the table.)*
25 **DAN RAPTURE: I'm Dan Rapture.**
26 **MORLEY SAVIOR: I'm Morley Savior.**
27 **MIKE WORSHIP: And I'm Mike Worship. Tonight on *Final***
28 ***Minutes* we look at the lives of three believers of Jesus**

1   **Christ.** *(Optional: Tick tick tick)*
2   **LUKE LOGGER:** *(Enters.)* **Just kind of think of him as my**
3   **big buddy upstairs.** *(Exits. Optional: Tick tick tick)*
4   **LEANA LOGGER:** *(Enters.)* **It's just a personal thing, you**
5   **know? I keep it to myself.** *(Exits. Optional: Tick tick tick)*
6   **LADY ON THE STREET:** *(Enters.)* **I really want to live my**
7   **life for Jesus, but I seem to have trouble.** *(Exits.*
8   *Optional: tick tick tick)*
9   **MORLEY SAVIOR: As we look at Christians' relationships**
10   **with the Lord Jesus Christ, we find they differ as**
11   **much as types of Campbell's soups on our grocery**
12   **store shelves. Some are totally engrossed with a**
13   **fervency to serve their Lord; others seem to put him**
14   **on the side, as you would green beans with a steak**
15   **and potatoes dinner; and still others camouflage**
16   **their faith to almost nonexistence. Tonight we look at**
17   **two different types of believers on *Final Minutes.***
18   *(RICK LANGEFORD enters and paces back for forth.)*
19   **MIKE WORSHIP:** *(Standing)* **This is Rick Langeford, a man**
20   **of mystery, stalking the streets of this world as if he**
21   **belonged. An unsubmissive dangler refusing the**
22   **protection that is rightfully his, availing himself to the**
23   **Enemy as open prey. This man is fair game. But I warn**
24   **you: Approach with caution. You'll never know which**
25   **way he is swaying. He might be for you, he could be**
26   **against you. Rick Langeford. He's cool, he goes to**
27   **school, some call him a fool, but he's the Enemy's**
28   **tool. Rick Langeford, an Undercover Christian.**
29   *(Optional James Bond-type music)* **We talked to Rick at**
30   **his pseudo-hip bachelor pad just outside of Cleveland,**
31   **Ohio.** *(MIKE WORSHIP crosses to RICK LANGEFORD.)*
32   **Rick, how long have you been a Christian?**
33   **RICK LANGEFORD: Oh, I don't know. I guess about all**
34   **my life.**

1 MIKE WORSHIP: **Surely there was a time or day when you**
2 **committed your life to Jesus.**
3 RICK LANGEFORD: **Well...about six years ago I went**
4 **forward after a preacher gave an altar call. Is that**
5 **what you mean?**
6 MIKE WORSHIP: **I don't know. Is it?** *(Laughs.)* **We asked**
7 **you, ya see?**
8 RICK LANGEFORD: **OK, I guess that would be it.**
9 MIKE WORSHIP: **Did your life change at that point?**
10 RICK LANGEFORD: **Well, yeah...**
11 MIKE WORSHIP: **In what way?**
12 RICK LANGEFORD: **I bought a couple of T-shirts.**
13 MIKE WORSHIP: **T-shirts?**
14 RICK LANGEFORD: **Yeah, you know – the kind with Bible-**
15 **type sayings on them. Oh, and I got a bumper sticker.**
16 MIKE WORSHIP: *(Aside)* **As we were packing up after our**
17 **first interview with Rick Langeford, a non-Christian**
18 **friend of Rick's dropped by. Unknown to Rick at the**
19 **time, our cameraman recorded a portion of their**
20 **conversation from the other room.** *(MURRAY enters.)*
21 MURRAY: **Hey, Rick, what are those guys from *Final***
22 ***Minutes* talking to you about?**
23 RICK LANGEFORD: **Hi, Murray. Oh, they wanted to ask me**
24 **about church-type things.**
25 MURRAY: **Why? Are you into that Jesus stuff?**
26 RICK LANGEFORD: **Actually, they just wanted my ad-**
27 **vice on how churches could improve themselves,**
28 **you know.**
29 MURRAY: **Oh, I see. Boy, for a minute there I thought**
30 **you'd gone religious on me.**
31 RICK LANGEFORD: **Well...**
32 MURRAY: **Yeah, that Christian junk is so stupid. I can't**
33 **believe people believe that stuff.**
34 RICK LANGEFORD: **Well, to each his own.**

1   **MURRAY: Yeah, that's right. "Do your own thing." That's**
2   **our philosophy, huh? Anyway, we're having an all-**
3   **night fraternity party Saturday night. Lots of booze.**
4   **Want to come?**
5   **RICK LANGEFORD: Ah, no, I've got to get up early Sunday**
6   **morning for church.**
7   **MURRAY: For what?**
8   **RICK LANGEFORD: I mean...**
9   **MURRAY: Did you say church?** *(Running out the door)* **Wait**
10   **till I tell the gang!**
11   **RICK LANGEFORD: Oh, no!** *(Interview resumes.)*
12   **MIKE WORSHIP: Would you say that your life is a witness**
13   **for Christ?**
14   **RICK LANGEFORD: I'm not sure what you mean.**
15   **MIKE WORSHIP: Well, is...**
16   **RICK LANGEFORD: I scraped off the bumper sticker, if**
17   **that's...**
18   **MIKE WORSHIP: No...let me put it this way: Do you share**
19   **your faith with others?**
20   **RICK LANGEFORD: It's just a personal thing with me. I**
21   **keep it to myself.**
22   **MIKE WORSHIP: Jesus said that if you confess me before**
23   **man, I'll confess you before my Father,** (Matt. 10:32,
24   author's paraphrase) **but if you don't...**
25   **RICK LANGEFORD: Once this girl and I talked about**
26   **angels and heaven and that sort of thing.**
27   **MIKE WORSHIP: Have you ever *led* someone to the Lord?**
28   **RICK LANGEFORD: I've talked to people and had them**
29   **say God or Jesus. Usually they follow it with a cuss**
30   **word, but hey, halfway there is better than nothing,**
31   **right?**
32   **MIKE WORSHIP: I have a hard time agreeing with that.**
33   **RICK LANGEFORD: Look, I'm just not Billy Graham. I'm**
34   **not into discussing my religion.**

1 **MIKE WORSHIP: Jesus said that he gives you the Holy**
2 **Spirit for the power to be a witness.**
3 **RICK LANGEFORD: OK, OK. I'll buy another bumper**
4 **sticker.** *(RICK LANGEFORD exits.)*
5 **MIKE WORSHIP:** *(Aside)* **Rick Langeford, salty as a water-**
6 **melon, with a candle burning under a bushel, with**
7 **the magnitude of the San Francisco fire. Rick**
8 **Langeford, walking with peace that bypasses all**
9 **understatements. He's real and he lives in your area.**
10 **Rick Langeford, Undercover Christian. What a**
11 **bummer.** *(MIKE WORSHIP returns to his seat. Optional:*
12 *Tick tick tick)*
13 **DAN RAPTURE:** *(Standing)* **My search for a stereotype of an**
14 **unfortunate segment of Christian believers brought**
15 **me to Smockerville, Arkansas, a small community**
16 **just west of Pine Bluff. It was here I met not just one**
17 **interviewee, but two: Luke and Leana Logger.**
18 **Husband and wife for five years, Luke and Leana**
19 **were raised in church, enduring sermon after**
20 **sermon, but unfortunately never hearing the Word of**
21 **God, the Bible. A typical day in the life of Luke Logger**
22 **consists of a hard day at the factory, home to one of**
23 **Leana's home-cooked dinners at their quaint apart-**
24 **ment, then off to one of their many church functions.**
25 **The Loggers are very distinct and unique individuals.**
26 **You can recognize them by the very large wooden**
27 **protrusions hanging in their eyes. Luke's is in his left,**
28 **Leana's in her right.** *(LEANA LOGGER enters and sits.)*
29 **LUKE LOGGER:** *(Enters.)* **Hello, Leana, I'm home.**
30 **LEANA LOGGER: I'm in the kitchen, Luke. How was work?**
31 **LUKE LOGGER: A real bum time. I had to work all day**
32 **long in the warehouse with Leo McCorkle,** *alone!* **All**
33 **he did was talk about other people. On and on.** *(Crash)*
34 **Oh, I'm sorry, I didn't see it.**

1   **LEANA LOGGER:** Yeah, Leo's like that. He's always finding
2   people's faults.
3   **LUKE LOGGER:** And who's he to talk? He's got so many.
4   *(Crash)* **Oh, no.**
5   **LEANA LOGGER:** Don't worry. The other day I saw this girl
6   walk into church. Miss Glamour Girl. Dressed to kill.
7   You should've seen her.
8   **LUKE LOGGER:** I did.
9   **LEANA LOGGER:** Well, the second I saw her and how she
10   looked, I knew old Leo would start staring. So I
11   looked for him and sure enough, he was bug-eyed.
12   **LUKE LOGGER:** Sounds like Leo. And you know what else?
13   He's a real klutzo. The other day I was drinking a
14   cola...
15   **LEANA LOGGER:** One of the ones you get free from that
16   broken dispenser?
17   **LUKE LOGGER:** Yeah. It's been broken for a week now and
18   the supervisor hasn't noticed it. Anyway, Leo spilled it
19   all over my shirt. It was my good bowling shirt, too.
20   I'm not going to forget it, either! *(Telephone rings.)*
21   **LEANA LOGGER:** I'll get it. *(Crash, spill)* **Hello. Oh, hi, Leo.**
22   Luke and I were just talking about you.... C'mon, Leo,
23   shame on you for even thinking that. What could we
24   say about our buddy Leo that's bad? Oh, OK, that'll be
25   okey-dokey. *(Hangs up.)*
26   **LUKE LOGGER:** What did old klutzo want?
27   **LEANA LOGGER:** He said he would like to give us a ride to
28   church so we wouldn't have to get the car out again.
29   **LUKE LOGGER:** Oh boy, after all day with him, then again
30   tonight, that's like spending eternity with him.
31   **DAN RAPTURE:** *(Aside)* **After viewing Luke and Leana's**
32   **lifestyles, we decided to have a personal conversation**
33   **with them.** *(DAN RAPTURE crosses to the LOGGERS.)*
34   **You say you are both Christians?**

1   LUKE LOGGER: Yes, we are.
2   DAN RAPTURE: What kind of relationship do you have
3   with Jesus?
4   LUKE LOGGER: I just think of him as my big buddy
5   upstairs.
6   DAN RAPTURE: Do you read the Bible?
7   LEANA LOGGER: No. We don't understand it.
8   DAN RAPTURE: Why not?
9   LUKE LOGGER: I don't know. We've never seemed to
10   think about it.
11   DAN RAPTURE: Well, the Bible says that when you are
12   born again you become spiritually minded, so that
13   you can understand the Word of God.
14   LEANA LOGGER: Maybe it's the thees and thous.
15   DAN RAPTURE: There are simpler versions.
16   LUKE LOGGER: We're waiting for it to come out in a comic
17   book edition. *(Laughs. Knocks over microphone.)*
18   LEANA LOGGER: Oh, I'm sorry, Mr. Rapture. I bumped
19   the microphone.
20   DAN RAPTURE: Actually, that brings up a question. Is
21   there anything you can do with those huge logs in
22   your eyes?
23   LUKE and LEANA: *(Together)* What logs?
24   DAN RAPTURE: Those planks. You know, you keep
25   knocking things over with them.
26   LUKE LOGGER: Oh, we hadn't noticed.
27   LEANA LOGGER: Are they uncomely?
28   DAN RAPTURE: Rather odd, I'd say.
29   LUKE LOGGER: Oh, we'll have to look into them sometime.
30   DAN RAPTURE: Well, you do look into them – constantly!
31   LEANA LOGGER: Hmmm. They never seemed to bother us.
32   DAN RAPTURE: Oops....
33   LUKE LOGGER: What happened?
34   DAN RAPTURE: Oh, I wear contact lenses, and one just

1   **popped out. Can you see it anywhere?**

2   **LEANA LOGGER: Is this it?**

3   **DAN RAPTURE: No, that's my hat.**

4   **LUKE LOGGER: You know, the whole time we were**
5   **talking, I could see that little rascal was gonna give**
6   **ya trouble.**

7   **LEANA LOGGER: Well, what's that thing over there?**

8   **DAN RAPTURE: No, no. Don't pull that, it's a microphone**
9   **cord.** *(Crashes. The LOGGERS stumble Off-stage. Aside)*
10   **The Loggers, Luke and Leana, two hypocritical**
11   **Christians who aren't even hearers of the Word, let**
12   **alone doers. They roam around looking outward**
13   **blindly, never looking inwardly. Afraid what they may**
14   **find? Maybe. Maybe not. Let God be the judge. Chances**
15   **are they wouldn't recognize the problems if they were**
16   **right in front of their noses. A sad fact, they miss the**
17   **joy that comes from obedience to God's Word. As John**
18   **15:3 says, "And now you are clean through the Word."**
19   (Author's paraphrase) **Luke and Leana Logger, ready for**
20   **the Biz bag?** *(He returns to his seat.)*

21   **MIKE WORSHIP: Our search for individuals who truly**
22   **portray the kind of life that Jesus taught about goes**
23   **on. Where will we find it? In your town, your home,**
24   **your life? Hopefully. If so, we'll find many more**
25   **shining lives before we reach the final minute.**

26   **DAN RAPTURE: I'm Dan Rapture.**

27   **MORLEY SAVIOR: I'm Morley Savior.**

28   **MIKE WORSHIP: And I'm Mike Worship. Join us next week**
29   **on Final Minutes...maybe.** *(Optional: Tick tick tick)*

30

31

32

33

34

PEOPLE SAY THE DARNDEST THINGS

By Dan Rupple

1   ***CAST:*** Announcer (On-stage or off), Jim Kennedy, Delbert
2   Bartley, Bible Lady, Art Langtree, Larry Nelson, Barb
3   Henderson, Carol (Off-stage voice).

4   ***SETTING:*** A game show.

5   ***PROPS:*** Microphone for ANNOUNCER, Bible for BIBLE LADY.

6   ***COSTUMES:*** Suits for JIM and ANNOUNCER, and normal
7   attire for everyone else.

8   ***SOUND EFFECT:*** Beep, taped conversation between ART and
9   CAROL.

10

11   **ANNOUNCER: Ladies and gentlemen, travel with us now,**
12   **beyond the clouds, beyond the galaxies, right through**
13   **and into heaven itself, as we go before the glorious**
14   **mighty judgment seat of God. Yes, let's begin televi-**
15   **sion's most revealing game show...*People Say the***
16   ***Darndest Things*. And now, here's our host, Jim**
17   **Kennedy. Jim-O?** *(JIM enters.)*

18   **JIM: Thank you, thank you, and welcome to *People Say the***
19   ***Darndest Things*. Just a quick review of the rules for**
20   **our new viewers. Our contestants have all been**
21   **informed of the rules for many years, so no excuses**
22   **and no alibis are permitted. All judgments are**
23   **reserved for God himself through the authority of his**
24   **Word. So, with that established, let's meet our first**
25   **contestant.**

26   **ANNOUNCER: Jim, our first contestant is a mechanic from**
27   **Buffalo, New York. Audience, welcome Delbert**
28   **Bartley.** *(DELBERT enters.)*

1   **JIM: Welcome, Delbert, to *People Say the Darndest Things*.**
2   **How ya doing?**
3   **DELBERT: Not so good. I'm a little nervous.**
4   **JIM: Well, Delbert, after looking at your file, I'd say you**
5   **have plenty of reason to be. Delbert, I want you to**
6   **know that you hold a *People Say the Darndest Things***
7   **record, 'cause in your lifetime, you took the name of**
8   **the Lord in vain, either by cursing God or by using the**
9   **name of Jesus 617,542 times.**
10   **DELBERT: Oh, *(——— Beep).***
11   **JIM: Make that 617,543 times.**
12   **DELBERT: Now wait a second. I said "God bless you" to a**
13   **lotta people too, especially when people sneezed, you**
14   **know. Doesn't that sorta even out?**
15   **JIM: I don't think so, Delbert. OK, it's time for the ruling,**
16   **and Scripture says...Matthew 12:34-37.**
17   **DELBERT: Uh, what's that say?**
18   **BIBLE LADY: "Out of the abundance of the heart the**
19   **mouth speaks. I say to you that every idle word that**
20   **men shall speak, they shall give account thereof in the**
21   **day of judgment. For by your words you shall be justi-**
22   **fied, and by your words you shall be condemned."**
23   (Author's paraphrase)
24   **JIM: Thank you, Bible Lady.**
25   **DELBERT: Condemned?**
26   **JIM: Yeah, looks like you're in trouble, but thanks for being**
27   **on the show. Now just go right on through the judg-**
28   **ment door for God's sentencing. *(Exit DELBERT.***
29   ***Applause)* Boy, sure sounds like Delbert had quite a**
30   **bad heart and far too many idle words. Well, let's meet**
31   **our next contestant.**
32   **ANNOUNCER: Jim, our next contestant was an operations**
33   **supervisor in Omaha, Nebraska. Audience, welcome**
34   **Art Langtree. *(ART enters.)***

1   **JIM: Welcome, Art**

2   **ART: Thank you, Jim, thank you.**

3   **JIM: How ya doing?**

4   **ART: I'm doing great.**

5   **JIM: Feeling pretty assured of yourself, huh?**

6   **ART: Oh, let me tell you, Jim, I keep a close watch on this**

7   **mouth of mine.**

8   **JIM: Well, OK, Art, let's look at your file. Oh, Art, I see a**

9   **few slips.**

10   **ART: What do you mean?**

11   **JIM: We're gonna go back to March 8, 1974 – the place,**

12   **your living room. Let's run the tape.**

13   **ART:** *(Looks above audience's heads.)* **Monitor up here?**

14   **JIM: Yeah.**

15   ***PRE-RECORDED INSERT***

16   **ART: Carol, I'm tired of asking you. Where's my bowling**

17   **ball?**

18   **CAROL: I told you, it's in the closet.**

19   **ART: It is not. I'm looking in the closet, and I... Oh** *(Beep)*

20   **women! I just...** *(Ball drops.)* **Oh, you...** *(Beep)* **Oh, my**

21   *(Beep)* **toe.**

22   ***END INSERT***

23   **JIM: There you have it, Art. Pretty convicting.**

24   **ART: OK, so I blew it once. Did you have to play it in public?**

25   **Look, I was in the closet. I didn't hurt anyone.**

26   **JIM: Well, Art, that wasn't the only time. I've got a list, if**

27   **you care to see any more.**

28   **ART: Uh, no, no, that's OK.**

29   **JIM: Well, let's get a ruling – and the Scripture says...Luke**

30   **12:3.**

31   **BIBLE LADY: "Therefore, whatever you have spoken in**

32   **darkness shall be heard in the light; and that which**

33   **you have spoken in the ear in closets shall be**

34   **proclaimed upon the housetops."** (Author's paraphrase)

1 **JIM: I'm sorry, Art, but you've been a good sport. Go right**
2 **on through for sentencing. Thanks again.** *(Exit ART.)*
3 **Before we move on, we got a couple of letters asking**
4 **about what happened to Harry Garner, the man who**
5 **throughout his life vehemently denied that Jesus is**
6 **Lord. As you recall, Harry received a Philippians 2:10**
7 **and 11. Bible Lady?**
8 **BIBLE LADY: "At the name of Jesus every knee shall bow,**
9 **and every tongue confess that Jesus Christ is Lord."**
10 (Author's paraphrase)
11 **JIM: We can report that Harry is now on his knees, admit-**
12 **ting that Jesus is Lord. Sadly, too little, too late for**
13 **Harry. And now for our next contestant.**
14 **ANNOUNCER: Right, Jim-O. Next guest is a man previously**
15 **from Cedar Rapids, Michigan. Let's welcome to *People***
16 ***Say the Darndest Things* – Larry Nelson.** *(LARRY enters.)*
17 **JIM: Welcome, Larry.**
18 **LARRY: Thank you, Jim. It's great to be here.**
19 **JIM: Oh, it is?**
20 **LARRY: Sure, Jim. I went to church every Sunday, I raised**
21 **four hundred dollars for the stained glass fund, and I**
22 **saw the movie *Five Commandments* ten times.**
23 **JIM: Oh, impressive, Larry, but your file isn't spotless. I'm**
24 **sorry. You've got quite a few offenses.**
25 **LARRY: Huh? Maybe there's a mistake.**
26 **JIM: No. Take April 10, 1976, at the Elks Lodge, for**
27 **instance.**
28 **LARRY: I don't remember that day in particular.**
29 **JIM: Does the line "Did you hear the one about the travel-**
30 **ing salesman?" ring a bell?**
31 **LARRY: Oh, well, yeah...**
32 **JIM: Should we read the rest of the story?**
33 **LARRY: No, that's OK, but hey, it was just the guys, you**
34 **know. A few beers. We were just kidding. We always**

1   told jokes like that.

2   JIM: Well, OK, Larry, let's see. And the Scriptures
3   say...James 1:26.

4   BIBLE LADY: "If any man among you seems to be religious
5   but doesn't bridle his tongue, he deceives himself and
6   his religion is in vain." (Author's paraphrase)

7   JIM: Thank you, Bible Lady.

8   LARRY: Vain? After every Sunday having to get up and go to
9   that boring church?

10   JIM: Larry, you'll have to tell it to the judge, and thank you
11   for being on *People Say the Darndest Things*. Don?
12   *(Exit LARRY.)*

13   ANNOUNCER: Jim, our final contestant is a telephone
14   repair person from Whittier, California. Audience,
15   welcome Barb Henderson. *(BARB enters.)*

16   JIM: Welcome, Barb.

17   BARB: Praise the Lord, Jim. It's a privilege and an honor to
18   be here.

19   JIM: Great! Well, let's open your file and see what you've said.

20   BARB: OK.

21   JIM: Boy, Barb, it's empty. Not one word. Congratulations!
22   *(Applause)*

23   BARB: Thank you, but I can't take any credit. Ya see, I've
24   said plenty of bad things in my day – you know, lost
25   my temper or didn't bridle my tongue. But being a
26   Christian, Jesus took all the judgment for me, so my
27   file's clean.

28   JIM: Yeah, just like you never said one wrong word. That's
29   great. And Don, what do we have for Barb?

30   ANNOUNCER: Well, Jim, for Barb, there's joy, peace, and
31   happiness for eternity, and not just any eternity, but
32   eternity with God himself.

33   BARB: Praise the Lord.

34   JIM: Well, that's our show, once again proving that

1　　　　　　**Proverbs 13:3 says:**

2　　**BIBLE LADY: "He that keeps his mouth keeps his life; but**

3　　　　　　**he that opens wide his lips shall see destruction."**

4　　　　　　(Author's paraphrase)

5　　**JIM: This is Jim Kennedy on behalf of the Bible Lady,**

6　　　　　　**saying good night and see you all sometime on *People***

7　　　　　　***Say the Darndest Things.***

8

9

10

11

12

13

14

15

16

17

18

19

20

21

22

23

24

25

26

27

28

29

30

31

32

33

34

PILGRIM RACE

By Dan Rupple

1　**CAST:** Robbie Robenowitz, Jim Spencer, Norman Miller.

2　**SETTING:** A track meet.

3　**PROPS:** Microphone for ROBBIE.

4　**COSTUMES:** Suit for ROBBIE. Shorts, tank tops and running

5　　　shoes for JIM and NORMAN.

6

7　*(ROBBIE is at Center Stage holding his microphone.)*

8　**ROBBIE: Hello, sports fans. Robbie Robenowitz here at**

9　　　**the Pilgrim Race. I'm standing right at the finish line,**

10　　**hoping to speak with today's winning runner.**

11　　**According to our scouts, the runners have passed the**

12　　**final turn, so we should be seeing the winners at any**

13　　**time. Reports show John Maybury, Alex Hawkins and**

14　　**Linda Ferguson leading the pack, with Jim Spencer a**

15　　**distant fourth. The Pilgrim Race differs from a**

16　　**straight marathon run because of its constant obsta-**

17　　**cles and its important road selection decisions. And**

18　　**here they come now. It's Hawkins out in front,**

19　　**followed by Maybury and Ferguson. But wait a**

20　　**minute! Spencer is gaining. He's passed Ferguson**

21　　**and Maybury. Hawkins is losing steam. Spencer, Jim**

22　　**Spencer is the leader.** *(JIM runs On-stage.)* **Hawkins,**

23　　**Ferguson and Maybury round out the front four. I've**

24　　**got Jim here now. Jim! Congratulations on your victory.**

25　**JIM: Thank you, but praise the Lord!**

26　**ROBBIE: You had a great run. It shows great mental, phys-**

27　　**ical and most of all, spiritual strength.**

28　**JIM: Well, I can do all things through Jesus Christ, Robbie.**

1   He gives me strength.

2   ROBBIE: Jim, training is such an important part of any
3   race. What's your method?

4   JIM: Well, Robbie, I start with a good diet. You've got to eat
5   right. I have well-balanced meals – you know, meats,
6   milk, and so on.

7   ROBBIE: Could you describe a usual breakfast?

8   JIM: Sure. I'll start with something meaty, say Romans,
9   then maybe a side of Proverbs and a big glass of living
10   water, then a Psalm or two for dessert.

11   ROBBIE: You have that every day?

12   JIM: Not in that particular order, Robbie. I eat my way
13   right on through the entire Bible. Each book has
14   different nutrients.

15   ROBBIE: How about exercise?

16   JIM: Very important, Robbie. You know, you can't just be an
17   eater of the Word, but you must be a doer also. Well,
18   right before breakfast, I do my spiritual calisthenics.

19   ROBBIE; Spiritual calisthenics?

20   JIM: Sure, you know – my devotions, praise, prayer, inter-
21   cession. All very important to keep each part of the
22   body strong and active.

23   ROBBIE: And diet and devotions are what wins the race?

24   JIM: Partly. That just begins the day. But then throughout
25   the day I do numerous exercises to keep fit.

26   ROBBIE: Fit for the Master's use, right?

27   JIM: Right on, Robbie.

28   ROBBIE: What kind of exercises do you do, Jim?

29   JIM: Well, they vary. You know, fellowship, tithing,
30   witnessing, Bible study, worship, that sort of thing.

31   ROBBIE: All that training. It must take a lot of discipline.

32   JIM: That's what it's all about, Robbie. To run the race, to
33   win, or to fight the good fight, you've got to be disci-
34   plined. Why do you think they call us disciples?

1   **ROBBIE: How do you keep motivated?**

2   **JIM: Robbie, the secret is keeping your eyes on the finish**

3   **line, not being distracted by anything off the course,**

4   **and then striving to obtain the prize.**

5   **ROBBIE: Well, obtain you did. Thank you, Jim, for talking**

6   **with us.**

7   **JIM: Thank you, Robbie.** *(NORMAN stumbles in.)*

8   **ROBBIE: And now the final race contestants have just**

9   **crossed the line, and I'm talking with Norman Miller,**

10   **the loser. Norman, you finished last in the Pilgrim Race.**

11   **NORMAN: OK, Robbie, you don't have to rub it in. I'm**

12   **dying already.**

13   **ROBBIE: Jim Spencer just told us of his rigorous training**

14   **schedule and self-discipline. How about you?**

15   **NORMAN: Well, Robbie, the Trainer said "Come unto me**

16   **and I'll give you rest," so I took it.**

17   **ROBBIE: Took what?**

18   **NORMAN: Rest! Lots of it, Robbie. I figured thirteen hours**

19   **of sleep a day kept me more alert for the hours I was**

20   **awake. It didn't work, though. Oh boy, I need a bed. I**

21   **blew it, Robbie. Too much junk food. All I fed on was**

22   **Christian records, personal testimonies, and an occa-**

23   **sional fix of Scripture cards. All milk, but no meat,**

24   **Robbie. I was a spiritual vegetarian.**

25   **ROBBIE: Surely you exercise?**

26   **NORMAN: I'd put in an hour of pew-warming on Sunday,**

27   **by I guess that wasn't enough. I feel like a walking**

28   **Ben-Gay commercial. Well, except my hand.**

29   **ROBBIE: Your hand?**

30   **NORMAN: Yeah, that got a lot of exercise. You know,**

31   **turning on the TV, changing channels, flipping**

32   **through the TV Guide, switching on the radio, tuning**

33   **in the stations. All that was very demanding.**

34   **ROBBIE: And did that help you in the race today?**

1   **NORMAN: No, I'm afraid not, Robbie. Look, I got to run –**

2   **uh, crawl.** *(Crawls Off-stage, then yells.)* **Does anyone**

3   **have a milkshake?**

4   **ROBBIE: Well, that's the report from the Pilgrim Race.**

5   **Joe, back to you in the booth.**

6

7

8

9

10

11

12

13

14

15

16

17

18

19

20

21

22

23

24

25

26

27

28

29

30

31

32

33

34

LEAVE IT TO SQUIRRELLIE

By Dave Toole

1 **CAST:** Narrator (On-stage or off), Jane, Warren, Willie,
2   Squirrellie, Freddie, Wiley, Lonnie.
3 **SETTING:** The Cheever household. The stage should have
4   two suggested sets: the Cheever kitchen at Stage Left, and
5   Willie and Squirrellie's bedroom at Stage Right. The
6   school scene takes place Upstage Right away from the
7   boys' bedroom area. There should be a partition between
8   the two main areas — ideally, with a door. The boys'
9   bedroom should contain two beds (or tables made up to
10   resemble beds) at the minimum. The kitchen area
11   should contain a table that has been set and an area with
12   assorted bowls and utensils for JANE's cooking.
13 **PROPS:** Chain with Christian fish symbol on it, Bible and
14   textbook for SQUIRRELLIE; suitcases with clothes inside
15   for SQUIRRELLIE and WILLIE; coffee pot and covered
16   dish (the "roast" for JANE).
17 **COSTUMES:** Fifties-type attire for all. JANE should wear a
18   dress, heels, pearls and an apron. WARREN wears a suit.
19   The boys and their friends should dress casually.
20 **SOUND EFFECTS:** School sounds.
21
22 **NARRATOR:** *Leave It to Squirrellie*, **with Hugh Budford,**
23   **Barbara Billingsworth, Tommy Dow and Jerry**
24   **Smathers – he's Squirrellie.** *(Lights up, Stage Left.*
25   *Enter JANE and WARREN.)*
26 **JANE: Warren, we'd better hurry if we don't want to be**
27   **late. Are the boys ready?**
28 **WARREN: Well, I hope so, dear. They've had almost an**

Leave It to Squirrellie

1   **hour to pack.** *(Calling Off-stage)* **Boys, let's hurry. We**
2   **don't want to be late.**
3   **WILLIE and SQUIRRELLIE:** *(Together from Off-stage)* **OK, Dad.**
4   **JANE: Warren, I'm worried about Squirrellie. Are you sure**
5   **he'll be all right? It's his first time away from home.**
6   **WARREN: Now, Jane, we've been all through this before. This**
7   **church camp is just what he needs. Swimming, horse-**
8   **back riding, camping – all the things a boy his age loves.**
9   **JANE: Well, I don't know...**
10 **WARREN: Of course not, dear – you were never a little boy.**
11   **Besides, it's only one week.**
12 **JANE: Guess so...** *(Enter WILLIE from darkened bedroom.)*
13 **WILLIE: OK, Dad, I'm ready to go.**
14 **JANE: Willie, did you remember your toothbrush?**
15 **WILLIE: Uh-huh.**
16 **JANE: And the number where we can be reached?**
17 **WILLIE: Yeah.**
18 **JANE: Don't forget to do just what Dumpy's parents tell**
19   **you to.**
20 **WILLIE: Gee, Mom, how's a guy supposed to have any fun?**
21 **JANE: Never mind. Just mind your manners.**
22 **WILLIE: Sure, Mom.**
23 **WARREN: Say, is Squirrellie ready yet?**
24 **WILLIE: Oh yeah, Dad, he's been packed for half an hour.**
25   **He's just up there mopin' around. You know how kids**
26   **are.**
27 **JANE: Oh, Warren, maybe you should go upstairs and talk**
28   **to him.**
29 **WARREN:** *(Lights fade out.)* **Oh, all right.** *(Knock at door.*
30   *Lights up Stage Right.)* **Squirrellie? OK if I come in?**
31 **SQUIRRELLIE: Sure, Dad.**
32 **WARREN:** *(Enters.)* **What's the matter, son?**
33 **SQUIRRELLIE: I dunno, Dad. I guess I'm not as sure as**
34   **you are that this is a good idea.**

1 WARREN: Oh, now, Squirrellie, I know just how you feel.
2 You know, I remember my first time away from
3 home. I was supposed to spend a week with your
4 great aunt Harriet.
5 SQUIRRELLIE: The one with the big nose?
6 WARREN: Uh...yes. Anyway, I thought it would be the
7 longest week I'd ever spent because I didn't know
8 anybody where she lived. But you know what? It
9 turned out to be a great time. There were lots of kids
10 to play with. I just had to meet them.
11 SQUIRRELLIE: Yeah, I guess so. But your parents didn't
12 make you spend a week at church.
13 WARREN: Squirrellie, you're not spending the week at
14 church. You're spending it at camp. We went over the
15 brochure together. You saw for yourself how much
16 there is to do. Besides, church isn't such a bad thing.
17 SQUIRRELLIE: Then how come you and Mom don't go?
18 WARREN: Ah...well...your mother and I work all week, and
19 after we get all the work done around the house on
20 Saturday, Sunday's the only day we can take it easy.
21 Even the Bible says you should take one day off, right?
22 SQUIRRELLIE: I guess so.
23 WARREN: All right! Now, you go ahead and get your things
24 together, and I'll see you downstairs.
25 SQUIRRELLIE: Dad...
26 WARREN: Yes?
27 SQUIRRELLIE: Did you really have a good time at Aunt
28 Harriet's?
29 WARREN: Why sure, and I think you're gonna have a good
30 time at camp, too. Now, let's hurry up – your mother's
31 waiting.
32 SQUIRRELLIE: OK, Dad. *(WARREN and SQUIRRELLIE exit.)*
33 *(Lights fade out. Optional music. Music fades, lights up*
34 *Stage Left. The Cheever family enters coming home from*

1   *vacation, one week later.)*

2 **WARREN: Now, boys, be sure and put all your things away**

3   **neatly.**

4 **JANE: And just put your dirty clothes in the hamper, OK?**

5 **SQUIRRELLIE and WILLIE:** *(Together)* **OK, Mom.** *(Boys*

6   *cross to darkened room.)*

7 **JANE: Ah, it's great to be back and see the boys, isn't it?**

8 **WARREN: Well, it should be – you worried about them all**

9   **week.**

10 **JANE: Now, Warren Cheever, that's not true. It's just that**

11   **this was Squirrellie's first time away from home and**

12   **all and...oh, he did seem to enjoy it, didn't he?**

13 **WARREN: Well, I hate to say I told you so, but...**

14 **JANE: Oh, Warren, really!** *(Both exit.)*

15 **WARREN:** *(While leaving)* **Sorry, dear, sometimes facts are**

16   **hard to deal with.** *(Lights out Stage Left, up Stage Right.*

17   *WILLIE and SQUIRRELLIE are putting their things away.)*

18 **SQUIRRELLIE: Yeah, it was really neat, Willie. They had**

19   **boats and horses and a really nifty water slide. We**

20   **played kickball and baseball and volleyball and went**

21   **swimming, and one day Mr. Frazier took us for a hike**

22   **and we saw some deer and some squirrels and we had**

23   **a bonfire and roasted hot dogs and marshmallows**

24   **and everything!**

25 **WILLIE: Sounds pretty cool, Squirrel. Did you make any**

26   **new friends?**

27 **SQUIRRELLIE: Oh, yeah, there were lots of kids to play**

28   **with. It was really great, Willie. What did you do all**

29   **week?**

30 **WILLIE: Ah, Dumpy's dad had the measles, so we didn't do**

31   **much over there. We mostly hung around Rollin's**

32   **Bluff with Freddie and watched the dump trucks**

33   **load up with dirt. Hey, what's that?**

34 **SQUIRRELLIE: What's what?**

1   WILLIE: That thing around your neck.

2   SQUIRRELLIE: Oh, you mean this thing?

3   WILLIE: Yeah.

4   SQUIRRELLIE: It's sort of a fish.

5   WILLIE: Let me see it. I X O Y E? What's that mean?

6   SQUIRRELLIE: Well, it means I got...borned again, kinda.

7   WILLIE: Born again? You mean you're a Christian?

8   SQUIRRELLIE: Well, yeah, I think so.

9   WILLIE: Boy, Squirrellie, does Dad know about this?

10   SQUIRRELLIE: No. Do you think he's gonna holler at me
11   and stuff?

12   WILLIE: I dunno, Squirrellie. You've never done anything
13   like this before. What would make you go and do a
14   goofy thing like that?

15   SQUIRRELLIE: I dunno, Willie. They were all just
16   studying the Bible, and they read a part that said if I
17   didn't, I would go to hell, and that if I didn't want to
18   go, what I had to do was repent from all the bad stuff
19   that I did and accept Jesus as my Savior and live my
20   life for him, and I could go to heaven.

21   WILLIE: What does all that mean?

22   SQUIRRELLIE: Well, it means that instead of doin' all the
23   things that I want to do, I should only do the things
24   that the Bible says to do, like be nice to people and not
25   be selfish and pray and read the Bible every day.

26   WILLIE: Sounds kinda creepy, if you ask me.

27   SQUIRRELLIE: Well, I know it does at first. I didn't think
28   I was going to like readin' my Bible every day, because
29   it always sounds so boring when Reverend Watkins
30   reads it. But really, I like it now.

31   WILLIE: You got a Bible?

32   SQUIRRELLIE: Yeah, they gave it to me at camp. *(Picks up*
33   *Bible.)* Look, it's got pictures and maps and it's
34   written so I can understand what it means.

1   **WILLIE: Mmmm, that's kinda neat.**

2   **SQUIRRELLIE: Yeah, and they got a prayer group and a**

3   **believers club and lots of other things to help me**

4   **grow in the Lord. At first I thought it was dumb to be**

5   **a Christian because it wasn't any fun, but it's really**

6   **pretty neat, huh, Willie?**

7   **WILLIE: Ah, I guess so. So long as you like it. I wouldn't do**

8   **it, though.**

9   **SQUIRRELLIE: Why not, Willie?**

10   **WILLIE: Because, Squirrellie, if I stopped doin' all the**

11   **stuff I'm not supposed to be doin', I wouldn't have**

12   **anything left to do.**

13   **SQUIRRELLIE: Willie, can I pray for you?**

14   **WILLIE: I guess so, but why would you want to do that?**

15   **SQUIRRELLIE: 'Cause I really love you, Willie. You're the**

16   **best brother a guy ever had.**

17   **WILLIE: Ah, cut it out, Squirrellie.** *(Lights out Stage Right,*

18   *up Stage Left.)*

19   *(Midmorning a few days later)*

20   **JANE: More coffee, dear?**

21   **WARREN: Huh? Oh, yes, please.** *(JANE pours.)* **Thank you,**

22   **dear.**

23   **JANE: Let me feel your forehead again. Oh, you seem all**

24   **right, but what I can't understand is how in the world**

25   **four grown men could manage to fall into the lake**

26   **while playing golf.**

27   **WARREN: Well, it wouldn't be so hard to understand if**

28   **you ever rode with Fred Rutherford. I could almost**

29   **swear he drove that golf car straight into the lake on**

30   **purpose.**

31   **JANE: But didn't you say the accelerator got stuck on him?**

32   **WARREN: I'm not so sure.** *(Door knock)* **I'll get it.** *(Walks*

33   *over to door and opens it.)*

34   **FREDDIE:** *(Off-stage)* **Oh, good morning, Mr. Cheever,**

1   **Mrs. Cheever.**

2   **WARREN: Ah, good morning, Freddie.** *(Enter FREDDIE.)*

3   **FREDDIE: My, Mrs. Cheever, you sure look lovely today.**

4   **JANE: Thank you, Freddie.**

5   **FREDDIE: Quite a nice day, isn't it?**

6   **WARREN: Well, for some of us.**

7   **FREDDIE: You know, as I was out on my paper route this**

8   **morning, I just couldn't help but notice the awesome**

9   **beauty of this thriving community of ours.**

10   **JANE: Oh, I didn't know you had a paper route, Freddie.**

11   **FREDDIE: Oh yes, Mrs. Cheever. It's only a temporary situ-**

12   **ation, though. I felt it would be a good idea to get**

13   **some business experience in case someone offers me**

14   **a real job, like Mr. Cheever has.**

15   **WARREN: Well, that's very wise, Freddie. The boys are up**

16   **in their room.**

17   **FREDDIE: Thank you, sir. It's certainly a pleasure to see**

18   **both of you again. Perhaps now that I've got some**

19   **experience, Mr. Cheever, you and I can get together**

20   **and talk about business sometime. You know, man**

21   **to man.**

22   **WARREN: Well, we'll see about that, Freddie.**

23   **FREDDIE: Yes, we will. I'll be going up to see William now.**

24   **I certainly have enjoyed our little chat, sir.** *(FREDDIE*

25   *leaves.)*

26   **WARREN: I dunno, kinda different.** *(Lights out Stage Left,*

27   *up Stage Right. FREDDIE enters the boys' room.)*

28   **FREDDIE: Have no fear, handsome's here.**

29   **WILLIE: Oh, hi, Freddie.**

30   **FREDDIE: Hiya, men, what's shakin'?**

31   **WILLIE: Ah, nuthin' much. I was just gonna go over to**

32   **Stubby Ferguson's house and see his iguana.**

33   **FREDDIE: Oh yeah? Well, maybe you can get a date with**

34   **one of his lizards, huh? Hee-hee. Hey, what are you**

1   dressed up for, Squirt? You look like you just climbed

2   out from under a rock.

3   SQUIRRELLIE: Oh, I'm gonna go down today and help

4   paint the church.

5   FREDDIE: Paint the church? Who's makin' ya do that?

6   SQUIRRELLIE: No one's makin' me do it. I just want to,

7   that's all.

8   FREDDIE: You mean they ain't payin' ya? You're doin' it

9   for free?

10   SQUIRRELLIE: Well, yeah.

11   FREDDIE: Hey, Willie, I thought you were this guy's

12   brother. Squirrellie, let me tell you about churches.

13   They're a rip-off. My ol' man says they're the biggest

14   crooks in town. They don't have to pay for taxes or

15   anything. They just get people like you to do all their

16   work for free and keep all the money from the offer-

17   ings for themselves. And I hear some of those

18   offerings are over a million dollars.

19   SQUIRRELLIE: But that's not true, Freddie. Our church

20   doesn't have a million dollars. Some of the pastors

21   even have extra jobs just to feed their families.

22   FREDDIE: That's all a scam, Sam. You watch – one day

23   you'll wake up and they'll all be gone to the Bahamas

24   or somethin'.

25   WILLIE: Ah, lay off him, Freddie, will ya?

26   FREDDIE: OK, OK. Don't say I didn't warn ya. Christians

27   are nuthin' but a bunch of phonies.

28   WILLIE: Cut it out, Freddie. Why don't you wait for me

29   downstairs?

30   FREDDIE: Hey, don't get mad, Dad. I'm goin', I'm goin'! Hey,

31   St. Theodore, see ya later, eh? *(Exit FREDDIE Stage Left.)*

32   WILLIE: Sorry about that, Squirrellie. You know how

33   Freddie is.

34   SQUIRRELLIE: It's OK, Willie – he doesn't bother me. I

1   **know there's lots of people who say they're Christians**

2   **but really aren't. What I don't understand is how God**

3   **can love a guy like Freddie. He must be an awfully big**

4   **God.**

5   **WILLIE: Yeah, I guess so.** *(Lights out. Lights up Stage Right.)*

6   *(It is two days later. SQUIRRELLIE is on his hands and*

7   *knees.)*

8   **SQUIRRELLIE: Sit, sit. C'mon, boy, sit. C'mon now. There**

9   **you go! There you go! Roll over. C'mon now, roll over.**

10   **C'mon now, you just put your legs out like this and**

11   **roll over. C'mon, you can do it. Really, it's not hard. If**

12   **you want, you can just roll halfway over and play**

13   **dead.** *(Enter WILEY and LONNIE from Stage Left.)* **Oh,**

14   **hi, Wiley. Hi, Lonnie.**

15   **WILEY: Watcha doin', Squirrellie?**

16   **SQUIRRELLIE: Oh, I'm just tryin' to teach my frog,**

17   **Burpie, some tricks like that one at the carnival.**

18   **WILEY: Ah, c'mon, Squirrellie. You can't teach an old frog**

19   **new tricks. You got to get 'em when they're tadpoles.**

20   **You're just wastin' your time with that old thing.**

21   **LONNIE: Yeah, Squirrellie. Besides, guess what? Dean**

22   **Swainny's big brother is working at the Rialto today,**

23   **and guess what they're showin'?** *Berserk Busboy* **and**

24   *The Wild Vampires.* **They're rated R** *(Ooohs)* **and Dean's**

25   **brother says he can get us in for free. Wanna go?**

26   **SQUIRRELLIE: No, I don't think so, you guys.**

27   **LONNIE: Why not, Squirrellie? Afraid your parents will**

28   **find out?**

29   **WILEY: Or maybe you'd prefer to spend your day with a frog.**

30   **SQUIRRELLIE: No, it's not that. It's just that, well, I'm a**

31   **Christian now, and what you guys want to do is wrong.**

32   **LONNIE: Are you kiddin', Squirrellie? You know how long**

33   **you'll have to wait to get another chance like this?**

34   **Maybe ten years. And even then you'll have to pay five**

1   dollars. Today's free.

2   **SQUIRRELLIE:** But, Lonnie, those movies are *bad* movies.
3   They show all kinds of things you're not even
4   supposed to think about. And now that I'm a
5   Christian, I just can't go!

6   **WILEY:** Look, Squirrellie, me and Lonnie go to Sunday
7   school every week, too. You're not saying we ain't
8   Christians, are you?

9   **SQUIRRELLIE:** Well...

10   **LONNIE:** Remember, you're not supposed to judge other
11   people.

12   **SQUIRRELLIE:** Well, Lonnie, Wiley, it's not up to me to say
13   if you're really Christians. That's between you and the
14   Lord. All I know is, Christians just aren't supposed to
15   go to those kinds of movies.

16   **LONNIE:** Oh, yeah? Then how come Dean's brother saw
17   Mr. Hopkins there last night? Huh?

18   **SQUIRRELLIE:** The Mr. Hopkins who's in the choir?

19   **LONNIE:** Yeah.

20   **WILEY:** Listen, Squirrellie, are you comin' or not?

21   **SQUIRRELLIE:** I told you, Wiley, I can't go.

22   **WILEY:** Have it your way, Squirrellie. C'mon, Lonnie.

23   **LONNIE:** Yeah, let's go. Leave old frog face to his toad. *(Exit*
24   *WILEY and LONNIE Stage Left.)*

25   **SQUIRRELLIE:** Gee, Burpie, sometimes it's real hard to do
26   the right thing, huh? *(Lights out Center Stage. Lights up*
27   *Stage Right.)*
28   *(The next Monday. WILEY and LONNIE are standing*
29   *together. Enter SQUIRRELLIE. Sounds of school.)*

30   **SQUIRRELLIE:** Mornin', Wiley. Mornin', Lonnie.

31   **WILEY:** Hey, Lonnie, you see what I see?

32   **LONNIE:** Yeah, I see it.

33   **WILEY:** What is it?

34   **LONNIE:** A dirty rotten fink.

1   **WILEY: Yeah, that's what it is – a dirty rotten fink.**

2   **SQUIRRELLIE: Hey, you guys, what's wrong?**

3   **WILEY: What's wrong? Don't you play dumb with us,**
4   **Squirrellie Cheever. We know you told our parents**
5   **about the movies Saturday.**

6   **LONNIE: Dirty rotten fink.**

7   **SQUIRRELLIE: I didn't do that, you guys. Lonnie, Wiley, I**
8   **didn't tell on you guys. I didn't even know if you went**
9   **for sure.**

10   **LONNIE: Then who was it? Your frog?**

11   **WILEY: C'mon, Lonnie, let's get out of here.**

12   **LONNIE: Yeah.**

13   **LONNIE and WILEY:** *(Together)* **Dirty rotten fink, dirty**
14   **rotten fink, dirty rotten fink, dirty rotten fink, dirty**
15   **rotten fink, dirty rotten fink!**

16   **SQUIRRELLIE: Hey, you guys, I didn't say anything –**
17   **honest!**

18   **WILEY: Oh, yeah? Well, we ain't never talkin' to you again,**
19   **Squirrellie Cheever.**

20   **LONNIE: Yeah, you dirty rotten fink!**

21   **WILEY: Yeah!** *(Exit WILEY and LONNIE Stage Right.)*

22   **SQUIRRELLIE: Gee, Lord, I only did what was right. I never**
23   **knew it was gonna be this hard.** *(Lights out Stage Right.)*
24   *(It is later that night. Lights up Stage Left on Cheever*
25   *kitchen.)*

26   **WARREN: How much longer till supper, dear?**

27   **JANE: Oh, I'm sorry, Warren. The roast is just a little slow.**
28   **It'll be about five minutes.**

29   **WARREN: Anything I can do to help?**

30   **JANE: Not with dinner, but I was hoping you could talk to**
31   **Squirrellie. I'm worried about him. Ever since he**
32   **came back from that camp, he's been acting strange.**

33   **WARREN: How's that?**

34   **JANE: Well, he not only makes his own bed in the**

1   morning, but now he makes Willie's, too. He's done
2   all his homework, hasn't been late once all this week,
3   and this afternoon he asked if he could wash the
4   windows.
5 WARREN: Squirrellie? That *is* strange.
6 JANE: Do you think you could talk with him? After all, he
7   is your son.
8 WARREN: He usually is at these times. OK, I'll see what I
9   can do.
10 JANE: Thank you, honey. *(Kiss.)* I'm going upstairs to
11   freshen up. I won't be long. *(Exit JANE Stage Right.*
12   *Pause. Enter WILLIE and SQUIRRELLIE.)*
13 WARREN: Well, boys, how was school today? *(Pause)* Willie?
14 WILLIE: Ah, gee, it was fine, Dad. Mrs. Caruthers was sick
15   today, so we didn't have a test in history. Oh, and Rick
16   Murphy lost his shorts in the cross country meet
17   today and had to drop out of the race. That was kinda
18   funny.
19 WARREN: Yes, I can imagine. So, Squirrellie, how was
20   your day?
21 SQUIRRELLIE: I dunno, Dad. Not so good, I think.
22 WARREN: What happened?
23 SQUIRRELLIE: Lonnie and Wiley asked me to do some-
24   thing that I didn't wanna do. And when they asked me
25   to do it, I told them that I didn't want to do it. Then
26   they got mad at me, and they tried to make me do it
27   anyway. But I still wouldn't do it. So they decided they
28   would do it. But their parents found out they did it
29   and they got in trouble. Now they think that I told on
30   them, but I didn't tell on them, but they said that I
31   did, so now nobody at school will talk to me.
32 WARREN: What'd they do, Squirrellie?
33 SQUIRRELLIE: Gee, Dad, I can't tell you on accounta
34   they're my friends and everything. You're a grown-up

1   and if I did tell ya, then I really would be a squealer.

2   **WILLIE:** I can tell ya, Dad. Lonnie and Wiley snuck into

3   the Rialto Saturday to see a couple of dirty movies.

4   **SQUIRRELLIE:** Golly, Willie, how did you know that?

5   **WILLIE:** Everybody knows, Squirrellie. Dean Swanny told

6   Dumpy Rutherford, and Dumpy's mom found out

7   and called Wiley's parents.

8   **WARREN:** Well, Squirrellie, sounds like you did the right

9   thing.

10 **SQUIRRELLIE:** Yeah, I know, Dad, but I still feel bad for

11   Lonnie and Wiley – not because they got caught, I just

12   feel bad because they did it.

13 **WARREN:** Well, son, I'm sure their parents feel the same

14   way. *(Pause)*

15 **SQUIRRELLIE:** Dad?

16 **WARREN:** Yes, Squirrellie?

17 **SQUIRRELLIE:** Dad, there's something I should tell you

18   about.

19 **WARREN:** What is it?

20 **SQUIRRELLIE:** Do you remember last week when I went

21   up to camp with the church?

22 **WARREN:** Yes.

23 **SQUIRRELLIE:** Something happened at church that I

24   didn't tell you about. It's not because I didn't want to

25   tell you about it, 'cause I really did want to tell you

26   about it, but I was afraid if I told you about it, you

27   might get mad or something.

28 **WARREN:** What it is, son?

29 **SQUIRRELLIE:** Dad, I'm a Christian.

30 **WARREN:** Of course you are, Squirrellie – we all are.

31 **SQUIRRELLIE:** No, Dad, I don't mean *that* kind of

32   Christian. I mean a *real* Christian, like the ones in the

33   Bible. I study God's Word and pray every day and

34   everything, so I can know just what God wants me to

1   **do. I pray about school and my friends and you and**
2   **Mom and Willie, too.**
3   **WARREN: Squirrellie, are you saying we're *not* Christians?**
4   **SQUIRRELLIE: Gee, Dad, if you really were Christians,**
5   **then I wouldn't have had to go to camp to find out**
6   **about Jesus.**
7   **WARREN: Well...uh...**
8   **SQUIRRELLIE: Oh, it's OK, Dad. I'm *glad* I got to go to**
9   **camp. God's changed my whole life. That's why I**
10   **wanted to tell you and Mom and Willie about the**
11   **Lord, and Lonnie and Wiley, too.** *(Enter JANE, who*
12   *crosses with the roast.)*
13   **JANE: Well, the roast is finally done.** *(She places it on the*
14   *table.)* **Here we go.** *(She sits at the table.)* **Warren, do you**
15   **want to say grace?**
16   **WARREN: No, I think I'll let Squirrellie do it tonight.**
17   **SQUIRRELLIE: Lord, thanks for all the neat things you**
18   **give us, and this food. And we ask you to bless us, too.**
19   **And Lord, thanks for giving me a neat mom and a**
20   **neat dad and a neat brother, too. In Jesus' name,**
21   **amen.** *(Pause)* **Dad, you're not mad at me or anything,**
22   **are you?**
23   **WARREN: No, Squirrellie. In fact, I'm very proud of you.**
24   *(Enter FREDDIE, who immediately sits at the table.)*
25   **FREDDIE: Gee, Mr. Cheever, you want to pass the potatoes,**
26   **please?**
27   **WARREN: Ah, sure, Freddie.**
28
29
30
31
32
33
34

Specs O'Keefe in the Case of the Missing First Love

SPECS O'KEEFE IN THE CASE OF THE MISSING FIRST LOVE

By Dan Rupple

1	**CAST:** Narrator (On-stage or off), Specs O'Keefe, Sherman,
2	Barry Boyer (or Bambi Boyer)*, Librarian, Miss Waverly,
3	Mr. Johnson, Boy, Two Wrestlers, Ed Richardson.
4	**SETTING:** Various locations. Designate four different areas of the
5	stage as: 1) Specs' office, 2) a library, 3) a hotel lobby and 4)
6	the Fellowship Hall. The office should have a desk and a few
7	chairs; the library, a bookshelf and counter or table; the
8	hotel lobby, a desk or table; the Fellowship Hall, a small
9	table, podium or music stand to hold the directory.
10	**PROPS:** Bits of tissue for SPECS' face, a file for the
11	LIBRARIAN, papers ("reservations") and keys for MR.
12	JOHNSON, and a phone book or other large book for the
13	Fellowship Hall directory.
14	**COSTUMES:** A suit and glasses for SPECS, along with bits of
15	tissue stuck to his face to cover shaving nicks; goofy outfit
16	for SHERMAN, i.e., beanie, bow tie, jacket, knickers,
17	sneakers; shorts, tank tops, etc. for the TWO
18	WRESTLERS. Everyone else in normal dress.
19	**SOUND EFFECTS:** Office sounds, bell, prerecorded lines of
20	the LIBRARIAN, ED, BOYER and MR. JOHNSON.
21	
22	**NARRATOR: There are many different kinds of people**
23	**who make this world go 'round. Some say that Specs**
24	**O'Keefe is one of them. If you meet Specs in a church,**
25	**Sunday school, prayer closet, heaven or hell or**
26	**anywhere in between, be careful – this is where he**

*This role may be played by a male or female.

1   works. **Specs O'Keefe, Spiritual Eye. Today we join**
2   **Specs in *The Case of the Missing First Love.*** *(SPECS*
3   *enters and stands at Center Stage. He has bits of tissue*
4   *stuck to his face.)*
5   **SPECS: It was a dreary fall morning. As I awoke from my**
6   **slumbering sleep, I staggered into the bathroom only to**
7   **be greeted by the stare of a stone cold face and a razor to**
8   **my neck. It was a face I had confronted before, but with**
9   **the help of some menthol shaving cream, I usually was**
10   **able to conquer it – not without a few nicks and scrapes,**
11   **I might add. But anyway, shaving wasn't my only**
12   **problem that day. Many more were lying in wait as I**
13   **approached my office. It isn't easy being a spiritual eye.**
14   **Problems and dangers lurk around each bend, but**
15   **somebody's got to do it, and today that somebody is me.**
16   *(SPECS goes to his office area and sits at his desk. Door*
17   *opens. SHERMAN enters, door closes.)*
18   **SHERMAN: Morning, Specs.**
19   **SPECS: Hi, Sherman.**
20   **SHERMAN: Gee, Specs, what happened to your face?**
21   **There's about a roll of toilet paper on it.**
22   **SPECS: Ain't got time to explain, Sherman. There're more**
23   **important things on our agenda. By the way, what's**
24   **on the agenda today?**
25   **SHERMAN: Well, there's a man waiting in the outer office.**
26   **He says it's urgent.** *(Door opens. Office sounds. Door*
27   *closes. Enter BOYER.)*
28   **SPECS:** *(Taking tissue off face)* **Send him in and get rid of**
29   **this tissue.** *(Hands tissue to SHERMAN.)*
30   **BOYER: Hi, Mr. O'Keefe, my name's Barry Boyer.**
31   **SPECS: What can I do for you?**
32   **BOYER: Well, Mr. O'Keefe, I'm missing something, and**
33   **I'm hoping you can find it for me.**
34   **SPECS: Hmmm. Missing, you say. Now being a profes-**

1   sional detective, deductive reasoning leaves two
2   choices. It was either lost or stolen.
3   SHERMAN: How does he do it?
4   SPECS: Which is it, Mr. Boyer?
5   BOYER: I'm not sure, but I'd have to say lost.
6   SHERMAN: Why's that?
7   BOYER: Well, it's no good to anyone else.
8   SPECS: OK, let's stop beating around the bush. You keep
9   saying "it's." What is "it's"? Spell it out for me, Boyer.
10 BOYER: F-I-R-S-T...
11 SPECS: No, you don't have to actually spell it out. That's
12   just gumshoe talk for "tell it like it is."
13 BOYER: Oh. Well, I lost my first love.
14 SHERMAN: Your first love?
15 BOYER: For Jesus. It's not there anymore. It's gone. You've
16   got to help me, Mr. O'Keefe. I'm desperate. Without it,
17   everything else I do is pointless. *(Cries.)*
18 SPECS: Now, Mr. Boyer, don't worry about it. We'll find it.
19 SHERMAN: *(Offers wad of tissue from SPEC's face.)* **Want**
20   **some tissue?**
21 BOYER: *(Takes it.)* **Thank you.** *(Starts to use it, then recoils.)*
22 SPECS: Can you describe it, Mr. Boyer?
23 BOYER: What? The tissue?
24 SPECS: No, no. Your first love. Was it big, small?
25 BOYER: Oh, very big.
26 SPECS: And when did you get it?
27 BOYER: Well, I got it when I first became a Christian,
28   eight years ago. You know, I was a whole new person.
29   Kind of like that blind guy in the Gospels. "Once I was
30   blind, but now I see." It was like a huge weight had
31   been lifted off me. All of the guilt and shame. I real-
32   ized it was all forgiven because of Jesus. It was just
33   me and Jesus. That simple. All I could think about,
34   talk about, night and day, was Jesus. I was just over-

1   flowing with my first love.

2   **SPECS:** When did you first notice it missing?

3   **BOYER:** After about five years, I noticed it missing once in

4   awhile. But I always found it again. But this last year,

5   I haven't ever seen it. I'm afraid I've lost it once and

6   for all! *(Crying)*

7   **SPECS:** Well, we might as well get started. Sherman?

8   **SHERMAN:** Yes, Specs?

9   **SPECS:** You sit down with Mr. Boyer. I want a report of

10   everywhere he's been since he realized his first love

11   was missing.

12   **SHERMAN:** Right, Chief.

13   **SPECS:** Mr. Boyer?

14   **BOYER:** Call me Barry.

15   **SPECS:** Right. Barry, I want you to tell Sherman all you

16   can, then go home and stay there till we find your

17   first love.

18   **BOYER:** Stay at home? But I've got work to do.

19   **SPECS:** Without your first love, your work is useless. You

20   said so yourself.

21   **BOYER:** Yeah, you're right. *(Door opens. Exit BOYER. Door*

22   *closes.)*

23   **SHERMAN:** What are you doing, Chief?

24   **SPECS:** Me? I'm gonna finish shaving and get ready to find

25   something that Barry Boyer might not recognize if it

26   was staring him right in the face. *(Optional music. To*

27   *audience)* **After a lengthy discussion, my assistant,**

28   **Sherman, had completed a thorough report of Barry**

29   **Boyer's whereabouts prior to the loss of his first love.**

30   **I looked over the locations with my keen detective**

31   **eyes. Sure, he could've lost it anywhere, but due to my**

32   **incredibly well-tuned hunches, I narrowed down the**

33   **suspected places to a measly handful. Besides, this**

34   **show doesn't have the time or budget to go everywhere**

1   Barry Boyer had been. We decided to stop wasting
2   time with long introductions and follow up our first
3   lead. *(SPECS and SHERMAN cross to the library area.)*
4   SHERMAN: What is this, Specs – a library?
5   SPECS: Close but no cigar, Sherman. This is the first place
6   on Barry Boyer's list.
7   SHERMAN: The Bible Study Institute?
8   SPECS: The Bible Study Institute. Exactly, Sherman.
9   SHERMAN: What do people do here, Specs?
10 SPECS: Why Sherman, it's as clear as the egg on your face.
11   They study the Bible. *(LIBRARIAN enters to counter.)*
12 LIBRARIAN: May I help you?
13 SPECS: Yes. I'm Specs O'Keefe, and this is my assistant,
14   Sherman. We need a little information.
15 LIBRARIAN: Oh, well, you'll want the Concordance Room.
16   *(Calls MISS WAVERLY.)* Miss Waverly, show these
17   gentlemen to the Concordance Room.
18 SPECS: Uh, excuse me, but that won't be necessary. See,
19   we're not here to study the Bible right now. We came
20   to talk about one of your patrons.
21 LIBRARIAN: Oh, I understand. Who do you need to know
22   about?
23 SHERMAN: Barry Boyer.
24 LIBRARIAN: Barry Boyer? One second. I'll pull his file. Let
25   me see...Barnacle, Barney, here it is – Boyer. Oh, yes, I
26   remember Barry well. He was here quite frequently.
27 SPECS: We're looking for Barry's first love. He's lost it,
28   and we'd like to know if this could be where he left it.
29 LIBRARIAN: Yes, Mr. O'Keefe, I was aware that Barry had
30   lost his first love.
31 SPECS: How's that? Did he tell you?
32 LIBRARIAN: No, they never tell me. I just know. Their
33   entire motivation and study habits changes.
34 SHERMAN: Changes?

1   **SPECS: In what way?**
2   **LIBRARIAN: They don't seem to love the Word anymore,**
3   **but they use it more as a weapon.**
4   **SPECS: A weapon?**
5   **SHERMAN: A weapon?**
6   **LIBRARIAN: Yes, a weapon. You see, when Barry first**
7   **came in years back, he'd spend almost all of his time**
8   **in the Hunger and Thirst After God's Word Room. But**
9   **I guess he had his fill, because he slowly spent more**
10   **and more time in the Doubting About Questions and**
11   **Striving of Words Department. He'd only study the**
12   **Word to either argue about it or to know more than**
13   **his friends. I think it made him feel more spiritual.**
14   **SHERMAN: Boy, Barry Boyer sure sounds like a creep.**
15   **LIBRARIAN: No, no. Barry's really a good young man. I**
16   **just think he's having a little trouble right now.**
17   **SPECS: Understandable, trying to be a Christian without**
18   **his first love.**
19   **SHERMAN: It's like playing without a full deck.**
20   **SPECS: Precisely. We've got to find it.**
21   **LIBRARIAN: I sure hope you do, but I'm afraid you won't**
22   **find it here.**
23   **SPECS: Oh?**
24   **LIBRARIAN: Yes. I don't know where he did lose it, but I'm**
25   **sure it isn't here.**
26   **SPECS: But, Ma'am, this is a big building – so many rooms.**
27   **How can you be sure?**
28   **LIBRARIAN: Well, Mr. O'Keefe, we keep our first love in our**
29   **heart. So to lose it, we'd have to have our heart open.**
30   **SPECS: Yes?**
31   **LIBRARIAN: Barry never did. When he came to study the**
32   **Word, his mind was open, but not his heart. At least**
33   **not lately. Oh, there was a time Barry was so open to**
34   **God's Word, everyone could see it. But sadly, not**

1   **anymore. Yes, Mr. O'Keefe, I believe you'll have to**
2   **search elsewhere.**
3   **SPECS: Thank you. We will. You've been a great help.**
4   **Come along, Sherman.**
5   **SHERMAN: Right, Specs.**
6   **SPECS: We gotta visit the second lead on our list if we can**
7   **find it.**
8   **LIBRARIAN: Excuse me.**
9   **SPECS: Yes?**
10   **LIBRARIAN: May I suggest our Bible Map Room? You can**
11   **find anything there.**
12   **SPECS: Why, thank you.**
13   **LIBRARIAN: You're welcome.** *(LIBRARIAN exits.)*
14   **SPECS: We took the librarian's advice and went to the**
15   **Bible Map Room to find directions to the location of**
16   **our next search for Barry Boyer's missing first love.**
17   **We drove down Egypt Avenue, cut across Wilderness**
18   **Highway to save time, and got off on the Jordan Road**
19   **exit. It was quite a trip – seemed like it took forty**
20   **years – but finally we arrived at our Promised Land.**
21   **The Prayer Closet. A quiet, unassuming little**
22   **building, but what goes on inside is powerful. We**
23   **approached boldly with confidence.** *(SPECS and*
24   *SHERMAN cross to hotel lobby area.)*
25   **SHERMAN: Boy, Specs, it's dark in here.**
26   **SPECS: You're right, Sherman. Stay close to the light.**
27   *(Kick)*
28   **SHERMAN: *Owww!***
29   **CROWD: Shhh...Shhh...Be quiet!**
30   **SPECS: What happened, Sherman?**
31   **SHERMAN: I stumbled on a kneeler.**
32   **SPECS: Well, we all stumble sometimes. Be careful.** *(MR.*
33   *JOHNSON enters.)*
34   **MR. JOHNSON: We have many different rooms to choose**

1   **from, depending on your needs.**

2   **SPECS: Well, actually...**

3   **MR. JOHNSON: We have the Praise Rooms. They're real**

4   **nice to begin your stay with. Then we have the**

5   **Petition Rooms, the Intercession Rooms, and of**

6   **course, the Thanksgiving Room.**

7   **SPECS: That's great, Mr. Johnson, but you see...** *(BOY enters.)*

8   **MR. JOHNSON: Fine. Boy!** *(Bell)* **Show these gentlemen to**

9   **rooms 704 and 705.**

10   **BOY: Any luggage, sir?**

11   **SPECS: No, we...**

12   **MR. JOHNSON: Here are your keys.**

13   **SPECS: Wait a minute! Now if you'll listen for just a**

14   **second. You haven't heard a word I've said.**

15   **MR. JOHNSON: Yes, I'm so sorry. You see, that's one of the**

16   **biggest problems we have here at the Prayer Closet.**

17   **We seldom quit talking enough to listen. Please**

18   **accept my apology.**

19   **SPECS: No problem.**

20   **MR. JOHNSON: Now about those rooms?** *(Bell)*

21   **BOY: Any luggage, sir?**

22   **SPECS: We don't need rooms.**

23   **MR. JOHNSON: Oh, I'm sorry to hear that.**

24   **SHERMAN: Why?**

25   **MR. JOHNSON: Well, business is a little slow. People just**

26   **aren't praying like they used to – you know, like**

27   **during the revivals. Boy.** *(Bell)*

28   **BOY: Any luggage, sir?**

29   **MR. JOHNSON: Back then the Prayer Closet was over-**

30   **flowing.**

31   **SPECS: Hmmm. Sorry to hear that.**

32   **MR. JOHNSON: Yes, well, I'll keep praying. So how may I**

33   **help you?**

34   **SPECS: My name is Specs O'Keefe. I'm a spiritual eye. My**

1   **client, Barry Boyer, lost his first love. It's my job to**
2   **track it down. We're wondering if he lost it here.**
3 **MR. JOHNSON: What was his name?**
4 **SHERMAN: Barry Boyer.**
5 **MR. JOHNSON: Name doesn't ring a bell.** *(Bell)*
6 **BOY: Any luggage, sir?**
7 **MR. JOHNSON: I'll check the reservations.** *(BOY exits. TWO*
8   *WRESTLERS enter and start an informal match.)*
9 **SPECS: Uh, what are they doing?**
10 **MR. JOHNSON: Oh, they're wrestling in prayer. Mr.**
11   **Carmichael, watch your hip. We don't want it to pop**
12   **out of its socket again.** *(TWO WRESTLERS exit.)* **Yes,**
13   **here it is – Barry Boyer.**
14 **SPECS: Has he been here recently?**
15 **MR. JOHNSON: No, I'm afraid not. It seems he makes**
16   **quite a few reservations but never shows.**
17 **SPECS: Well, has he ever been here?**
18 **MR. JOHNSON: Oh yes, yes. According to his record, he**
19   **spent a lot of time here years back. He used every**
20   **room in the house. Quite a warrior, I guess. But then,**
21   **let's see, about a year and a half ago, he...oh yes, I**
22   **remember him. Of course, "Clock Watch" Boyer!**
23 **SHERMAN: "Clock Watch"?**
24 **MR. JOHNSON: Yes, he'd have to practically drag himself**
25   **in here, then all the while, he'd keep asking the time.**
26   **Never stayed until check-out. In fact, the most he'd**
27   **stay would be, oh, five minutes, and then half of that**
28   **was spent asking what time it was.**
29 **SPECS: So you don't think he lost his first love here?**
30 **MR. JOHNSON: Oh no, although some people do.**
31 **SPECS: How's that?**
32 **MR. JOHNSON: Well, they stop coming to the Prayer Closet**
33   **out of love and start coming out of "duty," so to speak.**
34   **It becomes a real drag, and the first love gets lost.**

1   **SPECS: And Barry Boyer?**

2   **MR. JOHNSON: No, no, he never stayed long enough to get**

3   **his knees warm.**

4   **SPECS: Well, thank you, Mr. Johnson.**

5   **MR. JOHNSON: My pleasure. I'll be praying that you find**

6   **it. Remember, "Seek and you shall find, ask and it**

7   **shall be given to you."** (Matt. 7:7, author's paraphrase)

8   *(MR. JOHNSON exits.)*

9   **SPECS: Our client was well-remembered at the Bible**

10   **Study Institute and at the Prayer Closet, but ques-**

11   **tioning proved futile. Three days, and still no sign of**

12   **Barry Boyer's missing first love. No time to waste. I**

13   **choked down a quick Brussels sprout sandwich, and**

14   **Sherman and I scurried to our next hope for the**

15   **mysterious answer.** *(SPECS and SHERMAN cross to*

16   *Fellowship Hall area.)*

17   **SHERMAN: Well, here we are, Specs.**

18   **SPECS: Right on time, Sherman. I just ran out of intro-**

19   **duction. What's the name of this place?**

20   **SHERMAN: The Fellowship Hall.**

21   **SPECS: Aha, so this is Barry's hangout.**

22   **SHERMAN: Yep, he said he came here at least once a week.**

23   **SPECS: Great. I'll file that in my brain under R for**

24   **"Remember it."**

25   **SHERMAN: Boy, Specs, there's a lot of people here.**

26   **SPECS: That's right, Sherman. Good thing, too. One thing**

27   **every believer needs is fellowship. It's quite uplifting.**

28   **SHERMAN: Yeah, like they say, "Iron sharpens iron."**

29   **SPECS: Sherman, you've been studying.**

30   **SHERMAN: You betcha, every chance I get.**

31   **SPECS: This is a big place, Sherman. I wonder where to start.**

32   **SHERMAN: Specs, there's a directory right here.**

33   **SPECS: Good thinking, Sherman.**

34   **SHERMAN: Thanks.**

1   **SPECS: OK. Room 501, Bearing One Another's Burdens.**
2   **Room 508, Rejoicing Together. Room 721, Mutual**
3   **Encouragement. Room 843, Welcoming New**
4   **Believers. The list is virtually endless.**
5   **SHERMAN: Yes, but which room did Barry go to?** *(Enter ED.)*
6   **ED: Why, hello there. You two are new here, aren't cha?**
7   **SPECS: Yes, we are.**
8   **ED: The name's Ed Richardson, but everyone knows me as**
9   **Friendly Ed.**
10   **SPECS: My name's Specs O'Keefe, but everyone knows me**
11   **as Specs O'Keefe.**
12   **ED: It's a pleasure to meet you. Who's your awkward**
13   **friend here?**
14   **SHERMAN: My name's Sherman.**
15   **ED: Well, Praise the Lord. You know, God's been so good to**
16   **me, and I just rejoice in being able to meet new brothers.**
17   **SPECS: Mind if we ask you a few questions, Ed?**
18   **ED: Go right ahead. I'm here to serve. The Bible says if you**
19   **want to be great in God's kingdom, be the servant of**
20   **all. What do you need to know?**
21   **SPECS: Do you know a brother named Barry Boyer?**
22   **ED: Barry, sure do. Been coming here for a quite a few years.**
23   **SPECS: Where'd he hang out?**
24   **ED: Well, at first, he spent a good amount of time every-**
25   **where. Yes, sir, if fellowship in the Lord was to be had,**
26   **Barry'd be in the middle of it.**
27   **SPECS: How about lately? Which rooms has he been in?**
28   **ED: Well, lately, well, he hangs around out in the yard with**
29   **a few guys.**
30   **SPECS: What is the yard used for?**
31   **ED: Well, it isn't used, really. They just hang out and shoot**
32   **the breeze. Talk about baseball, movies, cars, anything**
33   **except the Lord. Well, I don't want to gossip. There's**
34   **enough gossip here in the name of fellowship.**

1   **SPECS: Good point.**

2   **ED: Though it really isn't gossip, Mr. Specs, because I did**

3   **go to Barry about it.**

4   **SHERMAN: About what?**

5   **ED: Well, about never talking about Jesus anymore. He**

6   **said that he and the guys spent so much time together**

7   **at the Bible Study Institute that afterward, when**

8   **they'd come here to the Fellowship Hall, they'd talk**

9   **about other things. Said it was like leaving it at the**

10   **office. Whatever that means.**

11   **SPECS: Hmmm. I see. Speaking of leaving, let's go. Thank**

12   **you, Ed.**

13   **SHERMAN: But Specs, we just got here.**

14   **SPECS: I've seen enough. His first love's not here. Come**

15   **along, Sherman.**

16   **ED: So long, Mr. Specs. Bye-bye, little buddy.** *(Exit ED.)*

17   **SHERMAN: Gee, Specs, how'd you know that Barry didn't**

18   **lose his first love at the Fellowship Hall?**

19   **SPECS: Sherman, love for God is spiritual. That means to**

20   **love something spiritual, he'd have to be spiritually**

21   **vulnerable.**

22   **SHERMAN: Sure, Specs. But the Fellowship Hall has spiri-**

23   **tual fellowship.**

24   **SPECS: True, Sherman, but none of Barry's fellowship**

25   **here was spiritual. It was all casual and natural, but**

26   **not spiritual.**

27   **SHERMAN: Well, even if he didn't personally have spiri-**

28   **tual fellowship, couldn't he still have left it there?**

29   **SPECS: No, Sherman. Barry wasn't even here.**

30   **SHERMAN: But he said he was.**

31   **SPECS: Yes, outside, but he never entered in.**

32   **SHERMAN: Yes, that's why there wasn't a room for casual**

33   **talking. That's why they met out back.**

34   **SPECS: Right. Oh yes, there's a place for casual talking,**

1   **but spiritual fellowship must be the priority. There's**
2   **no substituting.**
3 **SHERMAN: Sherlock Holmes, move over.**
4 **SPECS: We were getting nowhere fast in the search for**
5   **Barry Boyer's first love. Our list of suspected places**
6   **was rapidly diminishing with no apparent solution. It**
7   **seemed we were no closer than when we first started.**
8   **That might be fine for an amateur like Sherman, but**
9   **a professional like me is used to being hot on the**
10   **trail, ready for the payoff. Frustration wasn't my**
11   **usual cup of tea, and now I was taking the iced tea**
12   **plunge. I became obsessed. Either I would conquer**
13   **this case, or it would conquer me.** *(SPECS and*
14   *SHERMAN cross to SPECS' office.)* **Sherman, I've got it!**
15 **SHERMAN: Got what, Specs?**
16 **SPECS: The solution.**
17 **SHERMAN: You mean you've found Barry's first love?**
18 **SPECS: Well, yes and no.**
19 **SHERMAN: Well, which is it, Specs?**
20 **SPECS: I don't have it, but I know where it is. Sherman, I**
21   **want you to drive over to Barry's and bring him back**
22   **on the double.**
23 **SHERMAN: Gee, I've never had a double before. I usually**
24   **walk out or strike out. What're you going to do, Specs?**
25 **SPECS: Well, Sherman, as you know, I have you record**
26   **every interview we hold. I'm going to go through**
27   **those tapes and prepare my verdict.**
28 **SHERMAN: What a snooper!** *(SHERMAN exits.)*
29 **SPECS: Sherman headed out to get Barry, and I set to work**
30   **on the tapes. As I finished my final edit, the smell of**
31   **victory was in the air.** *(Door opens. Enter SHERMAN*
32   *and BOYER. Door closes.)*
33 **SHERMAN: Specs, I'm back. Gee, what smells?**
34 **SPECS: Victory, Sherman.**

1   SHERMAN: **Oh, I thought it was your aftershave.**

2   BOYER: **Mr. O'Keefe, Sherman says you've solved my case.**

3   SPECS: **Looks like it, Barry. Have a seat.**

4   BOYER: *(Sits.)* **How'd you ever find it? I thought all of your**
5   **leads were fruitless.**

6   SPECS: **Not so. They seemed fruitless at first because they**
7   **didn't have your first love. But that didn't mean they**
8   **didn't have the answer. Then it dawned on me. The**
9   **Bible says there is wisdom in a multitude of coun-**
10   **selors. And as I pieced together all they had said,**
11   **suddenly it began to make sense.**

12   BOYER: **So where did I lose it?**

13   SPECS: **Barry, that's just it. You didn't lose it.**

14   BOYER: **I didn't?**

15   SPECS: **Listen to this.**

16   LIBRARIAN: *(Prerecorded)* **We keep our first love in our**
17   **hearts...oh, but there was a time when Barry's heart**
18   **was so open to God's Word, everyone could see. But**
19   **sadly, not anymore.**

20   SPECS: **You see, Barry, it's still in your heart, but your**
21   **heart's not open. It's clogged – polluted with so much**
22   **other stuff that you can't even find your first love.**

23   BOYER: **Clogged? With what?**

24   SPECS: **Listen.**

25   ED: *(Prerecorded)* **...baseball, movies, cars, anything except**
26   **the Lord.**

27   SPECS: **Quite a comparison to how you were.**

28   BOYER: *(Prerecorded)* **It was just me and Jesus. I was just**
29   **overflowing with my first love.**

30   BOYER: **I can see it. I've complicated my relationship with**
31   **so many other interests. I haven't made Jesus the**
32   **priority like before. But how do I get him back?**

33   SPECS: **Well, that one took me a little longer, but then I**
34   **remembered what Mr. Johnson had said.**

1   MR. JOHNSON: *(Prerecorded)* **Remember, "Seek and you**
2   **shall find. Ask and it shall be given to you."** (Matt. 7:7,
3   author's paraphrase)
4   SPECS: **I realized you had the answer all along. We're**
5   **looking for something in your heart, and the Bible**
6   **says from the abundance of the heart, the mouth**
7   **speaks.** (Matt. 12:34, author's paraphrase) **So your very**
8   **words gave me the answer.**
9   BOYER: *(Prerecorded)* **You know, I was a whole new**
10   **person. Kind of like that blind guy in the Gospels.**
11   **"Once I was blind, but now I see." It was like a huge**
12   **weight had been lifted off me. All of the guilt and**
13   **shame. I realized it was all forgiven because of Jesus.**
14   SPECS: **Barry, the book of Revelations says, "Remember**
15   **therefore from whence thou are fallen, and repent,**
16   **and do the first works."** (Rev. 2:5)
17   BOYER: **Yeah, I see it now. I need to continually**
18   **remember what Jesus did in my life, how I got my**
19   **first love to begin with.**
20   SPECS: **If you dwell on what Jesus did and is doing in your**
21   **life, your love will be fresh every day.**
22   BOYER: **Mr. O'Keefe, how can I thank you? I can feel the**
23   **love already. I'm remembering what it was like when**
24   **I first repented and received God's love.**
25   SHERMAN: **Well, Specs, you solved another one.**
26   SPECS: **Yes, Sherman. It's so easy that it seemed compli-**
27   **cated. I just hope we don't have to find it again in a**
28   **few years. You know, Sherman, if you keep your eyes**
29   **on something constantly, you can't lose it.**
30   SHERMAN: **That's my boss.** *(Optional music)*
31
32
33
34

TIME WASTERS
Looks at Baseball

By Dave Toole

1 ***CAST:*** Narrator (On-stage or off), Tom Biggs, Doug Missilon.

2 ***SETTING:*** TV show on location in Cleveland, Ohio. Most of
3 the action takes place in DOUG's apartment, which is
4 decorated with baseball memorabilia, including various
5 signed baseballs, pennants, etc. Some of the dialog may
6 need to be adjusted, depending on available baseball
7 trinkets. Not everyone will have access to pencil sharp-
8 eners shaped like batting helmets! Also needed is a radio.

9 ***PROPS:*** Microphone and letter for TOM, leather display cases (or
10 some type of album) with baseball cards for DOUG.

11 ***COSTUMES:*** TOM should wear a suit. DOUG should wear a
12 baseball cap and a T-shirt or sweatshirt with a baseball
13 team's name on the front.

14 ***SOUND EFFECTS:*** Baseball game broadcast.

15

16 **NARRATOR: As the days grow shorter and shorter, Jesus**
17 **admonished us to redeem the time – to give our rela-**
18 **tionship with him top priority in our lives. The**
19 **people interviewed on this show feel there's only one**
20 **thing more important, and we're here to find out just**
21 **what that one thing is...**

22 TOM: *(Enters.)* **Hello, everybody, and welcome to *Time***
23 ***Wasters*. I'm your host, Tom Biggs, and today we're in**
24 **Cleveland, Ohio, in answer to a letter that reads:**
25 **"Dear Tom,**
26 **I watch your show every week and am always**
27 **amazed at the trivial things people put ahead of the**
28 **Lord. Surely we all waste the time God has given us to**

some degree, but I never thought I'd meet someone like the people you have on your show until last month, when a young man moved into the apartment next to mine. When I went over to meet him, I asked him if he was a Christian. He said yes, he was, and I believe he meant it, too, but when I invited him to church, he said he had to go to a baseball game. Over the past weeks it's always been the same excuse – baseball. He goes to the games, watches them on TV, has hundreds of videos of famous games and all kinds of books. He is as devoted to his games as anyone I have ever met. Perhaps he would be a good person to have on your show. I think so.

Signed, Mrs. Candice Brooks"

Well, Mrs. Brooks, with the recent surge in the popularity of sports, we couldn't agree with you more, and that's why we're here to interview Mr. Doug Missilon. *(TOM crosses over to DOUG's apartment. There is a baseball game on the radio.)* So, Doug, I understand you're a baseball fan.

DOUG: I sure am, Tom – have been since I got my first pack of baseball cards in second grade. That was almost fifteen years ago. Now I have one of the best collections in the country – over nine thousand cards. Babe Ruth, Lou Gehrig, PeeWee Reese – I got 'em all. Even a Honus Wagner! You know how much that's worth? Over half a million dollars! There's only nineteen in the whole world!

TOM: Boy, that does sound like a very impressive collection.

DOUG: Yeah, and I keep the good ones in these custom cases especially made for baseball cards.

TOM: Is that real leather?

DOUG: Sure is! I keep the rest in boxes at my parents' house. Say, do you know what day it is?

1   **TOM: Monday.**

2   **DOUG: It's Roger Hornsby's birthday. Do you know he has**

3   **the second highest lifetime batting average? .358. Ty**

4   **Cobb has the best – .366.**

5   **TOM: Oh, I thought Babe Ruth's was the best.**

6   **DOUG: Oh, no. Babe Ruth has the fourteenth best average**

7   **with .342, right behind Billy Hamilton.**

8   **TOM: Oh, I see. Well, you certainly know your game.**

9   *(Motions to baseballs.)* **What are all these things?**

10   **DOUG: Oh, stuff from the different games I've been to.**

11   **These baseballs over here are from different World**

12   **Series games. This one here was a home run ball hit**

13   **by Reggie Jackson, back when he was with the A's.**

14   **Over here are the different team pennants. Some of**

15   **them are real collector's items, too, like this one from**

16   **the Washington Senators, or this Milwaukee Braves.**

17   *(Or substitute other team names.)* **Both are in excellent**

18   **condition, too.**

19   **TOM: Say, what are those over here?**

20   **DOUG: Oh, those are just pencil sharpeners shaped like**

21   **batting helmets. I have the whole set – had to buy**

22   **almost a hundred boxes of Sugar Crispies to get them,**

23   **though. The funny thing about it is I hate Sugar**

24   **Crispies, but what else could I do?**

25   **TOM: What else indeed? Say, Doug, I wonder if we might**

26   **talk about something other than baseball for a minute.**

27   **DOUG: Sure, what?**

28   **TOM: Well, I understand from Mrs. Brooks next door that**

29   **you're a Christian. Is that right?**

30   **DOUG: Oh, you know Mrs. Brooks? What a nice lady. Yes,**

31   **I'm a Christian.**

32   **TOM: I hope you don't misunderstand me, but have you**

33   **ever thought baseball might be interfering with your**

34   **Christian faith?**

1 DOUG: Oh, no. How could it? Baseball isn't unchristian.
2   Why, even a lot of players are Christians – Orel
3   Hershiser, Dave Dravecky, Brett Butler...
4 TOM: No, Doug, I think you're missing my point. It seems
5   to me that baseball is more important to you than Jesus.
6 DOUG: Oh, no, Tom, not at all. Why, I plan to go to church
7   with Mrs. Brooks right after the season's over. In
8   fact, I already mentioned it to her. You can ask her if
9   you want.
10 TOM: What about in the meantime?
11 DOUG: The Lord's provided me with such great seats for
12   the rest of the season, I really wouldn't be a good
13   steward to waste them. And of course, I still have to
14   put up some shelves to keep my books in order and go
15   through my statistics and reorganize them... *(TOM*
16   *crosses to audience as DOUG wanders Off-stage.)*
17 TOM: You know, most people don't realize it, but by defin-
18   ition, an idol is anything you put before the Lord. In
19   Doug's case, the sport of baseball has taken up all his
20   time, money and aspirations. It's certainly the most
21   important thing in his life. Sadly enough, though,
22   Doug is not alone in his obsession with sports. With
23   people enjoying more and more free time, and with
24   the current emphasis on physical fitness, sports have
25   become more popular than ever before – which isn't
26   bad, as long as you keep the rest of your life in proper
27   perspective. This is Tom Biggs, hoping Jesus is always
28   as important to you as you are to him. So long for now.
29
30
31
32
33
34

TIME WASTERS
Looks at Bible Trivia

By Dave Toole

1 **CAST:** Tom Biggs, Bob, Tim.

2 **SETTING:** On location at a dorm on the campus of Bible U. in
3 Atlanta, Georgia. A partition divides the stage into two
4 dorm rooms: BOB's and TIM's. There is a door in the
5 partition.

6 **PROPS:** Microphone and letter for TOM, Bible for TIM to page
7 through while TOM interviews BOB.

8 **COSTUMES:** Suit for TOM. Casual attire for BOB and TIM.
9

10 *(TOM is Upstage Center. BOB and TIM are in their respec-*
11 *tive dorm rooms.)*

12 **TOM: Hello, and welcome to *Time Wasters*. I'm your host,**
13 **Tom Biggs, and today we're in Atlanta, Georgia, the**
14 **heart of the Bible Belt. Now some may think this is a**
15 **strange place for *Time Wasters* to come, but we're**
16 **here in response to this letter:**
17 **"Dear Tom,**
18 **Since I accepted the Lord Jesus as my Savior seven**
19 **years ago, I have felt a calling in my life to go into the**
20 **ministry. As soon as I graduated, I headed straight for**
21 **Bible college. I was very excited to get the chance to**
22 **attend seminary, and I naturally assumed the others**
23 **attending would share my excitement. Unfortunately,**
24 **that is not always the case. Many people here are not**
25 **seeking to serve the Lord Jesus at all, but to glorify**
26 **themselves through works by building up a lot of**
27 **knowledge about the things of God. If being a hearer**
28 **of the Word – even a student – but not a doer is a**

waster of time, surely these people qualify for your show.

Signed, Richard Logan"

Well, Richard, people try many things to reach God. Years of community service, struggling to be a good person, or even memorizing the Scriptures, and they're all useless unless you have a living relationship with the Lord Jesus Christ. To quote the prophet Isaiah, "Our works are as filthy rags before a Holy God." (Is. 64:6, author's paraphrase) *(TOM crosses over to BOB.)* So, Bob, how long have you been attending Bible U.?

BOB: Five years now. I'm doing my postgraduate work here.

TOM: Uh, what are you working on now?

BOB: I'm doing a study of a pigeon-toed Bible character. You know, it's amazing how many... *(Door flies open and TIM pokes his head inside.)*

TIM: Who's the oldest man in the Bible?

BOB: Methuselah. Ha! Genesis 5:27.

TIM: All right, who was the second oldest?

BOB: Ahhh...

TIM: Aha! Gotcha! That's one for me. *(Door slams.)*

BOB: Wait. Wait. Wait. *(Running to door)* I know this one. *(Opens door.)* It's Jerad. Genesis 5:20 or 5:21!

TIM: Come on, which is it?

BOB: Ah, Genesis 5:20.

TIM: Lucky guess.

BOB: Lucky nothing, that's one for me. *(Shuts door and returns.)* Sorry about the interruption.

TOM: That's quite all right. Who's your friend there?

BOB: Oh, that's Tim Simmons – just one of the guys.

TOM: Oh, I see. Does he pop in like that often?

BOB: No, no, not too often. It's just a little game we play.

TOM: Mmmm. Well, Bob, what's God been doing in your...

(Door opens.)

1   TIM: How many verses in the Bible?
2   BOB: 31,102 – 23,147 in the Old Testament and 7,955 in the
3   New. How many letters are there?
4   TIM: Letters, ah...2,728,100 in the Old Testament and
5   838,380 in the New Testament for a total of 3,566,480.
6   BOB: OK. How many words?
7   TIM: 773,69...5
8   BOB: Gotcha! 773,692!
9   TOM: Ah, excuse me, guys, could I interrupt here? I under-
10   stand your name's Tim. My name's Tom Biggs.
11   TIM: *The* Tom Biggs? Of the *Time Wasters* show?
12   TOM: Uh, yes, have you seen it?
13   TIM: I sure have. What are you doing here with Bob? He a
14   time-waster?
15   TOM: That's what we're here to find out, Tim.
16   TIM: What does he do?
17   TOM: We'll get to that in a moment. Right now I want to ask
18   about this game of yours.
19   BOB: Dueling Scriptures?
20   TOM: Whatever you call it. You guys must put in quite a lot of
21   time coming up with these questions, not to mention the
22   answers.
23   BOB: I suppose it all depends on how you look at it, Tom. Since
24   we're here at college to learn as much as we can about...
25   TIM: Wait a second. You don't think that playing Dueling
26   Scriptures is a waste of time, do ya? It's all about the Bible.
27   TOM: Well, Tim, anything that comes between you and your
28   relationship with the Lord is...
29   TIM: Learning about the Bible?
30   TOM: How about Jesus?
31   TIM: He's in there too!
32   BOB: Listen Tom, a Bible's a Bible. *(TIM and BOB shrug and*
33   *exit. TOM crosses to audience.)*
34   TOM: Religion. It's not a very popular word. And why

1   should it be? Religion is a lifetime of dedication and
2   work for nothing more than a chance for eternal life.
3   And yet, thousands of people every day reject the
4   work of Jesus for religion. Trusting in themselves
5   instead of the Lord. If only they knew the joy and
6   peace Jesus has to offer them. And you know, both
7   believers and nonbelievers can fall into this trap.
8   Whenever you rely on what you know or what you can
9   do, that's when you're in trouble. Just like Bob and
10   Tim, building up lots of Bible trivia instead of a rela-
11   tionship with the Lord. So often the enemy tries to
12   deceive us by convincing us to rely on ourselves,
13   rather than the Lord Jesus Christ. Think about it. And
14   may Jesus always be as important to you as you are to
15   him. So long for now!
16
17
18
19
20
21
22
23
24
25
26
27
28
29
30
31
32
33
34

TIME WASTERS
Looks at Hobbies

By Dave Toole

1   ***CAST:*** Tom Biggs, Dana Oberman.

2   ***SETTING:*** DANA's house in St. Louis, Missouri. There is a

3   large painting of a family tree hanging on the wall.

4   ***PROPS:*** Microphone and letter for TOM.

5   ***COSTUMES:*** Suit for TOM. Christian T-shirt for DANA.

6

7   *(DANA admires his painting. TOM is at Upstage Center.)*

8   **TOM: Hello, everybody, and welcome to *Time Wasters*. I'm**

9   **your host, Tom Biggs, and today we're in St. Louis,**

10   **Missouri, in answer to a letter that reads:**

11   **"Dear Tom,**

12   **Until recently I was unable to watch your show**

13   **because we had our prayer meeting the same night**

14   **you were on. Recently, though, we shifted to another**

15   **night and I was able to tune in. After watching one of**

16   **your shows, I realized I knew someone you'd want to**

17   **meet. His name is Dana Oberman and we have some**

18   **classes together at the local junior college. This guy**

19   **wears a lot of Christian T-shirts, but his *real* love is**

20   **genealogy. He spends so much time in his family tree,**

21   **he's beginning to look like Bonzo the Wonder Chimp!**

22   **Seriously, though, Dana is in real bondage to this**

23   **stuff. Maybe you can help.**

24   **Signed, Carl Sutton"**

25   **Well, Carl, up until recently genealogy was consid-**

26   **ered an unusual pastime, but ever since the success**

27   **of the TV shows *Roots* and *Shogun*, its popularity has**

28   **soared.** *(TOM crosses over to DANA.)* **This sure is an**

1   interesting wall painting.

2   DANA: Thank you, Tom. Most people have a little chart of
3   their family tree somewhere in the house, but as you
4   can see, this is hardly the usual little chart. Actually,
5   Tom, I didn't paint it – a friend of mine did. I just did
6   the research.

7   TOM: Well, it's very beautiful. You know, it must have cost
8   quite a bit of money to have someone so talented
9   come into your living room and paint something like
10   this on your wall.

11   DANA: No, no, not at all. I did a family chart for him and
12   his roommate. I do a lot of that for neighbors and
13   friends.

14   TOM: Oh, I see. Well, then, you do research into other
15   people's families, too?

16   DANA: Oh yeah. In fact, sometimes when I need a little
17   extra cash, I go down to the swap meet and take
18   orders from people down there. It's really kind of
19   fun. You never know what kind of person you'll meet.
20   Why, last week I did a chart for a guy named Bent.
21   Turns out this boy's family was real big out West.
22   Started a settlement in Colorado. They called it Bent's
23   Fort. It's still there today. Of course, it's only a tourist
24   attraction now.

25   TOM: Mmmm. That's really something.

26   DANA: Hey, maybe I can do your family sometime. It
27   wouldn't take me that long – a couple of weeks at the
28   most. All I need are your parents' names, birth dates
29   and birthplaces. Grandparents, uncles, aunts –
30   they'd be helpful too, but I don't really need them.
31   Oh, are you married? I'm gonna need that informa-
32   tion about your wife and stuff.

33   TOM: Well, Dana, I appreciate the offer, but I wouldn't
34   want to take up your time doing...

1   **DANA: No problem, Tom. I'd be happy to do it.**

2   **TOM: I'm sure of that, Dana. In fact, that's why I'm here.**

3   *(Pause)* **Don't you think you spend too much time with**

4   **all this?**

5   **DANA: Oh, gosh no, Tom, I only do it in my spare time. You**

6   **know, weekends, after work, before school, after**

7   **school, that kind of stuff. I'd never call in sick or miss**

8   **a class for it. It's just a hobby – a pastime.**

9   **TOM: It doesn't sound like there's much time left over for**

10   **the Lord.**

11   **DANA: But that's why I wear these T-shirts all the time.**

12   **See, this says "Jesus is Lord."** *(Or whatever slogan your*

13   *shirt says)* **I have two of these, and all kinds of others,**

14   **too! I think it's very important to be a witness for the**

15   **Lord wherever you go. In fact, this one guy I did a**

16   **chart for offered to make me some free shirts adver-**

17   **tising my services, but I said no way, I'm not putting**

18   **my light under a bushel.**

19   **TOM: But you *are* putting it under your family tree.**

20   **DANA: Huh?**

21   **TOM: Don't you see? God wants you to put in time**

22   **researching him and his ways and not, as the Bible**

23   **puts it, "endless genealogies."**

24   **DANA:** *(Pause)* **Maybe you're right, Tom. I hadn't thought**

25   **about that before. Maybe I should spend more time**

26   **with the Lord. I could take a course at the city college**

27   **next semester. They have one on the Bible as litera-**

28   **ture, you know. I could get into an intense study of**

29   **spiritual characters and numbers...** *(TOM crosses to*

30   *audience as DANA wanders off.)*

31   **TOM: Webster's Dictionary defines a hobby as "a pursuit**

32   **or interest engaged in for relaxation" and that's good,**

33   **because all of us need something to take our minds**

34   **off the cares of the day. Hobbies can be challenging**

and fun, but they can also be a real source of wasted time. Most hobbies take a lot of time and patience, which is fine, as long as it's not at the expense of other commitments in your life. As Christians, we have a commitment to our Lord and Master, Jesus Christ. If your arts and crafts or model airplanes are infringing on the time you spend with the Lord, maybe it's time you exchange your paint brush for your Bible and see what you've been missing. This is Tom Biggs, hoping Jesus is always as important to you as you are to him. So long for now.

TIME WASTERS
Looks at Housework

By Dave Toole

1   **CAST:** Tom Biggs; Diane Yeager; Steve — Sound Man; Alan —
2   Cameraman.
3   **SETTING:** DIANE's home in Carson City, Nevada. You can
4   add any number of decorator touches. Be sure to have
5   two cushions on the sofa (can be three chairs pushed
6   together with a blanket on top). The dialog may need to
7   be adjusted if your cushions do not have a raccoon and
8   chipmunk on them.
9   **PROPS:** Microphone and letter for TOM, two pieces of cake
10   on a plate and a glass of milk for DIANE.
11   **COSTUMES:** Suit for Tom, something fussy and overdone for
12   DIANE. Casual clothes for STEVE and ALAN.
13
14   *(TOM is at Center Stage. DIANE is bustling around in*
15   *her home.)*
16   **TOM: Hello, everybody. Welcome to *Time Wasters*. I'm**
17   **your host, Tom Biggs, and today we're in Carson City,**
18   **Nevada, in answer to a letter that reads:**
19   **"Dear Mr. Biggs,**
20   **My family and I are real fans of your show. We**
21   **always used to wonder where you got your guests**
22   **until last week, when we were at a friend's house.**
23   **This lady prides herself on having the cleanest,**
24   **neatest household in town. She literally dreams**
25   **about running through fields of wildflowers with a**
26   **vacuum cleaner! She spends her every waking hour**
27   **cleaning, scrubbing, and disinfecting. You can**
28   **imagine how surprised I was when she mentioned**

1   she was a Christian. I have tried to share with her

2   about how she spends her time, but to no avail. Tom,

3   this woman is truly a time-waster.

4   **Signed, Alvira Mason"**

5   **Well, Mrs. Mason, Satan will use anything to keep**

6   **us from the things of God – even worthwhile activi-**

7   **ties, like household chores. Your friend, Mrs. Diane**

8   **Yeager, is no exception.** *(Enter STEVE and ALAN. They*

9   *cross over to DIANE with TOM.)*

10 **DIANE:** **I'll be right with you. I just want to straighten**

11   **these two cushions here. I made them myself, you**

12   **know. I got the pattern out of** *Good Housekeeping* **–**

13   **what do you think?**

14 **TOM:** **They're very nice.**

15 **DIANE:** **Yes, so cute. Do you think I should put the one**

16   **with the chipmunk on top or the raccoon?**

17 **TOM:** **They're both nice.**

18 **DIANE:** **Thank you. Did you notice how shiny the eyes on**

19   **the chipmunk are? I had to go all over town to find a**

20   **pair of buttons that were just right.**

21 **TOM:** **They really are nice.**

22 **DIANE:** **The eyes on the raccoon are just regular buttons.**

23   **There, OK.** *(Sits in chair.)* **I'm ready to be interviewed.**

24   **Oh, this is exciting. Wait!** *(Gets up.)* **Do you like coffee**

25   **cake? I just got the greatest recipe** *(Goes Off-stage)* **for**

26   **coffee cake. They call it Herman Cake – isn't that**

27   **silly? Anyway, it takes ten days to make. You start off**

28   **with a yeast base, like sourdough bread, and each day**

29   **you add a new ingredient – some flour, some brown**

30   **sugar, some walnuts – oh, lots of things. And after ten**

31   **days – voilá!** *(Enters.)* **Herman's here. How's it look?**

32 **TOM:** **Very tasty, but I'm on a diet.**

33 **DIANE:** **Great. I'll get you a big glass of milk. Won't be a**

34   **second.** *(DIANE exits.)* **I go to this dairy across town to**

1   **get our milk. The young man there, he's so nice. He**
2   **gets us whole milk with cream. It's so good. Real**
3   **sweet, you know? Here we go.**
4   **TOM:** *(Aside)* **Listen, guys, I hate to disappoint her, but I**
5   **can't eat all this. Here, Steve, Alan. Go ahead, help**
6   **yourself.**
7   **STEVE and ALAN: Thanks, Tom. Mmmm, good stuff.**
8   **TOM: Take a big piece, here. Here she comes. Here she**
9   **comes.** *(DIANE enters.)*
10   **DIANE: Oh, I see you've almost finished your cake. Oh,**
11   **how is it?**
12   **TOM: Very good. Thanks for the milk.**
13   **DIANE: Oh, no trouble, you're welcome.** *(Sits.)* **Well, are we**
14   **ready?**
15   **TOM: I think so.** *(Pause)* **All right now, Mrs. Yeager...just**
16   **calm down here, this won't take long...**
17   **DIANE: Mrs. Yeager? Please, don't call me that – call me**
18   **Diane, everybody does!**
19   **TOM: OK, fine. Diane, just calm down here, don't get**
20   **nervous.** *(Pause)* **Diane...**
21   **DIANE: Yes?**
22   **TOM: I...I've noticed you take a distinct preoccupation**
23   **with your household chores.**
24   **DIANE: Well, Tom, you know what they say, "Cleanliness is**
25   **next to godliness."**
26   **TOM: I'm not so sure. Diane, I think you can reach a point**
27   **when a responsibility can become an obsession.**
28   **DIANE: Well, maybe you're right, Tom. I'm not so sure**
29   **about what you said, I just know that the Vatican is**
30   **kept nice 'n tidy – and what about the new glass**
31   **cathedral? You can bet your broom it gets a good deal**
32   **of Windex.**
33   **TOM: Yes, Diane, but you of course know your body is a**
34   **temple of the Holy Spirit. Shouldn't you give him**

1   some time to clean you up a bit?

2   **DIANE: Tom, I already shower every morning whether I**

3   **need it or not. How much cleaner could I be? You**

4   **know, I've been using Zest lately, and I've really**

5   **noticed it doesn't leave half the ring my old soap did.**

6   **I compared all the brands, and Zest leaves me so**

7   **squeaky clean. It's just so wonderful...** *(TOM crosses to*

8   *audience while DIANE, STEVE and ALAN exit.)*

9   **TOM: Unfortunately for Mrs. Yeager, the Bible does not**

10   **say, "Cleanliness is next to godliness." Instead, we**

11   **find in 2 Peter the way to godliness is "through the**

12   **knowledge of him that hath called us to glory and**

13   **virtue."** (2 Peter 1:3) **As Christians, we should always**

14   **be careful not to put our work for the Lord before our**

15   **relationship with him. Surely in an ungodly world**

16   **there is much to be done, but first we must always be**

17   **partakers of God's mercy and love. This is Tom Biggs,**

18   **hoping Jesus is always as important to you as you are**

19   **to him. So long for now.**

20

21

22

23

24

25

26

27

28

29

30

31

32

33

34

TIME WASTERS
Looks at TV

By Dave Toole

1   **CAST:** Tom Biggs; Harold Diddleman; (Optional) Steve —
2   Sound Man; (Optional) Alan — Cameraman.
3   **SETTING:** HAROLD's home in Santa Monica, California. You
4   need two chairs and a TV.
5   **PROPS:** Microphone and letter for TOM, cheese puffs, pret-
6   zels and remote control for HAROLD.
7   **COSTUMES:** Suit for TOM, sweats for HAROLD.
8
9   *(TOM is at Center Stage. HAROLD is in his home.)*
10   **TOM:** Hello, everybody. Welcome to *Time Wasters*. I'm
11   your host, Tom Biggs, and today we're in Santa
12   Monica, California, in answer to a letter from Ludlow,
13   Vermont, that reads:
14   "Dear Tom,
15   I am eighty-five years old and have been a
16   Christian for some sixty-odd years now, and in all my
17   days, I have seen some people waste time in thou-
18   sands of different ways. Even before I became a
19   Christian, I had little patience with people who didn't
20   make the most of every day. And as far back as I can
21   remember, I have never seen anything that can waste
22   more time for someone than a television. Seems to
23   me that's the main purpose of the thing, so why do
24   people watch it? I just don't understand. Anyway,
25   imagine my dismay when I got the chance to fly out to
26   California to meet one of my grandchildren for the
27   first time, only to find him addicted to that box. I
28   spent my whole vacation trying to talk to him, but I

1   **couldn't reach him. A friend told me you might be**
2   **able to help. After all, you're on TV, so maybe he'll**
3   **listen to you. Gratefully,**
4   **Signed, Mr. Diddleman"**
5   **Well, Mr. Diddleman, your letter expresses the**
6   **opinion of thousands of people around the nation,**
7   **and we couldn't agree more. Experts tell us excessive**
8   **TV viewing is responsible for many of our nation's**
9   **problems – physically, psychologically, and of course,**
10   **spiritually.** *(TOM crosses over toward HAROLD, calling*
11   *to him.)* **Harold.**
12   **HAROLD: Who is it?**
13   **TOM: Tom Biggs of *Time Wasters*.**
14   **HAROLD: Come on in.**
15   **TOM:** *(TOM enters.)* **Harold Diddleman? I'm Tom Biggs.**
16   **HAROLD: Right, right. Go ahead and have a seat. Want a**
17   **cheese puff? I'm just watching an old Sherlock**
18   **Holmes movie – Basil Rathbone, Nigel Bruce. Great,**
19   **just great.**
20   **TOM: Sounds good. Have you ever seen our show, *Time***
21   ***Wasters?***
22   **HAROLD: Not too much. I always watch *My Mother, the***
23   ***Car* that night. It's my favorite show. I never miss it.**
24   **TOM: Well, our show is kind of a human interest show. We**
25   **go to people's houses and film interviews with them.**
26   **HAROLD: Kind of like *That's Real Incredible People?***
27   **TOM: More like what we're doing right now, I'd say.**
28   **HAROLD: Oh, mmm, I'll have to record it on my VCR and**
29   **watch it sometime. It's great to be able to watch one**
30   **thing and tape another at the same time. It's a lot**
31   **easier than watching two or three sets at once. That**
32   **used to give me a headache. Want some pretzels?**
33   **TOM: No.**
34   **HAROLD: How did you pick me for your show?**

1   **TOM: Well, different people write in and...**

2   **HAROLD: Wait, wait, wait. I gotta see this part.** *(Pause)* **OK,**

3   **go ahead. What were you saying?**

4   **TOM: Your grandfather recommended you to us.**

5   **HAROLD: Grandpa Diddleman? Really? I thought he**

6   **hated TV. He was here for two weeks, telling me how**

7   **bad it was. He talked all the way through** *Casablanca.*

8   **Said it wasn't Christian.**

9   **TOM:** *Casablanca?*

10   **HAROLD: No, no. TV in general. I tried to tell him I**

11   **accepted the Lord on a TV, but he wouldn't listen.**

12   **TOM: You mean watching TV?**

13   **HAROLD: Yeah, right. Every Sunday morning I get all**

14   **three sets out and watch all the Christian programs.**

15   **TOM: At once?**

16   **HAROLD: Yeah, sure. Twenty-one shows in all, every**

17   **Sunday. I see 'em all. I guess you could say I attend**

18   **more church than most.**

19   **TOM: I don't know whether I could agree with that. How**

20   **does your wife feel about TV?**

21   **HAROLD: Oh, I'm not married.**

22   **TOM: Well, what I really want to know is how all this**

23   **affects your life – your family, friends, job?**

24   **HAROLD: Oh, I see. Well, most of my family lives back**

25   **East. My friends are all video buffs, and my TVs**

26   **support me.**

27   **TOM: How's that?**

28   **HAROLD: I'm an unemployed TV repairman. I fix an occa-**

29   **sional set now and again, but most of the time I just**

30   **live off my unemployment check. Hey, want to watch**

31   *King of Kings* **with Jeffrey Hunter later? We could**

32   **split a TV dinner.**

33   **TOM: I don't think so. Thanks anyway.** *(HAROLD shrugs*

34   *and exits while TOM crosses to audience.)* **The Bible**

1 tells us that Jesus is the Way, the Truth and the Life.
2 But to follow his way, we must first stand up and be
3 counted among his own. To learn the truth, we have
4 to make a daily effort to understand and apply his
5 word. And to live that life, we need to die to the things
6 of this world. Only then can we go from a watcher to
7 a winner in the game of life. This is Tom Biggs,
8 hoping Jesus is always as important to you as you are
9 to him. So long for now.
10
11
12
13
14
15
16
17
18
19
20
21
22
23
24
25
26
27
28
29
30
31
32
33
34

THE HAPPY FAMILY

By Dan Rupple

1   **CAST:** Narrator (On-stage or off), Grandpa, Milton, Billy.

2   **SETTING:** The sitcom home of the Happy family. GRANDPA

3   needs a rocker.

4   **PROPS:** None.

5   **COSTUMES:** Casual clothing suitable for the characters' various ages.

6

7   *(Optional music. GRANDPA sits in his rocking chair.)*

8   **NARRATOR: And now it's time for *The Happy Family*. The**

9   **family that lives just up the street from just about**

10   **everyone. Starring _____** *(Actor's name)*

11   **as Milton, _____** *(Actor's name)* **as**

12   **Gramps and _____** *(Actor's name)* **as the**

13   **irrepressible little Billy. Pull up a chair and join us,**

14   **won'tcha?** *(Enter MILTON.)*

15   **GRANDPA: Oh, Milton, thank goodness you're home.**

16   **MILTON: Hi, Dad.**

17   **GRANDPA: Have I got something to show you!**

18   **MILTON: What is it, Dad?**

19   **GRANDPA: I was in Billy's room today, and I found some-**

20   **thing.**

21   **MILTON: Marijuana? If my son's smoking marijuana, I'll kill**

22   **him.**

23   **GRANDPA: No, Milton, I'm afraid it's something worse.**

24   **MILTON: What?**

25   **GRANDPA: A Bible!**

26   **MILTON: Are you sure?**

27   **GRANDPA: Positive. It was under his mattress. I can't**

28   **believe it!**

1   MILTON: Wait a minute, Dad. Maybe he's just doing a book
2   report or something.
3   GRANDPA: No, Milton, that's not all. Yesterday I looked in
4   his room and he was praying. *Praying!* On his *knees!*
5   MILTON: Now, Dad, don't get excited. Maybe he was just
6   looking for something under his bed.
7   GRANDPA: Looking for what – his *Bible?* No, Milton, he was
8   praying. Praying? For what? He's got everything he's
9   ever needed.
10   MILTON: I've always said you spoiled that kid.
11   GRANDPA: Well, you can't let the neighbors think that we're
12   broke or something. And another thing – I don't like
13   those new kids he's hanging around.
14   MILTON: What do you mean, Dad? They're always friendly
15   to me.
16   GRANDPA: That's just it. Kids that are aren't supposed to be
17   nice. What happened to the smart-aleck delinquents he
18   used to hang around?
19   MILTON: Well, Dad, they seem to be happy.
20   GRANDPA: What right do they have to be happy growing up
21   in this armpit of a city with the smog and the crazy peo-
22   ple loose on the streets? And have you seen what Billy's
23   wearing now? A necklace with a fish on it.
24   MILTON: Wait a minute. A necklace?
25   GRANDPA: That's right.
26   MILTON: No son of mine is going to wear a necklace. I mean,
27   the long hair was one thing, but a necklace?
28   GRANDPA: He calls it a choker.
29   MILTON: Choker, boker! This is a disgrace to the family
30   name. Why didn't I make him join the football team?
31   GRANDPA: Billy doesn't like football, Milton.
32   MILTON: I don't care. Reggie White doesn't wear a necklace.
33   GRANDPA: Yes, he does, Milton. Remember that picture in
34   Sports Illustrated?

1   MILTON: What are we going to do, Dad? This could destroy
2   our home.
3   GRANDPA: I don't know, son.
4   MILTON: Maybe I should've roughed him up more when he
5   was little. You know, punched him in the nose.
6   GRANDPA: Why couldn't it have been marijuana? That I
7   could've handled. But a Bible!
8   MILTON: And a necklace!
9   GRANDPA: What will the guys at the shuffleboard courts
10   think?
11   MILTON: I've tried so hard to be a good father. *(Enter BILLY.)*
12   BILLY: Hi, Dad! Hi, Gramps!
13   MILTON: Billy, son, can we talk to you a minute?
14   BILLY: Sure, Dad. What's up?
15   MILTON: We found this in your room today, son.
16   BILLY: Oh yeah, my Bible.
17   GRANDPA: Is that all you have to say? My Bible! How do you
18   explain it?
19   BILLY: Well, I've been wanting to tell you about this.
20   GRANDPA: Tell us what? You're not sick, are you? The swine
21   flu?
22   BILLY: No, Grandpa, I'm not sick. I'm a Christian.
23   MILTON: What do you mean, a Christian?
24   BILLY: Jesus Christ is my Lord and Savior.
25   GRANDPA: Oh no, he's a Jesus freak!
26   MILTON: You're not going to shave your head or anything,
27   are you, son?
28   BILLY: No, Dad, you don't have to do anything like that. You
29   just have to be born again.
30   MILTON: Born again?
31   GRANDPA: Are you saying your mother didn't do it right the
32   first time? Nine months she put up with you.
33   BILLY: No, Grandpa. Not physically born again – spiritually!
34   GRANDPA: Billy, why are you doing this? To spite me?

1   **BILLY:** No, I love you.

2   **GRANDPA:** Well, you'd better, after all we've done for you.

3   **BILLY:** Yeah, but what have you done for Jesus? But he still

4   loves you. He loves you so much that he died for you.

5   And all he wants in return is for you to love him back.

6   **MILTON:** Are you sure you're not taking drugs?

7   **BILLY:** No, I'm not taking drugs.

8   **MILTON:** Well, why not? All the other kids are.

9   **BILLY:** I know. They're just looking for the answer. People

10   try all sorts of things: drugs, booze, sex...

11   **MILTON:** Watch yourself, young man!

12   **BILLY:** ...Money, but they'll never find it except through

13   Jesus.

14   **GRANDPA:** Well, maybe you're right, son. Your generation

15   definitely needs straightening out.

16   **BILLY:** No, Grandpa, it's not just my generation. It's your

17   generation, and yours too, Dad.

18   **MILTON:** Now wait a minute, you don't see me or any of my

19   friends smoking marijuana.

20   **BILLY:** Yeah, but Dad, are you really fulfilled? You're always

21   complaining about your job, the government, the

22   money...

23   **GRANDPA:** That's right, son, and you know how your ulcers

24   act up every time you pay the bills.

25   **MILTON:** I wouldn't have so many bills if you didn't have to

26   visit that dumb astrologer twice a month.

27   **GRANDPA:** Now, Milton, you can't talk to me that way. Zomo

28   the Great says that people are supposed to be nice to me

29   this month. After all, my third moon is in Saturn.

30   **MILTON:** What does that mean?

31   **GRANDPA:** I don't know, but it sounds official.

32   **BILLY:** See? Everyone is searching, and Jesus is the Way.

33   **MILTON:** The way to what?

34   **BILLY:** To everything. Heaven, true happiness, inner peace.

1   **GRANDPA: I don't know. For an Aries, you're sure showing a**
2   **lot of spunk.**
3   **MILTON: Grandpa, isn't it time for you to take your**
4   **medicine?**
5   **GRANDPA: No, Milton, it's only four-thirty.**
6   **MILTON: Well, take it anyway.** *(GRANDPA exits.)* **So what do**
7   **you mean by this born-again jazz?**
8   **BILLY: Dad, wouldn't you like a fresh start?**
9   **MILTON: Yeah, I would...but...no, son, I can't get involved in**
10   **some fad.**
11   **BILLY: I'm not talking about a fad, I'm talking about a rela-**
12   **tionship with the Lord.**
13   **MILTON: Son, I'm a lot older than you. I can't start over.**
14   **BILLY: Dad, the Bible says we're new creatures in Christ.**
15   **Old things are passed away, and all things become new.**
16   **MILTON: But there's so much to give up.**
17   **BILLY: But what are you holding on to? Worry, strife,**
18   **loneliness...**
19   **MILTON: All right, all right, you made your point. Ah, I don't**
20   **know, you might be right. Maybe there isn't anything**
21   **worth hanging on to. Oh, I don't know. Let me think**
22   **about it.**
23   **BILLY: OK, Dad.**
24   **MILTON: In the meantime, thanks, son.**
25   **BILLY: Sure, Dad.** *(Optional music)*
26   **NARRATOR: Will Milton accept Jesus as his Lord and**
27   **Savior? Can little Billy live up to the commitment he**
28   **has made? For the answers to these questions and**
29   **more, tune in next time when you'll hear Gramps say...**
30   **GRANDPA:** *(From Off-stage)* **What's this bit about old things**
31   **passing away?**
32   **NARRATOR: This is H. T. Prod, hoping that your family is a**
33   **happy family. Good night!**
34

P. & R. LUCRE TITHE SERVICE

By Dan Rupple

1   ***CAST:*** Phil T. Lucre.

2   ***SETTING:*** TV commercial set.

3   ***PROPS:*** None.

4   ***COSTUMES:*** Suit.

5

6   *(PHIL is at Center Stage.)*

7   **PHIL T. LUCRE: Hi. I'm Phil T. Lucre of P. & R. Lucre with**

8   **another one of our sixty-four reasons why you should**

9   **use P. & R. Lucre Tithe Service.**

10   **Have you ever considered whether to tithe ten per-**

11   **cent gross or ten percent net? I'm sure it crosses all of**

12   **our minds. Let's look at an example: Say for instance**

13   **you gross $350 a week. Do you tithe $35.00 or do you**

14   **wait until after you've rendered unto Caesar and tithe**

15   **$27.50.**

16   **The answer? Neither!**

17   **You are still missing many more legitimate tithe**

18   **deductions which can lead to substantial annual sav-**

19   **ings. Remember the friends you had over for dinner**

20   **Tuesday night? Did you talk about the Lord? Deduct**

21   **$2.**

22   **If you didn't talk about the Lord, grace before the**

23   **meal is adequate to justify a deduction.**

24   **Have you ever mailed a tract along with your house**

25   **payment? If you have, that makes it deductible. Take**

26   **a whole payment off. And don't forget to include**

27   **tracts with your utility bills, too. Those little fellas can**

28   **really add up.**

1 And these are just a couple of examples of justifi-
2 able tithe deductions. There are many more: Bible
3 covers, bumper stickers, wear and tear on pants legs
4 from prayer meetings, chicken for potlucks – the list
5 is endless.

6 We will instruct you on how to get the most for your
7 tithing dollar, and we know how important that is.
8 After all, God told us to be good stewards. How sad to
9 be in the same situation as the poor widow in the
10 Gospel. If she would've visited our office before she
11 threw in those two mites, we could've saved her half a
12 farthing. Now, how was she to afford groceries? Was
13 God going to provide? I don't think so! God helps
14 those who help themselves.

15 Friends, give us a call. You'll keep money that God
16 definitely doesn't want. How can a righteous God
17 build his kingdom on money that's rightfully yours? I
18 mean, you earned it! Right? You can't be a cheerful
19 giver if you're giving more than the law requires.

20 So when it comes time to tithe, seek ye first P. & R.
21 Lucre Tithe Service. We're located between where the
22 moth eats and rust corrupts. Call today! The money
23 you save won't be around forever.

24
25
26
27
28
29
30
31
32
33
34

BIG GEORGE,
LITTLE "G"

By Dave Toole

1   **CAST:** Ida Neudecker; George Neudecker; Bobby; TV
2   Announcer #1; TV Announcer #2; TV Announcer #3; Radio
3   Announcer #1 (Off-stage voice); Radio Announcer #2 (Off-
4   stage voice); Lucifer.

5   **NOTE:** This is the trickiest sketch of all to stage, as it was orig-
6   inally recorded for an album and not performed live. The
7   castle walls, the seven mink coats, and other items men-
8   tioned in the script would be much easier to imply or
9   pantomime than to actually stage. A minimalist
10   approach would be considerably less frustrating — per-
11   haps even a puppet show or Readers Theatre.

12   Comedian Steven Wright once said, "I wouldn't want to
13   have it all. I wouldn't know where to put it." This sketch
14   builds on that theme. Don't let the staging intimidate you.
15   Be creative! You won't want to miss this great sketch about
16   our selfish earthly wishes versus God's plan for our lives.

17   **SETTING:** This depends on how literally you wish to stage
18   this production. There are four different areas: the back-
19   yard (with garage, hammock or chaise lounge, and trash
20   can), the kitchen (with stove), the living room (with
21   couch and TV), and the bedroom (with lamp). You may
22   place a partition with a window and a door between the
23   backyard and house. A bare stage would work fine, with
24   areas designated to be the different rooms. Even the set
25   pieces may be pantomimed.

26   **PROPS:** Hedge clippers, piece of trash, bunch of bills, two rings,
27   seven mink coats, encyclopedia, and microphones for the
28   TV ANNOUNCERS. Again, pantomiming would suffice.

1   **COSTUMES:** Regular clothing for IDA, GEORGE and BOBBY.
2   Suits for the TV ANNOUNCERS. An all-black or all-red
3   outfit for LUCIFER.
4   **SOUND EFFECTS:** Popping noise, thunder, sirens, angry
5   crowd sounds, crying, doorbell, knocking.
6   **LIGHTS:** The lighting can really help with the flow of this
7   sketch, as GEORGE and IDA move around from one part
8   of their house to another. Even if you don't have access to
9   theatrical lighting, simply turning off the house lights
10   during the transition times helps.
11
12   *(GEORGE is puttering around in his yard. Enter IDA.)*
13   **IDA: Hello. I'm Ida Neudecker. See that man over there?**
14   **That's my husband, George. He used to have folks call**
15   **him "Big George." He doesn't anymore, though. And**
16   **that's what this story is about.** *(Exit IDA. GEORGE is*
17   *humming to himself.)*
18   **BOBBY:** *(Walking up)* **Afternoon, George. How're things at**
19   **the gas station?**
20   **GEORGE: Hey, hi ya, Bobby-boy. Things are fine down at**
21   **the station – just great. How you doin'?**
22   **BOBBY: Oh, fine, fine. Doin' some yard work, huh?**
23   **GEORGE: Yeah, got to weed the ol' flower beds, you know.**
24   **How 'bout you?**
25   **BOBBY: I've got to trim the hedge. Actually, I was wonder-**
26   **ing if I could borrow your hedge clippers if it's no**
27   **problem.**
28   **GEORGE: Oh, sure, sure. C'mon, let me get 'em for you.**
29   **They're out here in the garage.** *(Goes over to the*
30   *garage.)* **I think they're over by the workbench.**
31   **BOBBY: Say, George, ah, Karen and I were wondering...if**
32   **you and Ida aren't busy tomorrow, ummm, well,**
33   **would you want to go to church with us?**
34   **GEORGE: Aw, c'mon now, Bobby-boy, you know how I feel**

1   about that stuff. It's fine if you're into it. I've got noth-
2   ing against it, mind you. But, uh, I just don't buy it,
3   you know?

4 BOBBY: But George, how do you know until you check it
5   out?

6 GEORGE: *(Rummaging for clippers)* Oh, c'mon now, Bobby,
7   I know all about that stuff. I was raised in Sunday
8   school. I know all about God and Adam and Eve and
9   how God created the world and everything else. I just
10   have one question. If God is really in control of every-
11   thing, then how come we got so much trouble, huh?
12   Hey, c'mon, you got murders, rapes, earthquakes, dis-
13   ease. *(Spots clippers.)* Oh, here, here they are. All that
14   kind of trouble. Here, here're the clippers.

15 BOBBY: Oh, uh, thanks. But George, God's not responsible
16   for all that. The devil's the one who's really...

17 GEORGE: Oh, c'mon, Bobby. Look – I don't want to get
18   into it now. I've got too much to do here. You go on
19   ahead and clip your hedge out there. I'll be in the
20   backyard when you're done.

21 BOBBY: Well, OK, George, but if you ever change your
22   mind, you're always invited.

23 GEORGE: Oh, I know that, Bobby, and I really do appreci-
24   ate it. I really do. Well, see you later, huh?

25 BOBBY: OK. Thanks again for the clippers. *(Exits.)*

26 GEORGE: No problem. *(Pause)* Come to church? Not this
27   guy, no, sir. I get enough of that stuff on the TV. Oh
28   boy, these weeds are gonna take forever. Mmmm.
29   Think I'll lay down in the hammock for a while –
30   kinda build up my strength. Don't want to approach a
31   job like this all...all... *(Getting into hammock)* Oh,
32   swing my leg over...Ooops! Uh! There. Ahhh...Boy, I
33   just don't know. Hee-hee. God! What some people
34   believe. *(Yawns.)* You can bet your boots that if I were

1   **God, things would be different.** *(Drifts off to sleep.*
2   *Lights fade out. Optional time passage music. Lights up*
3   *on the Neudecker kitchen.)*
4   IDA: *(Calling out the window)* **George, dinner in five minutes.**
5   **GEORGE: Uh? Wha...oh, OK, dear. Oh boy. Ahhh** *(Sniff)*
6   **Must've dozed off there. Oh, better get up, get in the**
7   **house. Oh no, forgot to weed the garden. Doggone –**
8   **have to do it tomorrow.** *(Enters house.)* **Wish I didn't**
9   **have to do it at all.**
10   IDA: **Better wash up, dear. Dinner will be ready in a**
11   **minute. I'll toss this in the trash and we can eat.** *(Steps*
12   *out kitchen door and throws garbage in the trash can.)*
13   **The flower beds look great, honey.**
14   **GEORGE: I didn't do the flower beds, honey. I'm sorry.**
15   IDA: *(Steps back inside.)* **Then who did?**
16   **GEORGE:** *(Looks out the door.)* **Mmmm. Well, I guess I**
17   **must've done it before my nap. Hmmm!** *(Closes door.)*
18   **Well, I guess I don't have to worry about that any-**
19   **more. Oh boy, I'm starved. What's for dinner?**
20   IDA: **Tuna Helper.**
21   **GEORGE: Oh, again! Awww, I had my heart set on steak.**
22   **Boy, I wish we could have some steaks, potatoes...** *(IDA*
23   *looks into the stove, screams.)* **What is it? What's wrong?**
24   IDA: **T-bone steaks!**
25   **GEORGE: What?** *(Looks in the stove.)*
26   IDA: **George, George, how did you do it? Where did you get**
27   **those steaks? Where's the Tuna Helper?**
28   **GEORGE: I don't know, Ida. I don't know...**
29   IDA: **Well, you must know something, George. You can't**
30   **just magically change Tuna Helper into steaks. Now**
31   **how did you do it?**
32   **GEORGE: Wait a minute – maybe I can change things**
33   **magically.**
34   IDA: **What do you mean, George?**

1   **GEORGE: Well, Ida, I'm sure I didn't weed those flower**
2   **beds, but they're done. And I honestly didn't hide the**
3   **Helper, it must've just disappeared!**
4   **IDA: George, that's silly. You're not magic.**
5   **GEORGE: Oh, I'm not so sure, Ida. Maybe I am.**
6   **IDA: Oh, George, this is silly. You're not magic. Why – why,**
7   **you're not even lucky. Here, why drag this thing out?**
8   **Just try to change the steaks into lobsters.**
9   **GEORGE: Yeah! That's a good idea. Sure, Ida. Ohhh, let me**
10   **see...um, I wish those steaks were lobsters.** *(A loud pop*
11   *is heard. They both look into the stove — both react.)*
12   **IDA: Oh! George! You did it! You're magic! You're magic!**
13   **You're magic! You're magic! You're magic!**
14   **GEORGE:** *(With IDA)* **I'm magic! I'm magic! I'm magic!**
15   *(Pause)* **Ida! You know what this means? We ain't**
16   **broke no more! We're rich – *really* rich! Ho-ho-ho! I**
17   **can quit the gas station. Ha-ha-ha.**
18   **IDA: Oh, George, I'm so proud of you!**
19   **GEORGE: Oh-oh, Ida. This is so much fun. Hey! I wish I**
20   **had a million dollars!** *(Pop!)* **Wowee!** *(Both react.)* **This**
21   **is great! This is great!**
22   **IDA: George, look at all this money!**
23   **GEORGE: Oh, man alive! Let's see here. I wish I had a dia-**
24   **mond ring.** *(Pop!)*
25   **IDA: Oh, George, it's beautiful!**
26   **GEORGE: Oh, Ida, I'm sorry, dear. I wish you had a dia-**
27   **mond ring, too!** *(Pop!)*
28   **IDA: Oh, George, it's beautiful!** *(Kisses him.)* **I love you.**
29   **GEORGE: Aw, c'mon, Ida. Cut it out now. We got work to**
30   **do. C'mon, let's go to the living room. We need a couch**
31   **and a TV.** *(Exit IDA and GEORGE. Lights out.)*
32   **IDA:** *(From Off-stage)* **George, I'm tired. Can't we do this**
33   **tomorrow?**
34   **GEORGE:** *(From Off-stage)* **C'mon, Ida. We just gotta do the**

1   **clothes and the bedroom. We can do the bathrooms**

2   **and the garage tomorrow. Oh boy, this is fun.** (*Lights*

3   *up on IDA and GEORGE in the living room.*) **Oh, OK,**

4   **let's see here. I wish Ida had a mink coat.** (*Pop!*) **There**

5   **we are – how's that?**

6   **IDA: It's beautiful, George. Just like everything else.**

7   **GEORGE: I wish Ida had seven mink coats.** (*Pop! Pop! Pop!*

8   *Pop! Pop! Pop! Pop!*) **There we go. One for each day of**

9   **the week.**

10   **IDA: George, please. Let's stop. I love everything, but we**

11   **don't have room for it all.**

12   **GEORGE: Well, well, well then, we'll just get a new house.**

13   **What kind do you want? Two-story? A swimming**

14   **pool? Some tennis courts? Maybe a little...**

15   **IDA: George, it sounds like a mansion.**

16   **GEORGE: A mansion. Sure, we deserve a mansion. We**

17   **need a mansion. Yeah, yeah, a big one, too. The**

18   **biggest, in fact...yeah! Yeah! C'mon, Ida, I got an idea!**

19   **IDA: Oh, George, I'm tired. Do I have to?**

20   **GEORGE: C'mon, honey, you're gonna love this. Here we**

21   **go. Let's see the encyclopedia. OK, OK, yeah, yeah,**

22   **yeah, yeah! Here, here. Here we go. Let's see, uh, Ca to**

23   **De...** (*Sounds of pages turning*) **cars, carrots, cassons,**

24   **yeah, ha! Here it is, Ida, our new home – a castle!**

25   **IDA: George, really? It's gorgeous. I love it.**

26   **GEORGE: Oh, no sooner said than done. Watch this. Ho-**

27   **ho-ho-ho-ho. I wish my home was a castle. Just like**

28   **the one in the picture...only bigger.** (*Thunder, lights*

29   *flash. Stage note: Background of living room may be*

30   *quickly changed into stone walls during light flashes,*

31   *though this is not necessary if the action is mostly pan-*

32   *tomimed.*)

33   **IDA: Oh, George! Oh my, it's – it's wonderful.**

34   **GEORGE: Yeah, I kinda like it.** (*Knock at door*) **Oh, who**

1 **could that be?** *(Opens door.)* **Oh, hello, Bobby-boy.**
2 *(Sirens, angry crowds, crying)*
3 **BOBBY: George, George, what're you doin'? Where'd this**
4 **thing come from? George, this castle's crushed every-**
5 **thing for four blocks. It's gotta go, George. You gotta**
6 **get this thing out of here.**
7 **GEORGE: Oh no, I forgot. I'm sorry, Bobby. I didn't mean**
8 **no harm.**
9 **BOBBY: George, George, please! Just get rid of it!**
10 **GEORGE: Oh yeah, yeah. OK, ahhh, oh, I wish this castle**
11 **was gone!** *(Thunder, lights)*
12 **BOBBY: Oh, George, look at that. Everything's squished**
13 **flat. What're you gonna do?**
14 **GEORGE: It's OK, Bobby. It's OK. Just let me think for a**
15 **minute. Ahhh...Oh, OK, I wish everything was back to**
16 **normal.** *(Thunder, lights. Living room background*
17 *changes back.)*
18 **BOBBY: Oh, thanks, George. Thank you so much.**
19 **GEORGE: Well, that's OK, Bobby. My fault to begin with.**
20 **I'm real sorry.**
21 **BOBBY: That's OK, George. I'm gonna go home now and**
22 **make sure Karen and the kids are OK.** *(Walking off)*
23 **GEORGE: All right, Bobby. I'll see you tomorrow, buddy.**
24 *(Closes door.)* **Whew! That was close. I gotta learn to be**
25 **more careful.** *(Knock at door. GEORGE opens it.)*
26 **BOBBY: How did you do that?**
27 **GEORGE: Well, I don't really know how it works, but, well,**
28 **I just wished for it. That's where the castle came**
29 **from. All I had to do was wish for it. I sorta forgot**
30 **there wasn't any room for it.**
31 **BOBBY: George, George, this isn't good. This is wrong,**
32 **George. Man wasn't meant to do this kinda thing.**
33 **GEORGE: Aw, c'mon now, Bobby. I ain't hurtin' nothin'.**
34 **The castle was just a mistake. But you didn't see all**

1   the good stuff I made for me an' Ida. Stereos, a TV, a
2   computer, lots of stuff.

3 BOBBY: No, George, no. You don't understand. This is evil.
4   Your power is satanic.

5 GEORGE: Satanic? How do you know that? Look, I ain't no
6   witch. I'm only gonna use my power for good. After I
7   take care of me and Ida, I'm gonna save the world.
8   Feed the hungry, cure the sick, prevent earthquakes,
9   everything.

10 BOBBY: George, do you realize what you're saying? You're
11   saying that you're God. You can't do that.

12 GEORGE: Oh, now look, Bobby. I don't know anything
13   about God. All I know is I have the power to change
14   things, and it's my responsibility to try. In fact, it's my
15   destiny. *(Lights out. Optional time-passage music. TV*
16   *ANNOUNCER #1 enters Stage Left. Spotlight Stage Left.)*

17 TV ANNOUNCER #1: In addition to world peace, stable eco-
18   nomics, and his worldwide food programs, George
19   Neudecker, or "Big George," as he prefers to be called,
20   instituted a free beer program for all people eighteen
21   years and older, a three-day work week and forty-five
22   new professional football teams to extend the season
23   to a year-round schedule. He also scheduled six
24   Superbowls. *(TV ANNOUNCER #1 exits. TV ANNOUNC-*
25   *ER #2 enters Stage Right. Spotlight Stage Right.)*

26 TV ANNOUNCER #2: It was a visibly shaken Big George
27   who addressed the world today. It seems his much-
28   heralded abolition of disease and natural disasters
29   six weeks ago is still a source of major problems deal-
30   ing with overpopulation. Waste disposal, overcrowd-
31   ing and food distribution are only a few of the prob-
32   lems. As a New Jersey man put it, "What good is a
33   three-day work week if you've got to spend the whole
34   day waiting for food and two days to use the john?"

1   *(Spotlight Stage Right out. TV ANNOUNCER #2 exits. TV*

2   *ANNOUNCER #3 enters Stage Left. Spotlight Stage Left.)*

3 **TV ANNOUNCER #3: This is Jane Poleman. Open rebellion**

4   **today, as thousands of citizens took out their frustra-**

5   **tions over living conditions worldwide. Riots, looting**

6   **and violence were the order of the day. Big George**

7   **again claimed he was doing his best to keep up with the**

8   **problems, but as usual, the problems are coming faster**

9   **than the answers. Meanwhile, morticians staged a**

10   **demonstration to draw attention to the fact that busi-**

11   **ness there is down ninety-seven percent from this time**

12   **last year. A spokesman for the group said business is vir-**

13   **tually dead.** *(TV ANNOUNCER #3 exits. Spotlight out. Stage*

14   *lights up on the Neudecker bedroom.)*

15 **GEORGE:** *(Turns off TV.)* **What's wrong with all those peo-**

16   **ple, Ida? Don't they know I'm only trying to help? Why**

17   **do they hate me so much?**

18 **IDA: George, calm down. They don't hate you.**

19 **GEORGE: Sure they do. Don't they understand everything**

20   **I've done is for them? I haven't slept for two days try-**

21   **ing to help them. But do they care? Do they appreciate**

22   **it? No way. They riot, they kill, they steal, and worst of**

23   **all, they hate me. Well, I've had enough! If they don't**

24   **like the way I'm runnin' things, I'll show 'em. I wish**

25   **everything was back the way it was.** *(Thunder, lights.)*

26   **There!**

27 **IDA: Oh, George.** *(She hugs him and sobs.)*

28 **GEORGE: It's OK, Ida. I'm all right.** *(Pause)* **What the heck**

29   **– I was only trying to help. C'mon, honey, let 'em run**

30   **their own world. I'm going to bed.** *(Doorbell and knock-*

31   *ing)*

32 **IDA: Oh no, George, the reporters.**

33 **GEORGE: Aw, Ida, I'm too tired right now.** *(Doorbell and*

34   *knocking)*

1   IDA: But what can we do?

2   GEORGE: I don't...Wait a minute. I wish we couldn't be
3   found. *(Bell and knocking stop.)* There. There we go.
4   C'mon, Ida, last one in bed turns out the light... *(As*
5   *IDA switches off the lamp, lights go out. Time passage*
6   *music — lights fade up. Snoring, GEORGE wakes up,*
7   *then more snoring.)* Ida, Ida, honey. *(Snoring is inter-*
8   *rupted as IDA wakes up.)*

9   IDA: What is it, George?

10 GEORGE: Time to get up, sugar, it's 10:30. We must have
11   been more tired than we thought. Here. *(Stretches.)*
12   Oh, I'll just see how things are going here. *(GEORGE*
13   *turns the radio on.)*

14 RADIO REPORTER #1: So as of yet, we're not sure how
15   many have died, but it's surely in the thousands.
16   Bobby?

17 RADIO REPORTER #2: Thank you, Rich, for that live
18   report from New York, where the third devastating
19   earthquake in six hours has struck. Of course, New
20   York is not the only city struggling with disaster.
21   Montreal, Los Angeles, Tokyo, Peking...

22 IDA: George, oh no!

23 GEORGE: Quiet, Ida, quiet.

24 RADIO REPORTER #2: ...Moscow, Berlin, Rome, Paris,
25   London, all battling floods, fires, disease, storms and
26   every other imaginable disaster. The people have
27   stopped searching out Big George for help and have
28   begun blaming him for it all!

29 IDA: George, did you hear that?

30 GEORGE: Of course I heard it.

31 RADIO REPORTER #2: Meanwhile, attacks by wild ani-
32   mals have gotten... *(GEORGE turns the radio off.)*

33 IDA: Look, George, what are you going to do?

34 GEORGE: I'm not going to do anything.

1   **IDA:** But, George...

2   **GEORGE:** Ida, you heard that man. They blame *me* for all

3   of that. It's not my fault. They're the ones who didn't

4   want my help, remember? They hated me when I

5   helped them, and now they turn around and hate me

6   when I don't help them! What do they want from me,

7   anyway? Am I just supposed to sit here and do what-

8   ever *they* tell me to? So that's it, huh? So that's what

9   I'm supposed to do? Just sit around and be their lack-

10   ey? Huh?

11   **IDA:** *(Gently)* George, they're afraid. They don't know what

12   to think. All they know is they need help, and they

13   think you can help them. I know it's tough, but I think

14   you can, too.

15   **GEORGE:** But Ida...

16   **IDA:** Now, George. *(Getting up)* I'm going in to make you

17   some hot cocoa. You just stay here and think about it.

18   *(Walks out.)*

19   **GEORGE:** Oh. Oh golly, all this trouble. I only take one

20   night's sleep, just one night, and look what happens.

21   Oh, how did it all happen so fast?

22   **LUCIFER:** *(From Off-stage)* Perhaps I can explain. *(Enter*

23   *LUCIFER.)*

24   **GEORGE:** Huh? *(Startled)* Who are you? Where'd you come

25   from?

26   **LUCIFER:** Oh, I'm known by many names. I believe you

27   know me best as Lucifer.

28   **GEORGE:** The devil?

29   **LUCIFER:** *(Laughs.)* Oh, come now, Mr. Neudecker, or

30   should I say "Big George"? *(Laughs.)* Surely you've

31   heard of me. I mean, I am the Prince of the Power of

32   the Air, or are you one of those who don't believe?

33   **GEORGE:** Well, I'm not sure. I mean, I didn't. But I.... Say,

34   what are you doing here, anyway?

1   LUCIFER: Aha! At last, business. Very good. I'll keep it
2   short, Mr. Neu...Big George. I see you've been listen-
3   ing to the radio. I'm sure by now you have an idea of
4   the scope of my power.
5   GEORGE: You did all that?
6   LUCIFER: Well, I want to do more, but...
7   GEORGE: But what?
8   LUCIFER: That's the problem with being a prince —
9   there's always a king above you. If it wasn't for him,
10   there'd be no end to the things I'd do.
11 GEORGE: Well, how much more damage could you do?
12 LUCIFER: *(Chuckling)* Oh, you'd be surprised.
13 GEORGE: *(Getting angry)* And to think, after all the time
14   and effort I spend trying to fix things, and then *you*
15   come along and ruin it! Just who do you think you
16   are, buddy?
17 LUCIFER: The question is, Mr. Neudecker, just who do *you*
18   think you are? Prancing around the world with all of
19   your stupid, naive efforts to, as you put it, "fix things."
20   Well, what right do you have to meddle in such
21   affairs? You don't belong here. This is *my* world, at
22   least for a while. It was given to *me!*
23 GEORGE: By whom?
24 LUCIFER: By Adam and Eve! Or haven't you heard of
25   them?
26 GEORGE: You mean, in the Garden?
27 LUCIFER: That is precisely what I mean. You see, when
28   Adam and Eve chose to eat that apple, they were
29   rebelling against their Creator. They chose to sepa-
30   rate themselves from him and go their own way.
31 GEORGE: But they didn't choose to go with you.
32 LUCIFER: Ah, but they did, and so have many others. You
33   see, when men choose to go their own way, they
34   become easy prey. It's a lot like Simple Simon and

1   **the pie man, or a stray little puppy. I can do what-**
2   **ever I want with them, or have them do whatever I**
3   **want them to do. Most of the time, it takes very lit-**
4   **tle encouragement. Just like our friends in the**
5   **Garden.**

6   **GEORGE: Oh yeah? Well, I know how to fix you. I just wish**
7   **you weren't around, that's all.**

8   **LUCIFER:** *(Laughs.)* **Ho-ho. That is quite amusing, Mr.**
9   **Neudecker. It's perfectly impossible. You see, when**
10   **you received your powers, you also received certain,**
11   **ah, contractual agreements, entered into by your pre-**
12   **decessor. I am one of them.**

13   **GEORGE: How do I know you ain't lyin' to me? Huh? I'll**
14   **show you. I'll go back to the Garden of Eden and**
15   **make sure they don't eat that apple.**

16   **LUCIFER: Really, Mr. Neudecker, you're only...**

17   **GEORGE: No, you don't. You can't talk me out of it. I'm**
18   **goin' back to where it all started. I wish we could start**
19   **all over again.**

20   **LUCIFER: No! Mr. Neudecker, that's the wrong thing.**
21   **Everything will be destroyed. Ahhh...** *(Thunder, lights*
22   *go out.)*

23   **GEORGE:** *(In pitch dark with echo)* **Hey, who turned out the**
24   **lights? Where'd everybody go? Hey, what's going on**
25   **here? Ida? Ida, help! Help! Anybody! Everybody!**
26   **HELP! HELP! HELP! HELP! Where is everybody? Oh!**
27   **Oh.** *(Lights slowly fade up. GEORGE is asleep in his ham-*
28   *mock from the first scene. BOBBY is waking him.)*

29   **BOBBY: George, George, wake up. C'mon, George, wake up.**

30   **GEORGE: Huh? What? Oh, oh, Bobby, Bobby. What hap-**
31   **pened? What's goin' on? What's goin' on?**

32   **BOBBY: I don't know, George. I guess you had a bad dream**
33   **or something.**

34   **GEORGE: Oh, oh, oh boy, did I ever! Listen, Bobby, is it still**

1   **Saturday?**

2   **BOBBY: Well, yeah, George. Why?**

3   **GEORGE: I just wanna know if me and Ida can still go to**

4   **church with you tomorrow.**

5   **BOBBY: Well, sure, glad to have ya! Then after church I'll**

6   **give you a hand with those flower beds. Bet you wish**

7   **you didn't even have to do them at all, huh?**

8   **GEORGE: Don't say that, Bobby. Don't ever say that again!**

9   *(Enter IDA.)*

10   **IDA: Well, that's how George and I came to know the Lord.**

11   **It was almost five years ago. Isn't it a blessing to know**

12   **God really is in control? I think so, and so does George.**

13

14

15

16

17

18

19

20

21

22

23

24

25

26

27

28

29

30

31

32

33

34

KING ME
First Encounter

By Dan Rupple

1 **CAST:** Narrator (On-stage or off), Guard (First Encounter
2 only), King Me, King of Kings.
3 **SETTING:** The imaginary land of Uzbuzz. There is a throne
4 Center Stage (a chair with streamers, a cushion, a
5 footrest, etc.). The Fifth Encounter calls for a closet. This
6 is most easily accomplished if there is a door at one side
7 or another of your playing area.
8 **PROPS:** Telephone (may be placed on a small table beside the
9 throne) and assorted things, including a few small chairs
10 that KING ME stuffs into the closet.
11 **COSTUMES:** A uniform for the GUARD, a crown (may be
12 made of cardboard) and gaudy robe for KING ME, and a
13 biblical robe and sandals for KING OF KINGS.
14
15 *(Optional music. KING ME is sitting on his throne.)*
16 **NARRATOR: Once upon a throne, there sat a stubborn**
17 **king named Me. King Me ruled a declining kingdom**
18 **in the low-rent district of the land of Uzbuzz. He sat**
19 **on his throne, hopelessly watching the ruin of his**
20 **beloved empire. Then one day, one of his subjects**
21 **announced the arrival of a visitor who sought an**
22 **audience with His Majesty. Let's join them now in**
23 **episode one of *King Me*.** *(GUARD enters.)*
24 **GUARD: Your Majesty, there is a man at the gate who**
25 **desires to speak with you. He says it is urgent and**
26 **most important.**
27 **KING ME: I'm too busy. Besides, what could he tell me of**
28 **any importance? I've got everything under control.**

1   Get rid of him.

2   NARRATOR: The man went away, but because of his great
3   love and concern for the King, he came back every
4   day, until finally the King grew weary of the constant
5   harassment.

6   GUARD: Your Majesty, that man is at the gate again.

7   KING ME: Why won't this man stop this perpetual pestering?
8   Haven't I got enough problems? The walls of my king-
9   dom are in shambles, my people are thirsty from the
10   drought, and with the power shortage, everyone's stum-
11   bling over each other in the dark – and then this dude.
12   What's he selling – fire insurance?

13 GUARD: Well, what do you have to lose, Your Majesty?

14 KING ME: Watch your remarks. What's this man's name?

15 GUARD: He says it's King of Kings.

16 KING ME: Oh, all right, send him in. Who knows, maybe
17   he'll be good for a laugh or two. I dunno, we'll see.

18   *(KING OF KINGS enters.)*

19 KING OF KINGS: Greetings.

20 KING ME: Now listen, fella. Day after day you've been bug-
21   ging me, pestering me, trying to get me to listen to
22   you. What's the deal?

23 KING OF KINGS: Well, I've noticed your kingdom's having
24   a few problems.

25 KING ME: Listen, buddy, things are tough everywhere. Have
26   you seen Lenny's kingdom next door? The whole king-
27   dom's drunk by breakfast, and they're flat broke. Always
28   borrowing my stuff, too. I still haven't seen my lawn
29   mower since I loaned it to him. Why don't you bug
30   Lenny? Yeah, and while you're there, get my mower.

31 KING OF KINGS: Never mind Lenny. You're in sad shape,
32   friend.

33 KING ME: Look, it's easy to criticize. It's not easy ruling a
34   kingdom, especially in Uzbuzz – having to make all

1   the decisions and to cope with all the pressures.

2   Someday you'll have a kingdom, and then you'll be

3   able to relate.

4   **KING OF KINGS:** Oh, I know all about kingdoms. As a mat-

5   ter of fact, that's one of the reasons I'm here. You see,

6   I'm building a kingdom and I want you to be a part

7   of it.

8   **KING ME:** Oh, now I get your angle. You're a real estate

9   agent, huh?

10   **KING OF KINGS:** No, I'm a Savior.

11   **KING ME:** Oh. I don't need a Savior. Look, just because

12   things are tough right now doesn't mean I need to

13   panic and throw in the towel. I'm not selling out!

14   **KING OF KINGS:** Suit yourself. But if you think things are

15   bad now, wait till the fireball hits. But if you're not

16   interested...

17   **KING ME:** Wait a minute – the fireball? What's the fireball?

18   **KING OF KINGS:** You obviously haven't been listening to

19   the warnings. All the kingdoms in Uzbuzz have been

20   warned since long ago about the large fireball that's

21   rolling this way.

22   **KING ME:** Oh, yeah, yeah, I heard about that, but I never

23   worried about it. I don't believe in it. As a matter of

24   fact, we used to joke about it...How 'bout this: How

25   many fireballs does it take to screw in a light bulb?

26   Three – one to hold the bulb and two to hold the

27   asbestos gloves. You get it? You get it?

28   **KING OF KINGS:** I'm afraid you won't be laughing when

29   it comes.

30   **KING ME:** You mean it's for real? Well, look, I figure with

31   the kingdom walls it'll just bounce off.

32   **KING OF KINGS:** No, your walls are so weak they're

33   useless.

34   **KING ME:** Well, we'll rebuild the wall.

1   **KING OF KINGS:** With your power shortage, your builders
2   can't even see the wall.
3   **KING ME:** Look, we've got the finest fire department in the
4   land. If it comes, we'll douse it.
5   **KING OF KINGS:** You forgot the drought. You don't even
6   have any water.
7   **KING ME:** Yeah, well, what do you suggest?
8   **KING OF KINGS:** Allow me to sit on your throne.
9   **KING ME:** On my throne?! What can *you* do?
10   **KING OF KINGS:** I will give you the light of the world,
11   water so you will never thirst again, and I will rebuild
12   your walls with solid rock.
13   **KING ME:** What makes you so special? What makes you
14   think that you can do something I can't?
15   **KING OF KINGS:** Because I built this kingdom, Me, and
16   Lenny's kingdom, and all the other kingdoms as far as
17   the eye can see. But my subjects were deceived by a lying,
18   wicked prince who wanted my throne. I let the people
19   choose their king, and they chose Prince Darkness.
20   **KING ME:** Prince Darkness...yeah, I think his name was on
21   the lease when I took this kingdom.
22   **KING OF KINGS:** Yes, but the problem is Prince Darkness
23   had a death sentence out on him from my
24   Father...Now the fireball that's coming for Prince
25   Darkness will take not only him, but all of his sub-
26   jects, too.
27   **KING ME:** Gee, that means me? But what can I do? I signed
28   the lease.
29   **KING OF KINGS:** If you give your kingdom over to me, the
30   lease is void. Do you see? I'm the True Owner of all of
31   Uzbuzz.
32   **KING ME:** How can I be sure you're telling me the truth?
33   **KING OF KINGS:** Believe and receive, and you will know
34   even as you are known. (1Cor. 13:12)

1　　**KING ME:** You sure Lenny didn't put you up to this?

2　　**KING OF KINGS:** The choice is yours, King Me.

3　　**KING ME:** Hmmm. King of Kings, I do believe you. So, uh,

4　　　　here's my crown – *(Starts to hand it to KING OF KINGS)*

5　　　　it's yours. I hope it fits. If not, we could adjust the

6　　　　band or line it with Kleenex.

7　　**KING OF KINGS:** I don't need your crown. I'll just take

8　　　　your throne. *(Optional music. KING ME gets up from his*

9　　　　*throne and KING OF KINGS sits on it.)*

10　**NARRATOR:** And so King Me received King of Kings as

11　　　Lord of his kingdom. But King of Kings has more in

12　　　mind for King Me than he first expected. Tune in

13　　　tomorrow as King Me goes through a period of adjust-

14　　　ment and we hear him say...

15　**KING ME:** Now where do I sit?

16

17

18

19

20

21

22

23

24

25

26

27

28

29

30

31

32

33

34

KING ME
Second Encounter

By Dan Rupple

1 (*Optional music. KING OF KINGS sits on the throne.*
2 *KING ME stands beside him, pouting.*)
3 **NARRATOR: When we last left King Me, he had just com-**
4 **pleted his first of many encounters with King of**
5 **Kings. King of Kings warned King Me of the immi-**
6 **nent doom of his and every other kingdom in Uzbuzz**
7 **leased from Prince Darkness. It seems King of Kings'**
8 **Father had put a death sentence on Prince Darkness**
9 **for leading a revolution against his rightly rule. In his**
10 **love, King of Kings offered King Me a pardon on the**
11 **condition that King Me surrender his throne to him.**
12 **King Me agreed and relinquished rule. Let's go into**
13 **the throne room now and join them in episode two of**
14 ***King Me.***
15 **KING OF KINGS: Good day, King Me.**
16 **KING ME: What's so good about it, King of Kings?**
17 **KING OF KINGS: Well, it's beautiful out, and the kingdom**
18 **is slowly but surely being restored. It's time to rejoice.**
19 **KING ME: You rejoice. I'm gonna soak my feet.**
20 **KING OF KINGS: What's gotten into you today?**
21 **KING ME: It's not just today – it's every day. Day in and day**
22 **out, stand, stand, stand while you sit on my throne.**
23 **Why can't I sit there for a while?**
24 **KING OF KINGS: That was the condition. I must have full**
25 **control of your throne – not just when it's convenient**
26 **and you feel like standing, but all the time.**
27 **KING ME: Well, I'm getting tired. Now where do I sit? My**
28 **feet are swelling. They're gonna look like snow shoes**

1 before the week's over. Yesterday I had to go over to
2 Lenny's kingdom and borrow his Odor Eaters. Boy,
3 Lenny doesn't have to stand.
4 **KING OF KINGS:** Never mind about Lenny.
5 **KING ME:** Well, he's sitting on his throne.
6 **KING OF KINGS:** But he's holding on. You don't know how
7 much I want his throne.
8 **KING ME:** Can you blame him? Have you seen his throne?
9 That velvet cushion, and a canopy with a sun roof. I'd
10 love to have it.
11 **KING OF KINGS:** Wait until the fireball comes. Then
12 would you want to sit on Lenny's throne?
13 **KING ME:** Well... *(Quietly)* no.
14 **KING OF KINGS:** What?
15 **KING ME:** No.
16 **KING OF KINGS:** Good, now always remember that.
17 **KING ME:** Well, look, isn't there something I can do
18 instead of stand? Maybe a Moped? I don't have to be
19 stationary, as long as I'm off my feet.
20 **KING OF KINGS:** Yes, there is something, King Me. You're
21 going to have to go to the cross.
22 **KING ME:** The cross?
23 **KING OF KINGS:** You must be crucified.
24 **KING ME:** You mean as in ouch-hurt pain? You mean as
25 in dead?
26 **KING OF KINGS:** Yes.
27 **KING ME:** Why?
28 **KING OF KINGS:** You are a king. By your very nature, you
29 desire rule. As long as you live as a king, you will
30 strive to regain the reign of your throne. So, King Me,
31 in order for me to rule this kingdom, you must get out
32 of the way.
33 **KING ME:** Come on, the fireball story was a little far out,
34 but this is radical. Tell you what – let's flip for it. If I

1   win, you do the cross bit.

2 KING OF KINGS: I've already done the "cross bit." That's
3   what gives me the right to sit on your throne. See, I
4   died so that all kingdoms could be released from
5   Prince Darkness's death sentence. Then I rose again
6   to reign on the thrones of all the kingdoms in Uzbuzz
7   that will open their gates to me.

8 KING ME: This is getting complicated. Will I rise again?

9 KING OF KINGS: You will die as a doomed king and be
10   reborn as my heir.

11 KING ME: Sounds like quite an ordeal, but I like the heir
12   angle. How long till I become your heir?

13 KING OF KINGS: As long as it takes.

14 KING ME: Well, OK, I guess I have no choice. You're right.
15   Tomorrow it's up on the cross. Well, see you later. I'm
16   going over to Lenny's to soak my feet.

17 KING OF KINGS: King Me, today is the day. Now is the
18   time.

19 KING ME: Yeah, but Lenny's expecting me. I don't want to
20   let him down.

21 KING OF KINGS: You're letting me down. The longer you
22   wait, the harder it will be to go to the cross.

23 KING ME: Come on, even in the movies they get a last
24   phone call.

25 KING OF KINGS: You decide which it will be.

26 KING ME: OK, I'll go to the cross. *(Aside)* Lenny won't
27   believe this. *(KING ME exits. Optional music)*

28 NARRATOR: And so King Me goes to the cross and gives
29   full rule of the throne to King of Kings. What will hap-
30   pen to the kingdom under King of King's rule? What
31   will King Me do on the cross? Join us tomorrow in
32   another revealing episode of *King Me.*

33

34

KING ME
Third Encounter

By Dan Rupple

1   *(Optional music. KING ME is sitting on his throne, tele-*
2   *phone in hand.)*

3   **NARRATOR: When we last left Uzbuzz, King Me was com-**
4   **plaining of being tired of standing while King of**
5   **Kings sits on his throne. King of Kings informed King**
6   **Me that he must get on the cross and die to his kingly**
7   **nature so that King of Kings could rule freely in the**
8   **Kingdom. Today as we join King Me, he is off the cross,**
9   **sitting back on the throne. Let's listen in as he talks with**
10   **his friend, Lenny, on episode three of *King Me*.**

11   **KING ME:** *(KING ME on telephone)* **And then he says, "Pass**
12   **the strawberry cheesecake?" Can you believe it? Oh**
13   **boy. So, anyway, how're things in your kingdom?**
14   **Sure, Lenny, but I've seen your walls...pretty shabby,**
15   **Len, old buddy. Have you noticed mine? Whadda you**
16   **mean, did I have help? Are you saying you don't think**
17   **I could've managed it myself?** *(Enter KING OF KINGS.)*

18   **KING OF KINGS: King Me?**

19   **KING ME: Uh...I've got to run. I'll call you a little later.**
20   *(Hangs up.)* **Good day, King of Kings.**

21   **KING OF KINGS: King Me? What are you doing back on the**
22   **throne? We talked about your place on the cross.**
23   **You're supposed to be dead.**

24   **KING ME: Yeah, I reckon, but do I have to go rancid?**

25   **KING OF KINGS: Dead is dead. Now, either you are or you**
26   **aren't, and you're not even close.**

27   **KING ME: Well, I had to make a phone call.**

28   **KING OF KINGS: I'll handle the calls, King Me. That's why**

1   it's by the throne. Notice I didn't install an extension
2   by the cross.
3 KING ME: You know, that's an idea. Maybe a touch-tone –
4   you know, the ones with the little musical beeps.
5   Lenny's got one of those. He can play "Mary Had a
6   Little Lamb" on it. 'Course he took the lessons.
7 KING OF KINGS: Let's not change the subject. Now, how
8   can I rule if you keep getting back on the throne?
9   Don't you want me to rule?
10 KING ME: Well, yeah, but...hey, wait a minute. Why can't
11   we both rule? You and me, fifty-fifty?
12 KING OF KINGS: King Me...
13 KING ME: OK, sixty-forty, but think of the possibilities.
14   We'd be a great duo! Laurel and Hardy, Rodgers and
15   Hammerstein, Tracy and Hepburn, you and me. Yeah,
16   yeah, why didn't I think of this before? Two heads are
17   always better than one.
18 KING OF KINGS: There can only be one King. Now, either
19   I rule or I don't rule. There's no compromise. A king-
20   dom divided shall not stand. (Matt. 12:25, author's
21   paraphrase)
22 KING ME: Stand against what – the great fireball?
23 KING OF KINGS: Among other things, yes. Time is short,
24   King Me. Your kingdom must be prepared.
25 KING ME: Time is short, time is short, prepare the king-
26   dom, build the walls, here comes the big, bad fireball.
27   That's all I ever hear. Well, where is it? When's it
28   coming?
29 KING OF KINGS: You're beginning to doubt. Check your
30   heart, King Me. Do you believe me, or do you disbelieve?
31 KING ME: Believe, I guess. I'm just impatient.
32 KING OF KINGS: All right now, the longer the fireball tar-
33   ries, the more kingdoms I can save.
34 KING ME: You mean you're ruling other kingdoms, too?

1   **KING OF KINGS:** Many. However, not as many as I desire.

2   **KING ME:** And other kings have to get on the cross, just
3   like me?

4   **KING OF KINGS:** Yes. It's easier for some than others.

5   **KING ME:** King of Kings, how can you sit on my throne
6   and other thrones all at the same time?

7   **KING OF KINGS:** My ways are past your finding out. Many
8   things are beyond your understanding.

9   **KING ME:** You know, King of Kings, you do have a way
10   with things. Hey, I've got an idea.... Why can't you
11   destroy this fireball? Or extinguish it? Couldn't you
12   get your Father to throw a gigantic spitball on it?

13 **KING OF KINGS:** No, the fireball must pass through all of
14   Uzbuzz and burn the chaff. Then my kingdom will be
15   pure. Don't try to stop it – just prepare. Strengthen
16   the things which remain. (Rev. 3:2)

17 **KING ME:** What remains?

18 **KING OF KINGS:** Give me back the throne, and you will
19   know.

20 **KING ME:** And for me, it's cross time, right?

21 **KING OF KINGS:** That's right, King Me, but take heart, for
22   the sufferings of the present can't even be compared
23   to the glory that will be revealed in the kingdom.

24 **KING ME:** Well, that's encouraging, but for now it's bum-
25   mer city. *(Optional music. KING ME exits. KING OF*
26   *KINGS sits on the throne.)*

27 **NARRATOR:** And so back to the cross for King Me, as King
28   of Kings once again assumes the throne. Is it for good
29   this time? Maybe yes, maybe no. Tune in tomorrow
30   for our next episode of *King Me.*

31

32

33

34

KING ME
Fourth Encounter

By Dan Rupple

1 *(Optional music. KING OF KINGS sits on the throne.)*

2 **NARRATOR: When we last left King Me, he was learning that**

3 **there was even more to believing King of Kings and hav-**

4 **ing his kingdom restored than he had first realized.**

5 **Daily he was seeing that King of Kings' place was on the**

6 **throne and that his place was on the cross, dying to his**

7 **kingly nature. Let us join King Me now as he learns**

8 **another lesson in episode four of *King Me.***

9 **KING ME:** *(Enters.)* **Hey, King of Kings, I have a question for**

10 **you.**

11 **KING OF KINGS: King Me, you're off the cross again.**

12 **KING ME: I had a question.**

13 **KING OF KINGS: You didn't have to leave the cross to ask a**

14 **question. You can ask me anything you want from the**

15 **cross.**

16 **KING ME: Well, I didn't want to yell.**

17 **KING OF KINGS: I would've heard you.**

18 **KING ME: No harm done – next time I'll know, but anyway,**

19 **while I'm here, what's going on tomorrow?**

20 **KING OF KINGS: Why are you worried about tomorrow?**

21 **We've got enough to work on today. I'll take care of**

22 **tomorrow.**

23 **KING ME: Yeah, yeah, I know – the lilies of the field, the spar-**

24 **rows, etc. We've been through all of that. But let's just**

25 **pretend it's tomorrow morning.**

26 **KING OF KINGS: King Me?**

27 **KING ME: C'mon, be a good sport. Now it's tomorrow morn-**

28 **ing. We get up, we have breakfast – you know, coffee,**

1   eggs, pancakes. I say, "What's happening today?" And
2   you say?

3 KING OF KINGS: I say let's talk about yesterday.

4 KING ME: No, you're supposed to tell me about tomorrow.

5 KING OF KINGS: There's no sense in telling you about tomor-
6   row if you're going to throw today away.

7 KING ME: Boy, you don't give up, do you? How can you be so
8   persistent?

9 KING OF KINGS: I'm very long-suffering. King Me, look, let's
10   get to the point. What's on your mind for tomorrow?

11 KING ME: Well, Lenny's coming over and, well, he doesn't
12   know about what you're doing here and all. I haven't
13   explained to him that you're on my throne...

14 KING OF KINGS: Why? Are you ashamed of me?

15 KING ME: Are you kidding? No, not at all, never. It's just that
16   Lenny doesn't really agree with all that stuff about
17   Prince Darkness and your right to reign, and...

18 KING OF KINGS: Well, this looks like a good time for me to
19   talk with him. Why don't you introduce me to him?

20 KING ME: I don't think that would be a good idea. See, you
21   don't know Lenny. I think you'd blow him away.

22 KING OF KINGS: Don't worry about *me* blowing him away.
23   It's the fireball that will blow him away if I don't save
24   him. You have told him about the fireball, haven't you?

25 KING ME: Are you kidding? He'd laugh me out of Uzbuzz. I've
26   got a reputation to uphold.

27 KING OF KINGS: The only thing you need to uphold is the
28   cross, and that reputation must be on it.

29 KING ME: Look, all I'm asking is for you to let me sit on the
30   throne, just while Lenny's here. I won't make any deci-
31   sions or anything.

32 KING OF KINGS: What about me?

33 KING ME: Take the day off. Go to a baseball game or a movie.
34   How about it?

1   **KING OF KINGS:** King Me, the throne is yours, whenever you
2   want. But if you take it, I leave. See, I'm either King *of*
3   all, or not King *at* all.
4   **KING ME:** No, I don't want you to leave.
5   **KING OF KINGS:** Then let me reign when Lenny comes.
6   **KING ME:** But he'll laugh at me. I'll probably never see him
7   again.
8   **KING OF KINGS:** Part of your calling as my heir is not only to
9   believe in me, but to suffer for my sake also. The right-
10   eous will always suffer persecution.
11   **KING ME:** Why?
12   **KING OF KINGS:** As others see your kingdom restored and
13   cleansed, it points out to them that their kingdoms are
14   filthy and doomed. Now, no one wants to admit they're
15   wrong, so they put you down.
16   **KING ME:** Hmmm. Those fools. Well, we'll see who has the
17   last laugh.
18   **KING OF KINGS:** King Me, don't hate them. Have compassion
19   and love for them.
20   **KING ME:** Why?
21   **KING OF KINGS:** Don't you realize that you were just like
22   them, in the same predicament, until I loved you enough
23   to save you?
24   **KING ME:** Yeah, OK, tomorrow when Lenny comes, you take
25   charge.
26   **KING OF KINGS:** King Me.
27   **KING ME:** Huh?
28   **KING OF KINGS:** I'm pleased with you.
29   **KING ME:** Oh. *(KING ME exits, beaming. Optional music)*
30   **NARRATOR:** And so King Me not only has sacrificed himself
31   for King of Kings, but now also for his friends. True love
32   is never greater than a man laying down his life for his
33   friend. (John 15:13, author's paraphrase) **Join us tomorrow**
34   **for the further adventures of *King Me*.**

KING ME
Fifth Encounter

By Dan Rupple

1 *(Optional music. The throne is empty. KING ME is shov-*
2 *ing things into a closet.)*

3 NARRATOR: Well, here we are one more time, looking in on the
4 growing relationship between King Me and King of Kings.
5 Day after day, lesson after lesson, King Me is slowly becom-
6 ing the heir of righteousness that King of Kings wishes for
7 him to be. But not without struggles, fights and disobedi-
8 ence, I might add. Even with all the progress, it seems that
9 King Me will never arrive – there's always another mark to
10 reach. Well, enough talk. Let's visit them now in the con-
11 cluding episode of *King Me.*

12 KING ME: *(To self)* Let's see if I could just squeeze this one in
13 here...and...uh, that one's sticking out. Maybe if I lift this.
14 Now the door won't close. Well, ah, this one should do
15 it...ummm...

16 KING OF KINGS: *(From Off-stage)* King Me? Where are you?

17 KING ME: Oh, oh, come on, go in. *(Slams door.)* There – whew!
18 *(Stands in front of door.)*

19 KING OF KINGS: King Me?

20 KING ME: Here I am. *(Enter KING OF KINGS.)*

21 KING OF KINGS: I've been looking for you.

22 KING ME: Yeah, I just had a project I was working on. No
23 problem. What can I do for you, King of Kings?

24 KING OF KINGS: Well...uh, what project were you working
25 on?

26 KING ME: Oh, it's nothing. Just a hobby – you know, some-
27 thing for my spare time. I'm finished though. Now,
28 what's up?

1   **KING OF KINGS: Could I see it?**

2   **KING ME: See what?**

3   **KING OF KINGS: Your hobby.**

4   **KING ME: Oh, well, you know it's funny** *(Laughs)* **but I can't**

5   **even remember where I put it. It wouldn't interest you**

6   **anyway.**

7   **KING OF KINGS: King Me, I care about everything you're**

8   **into. I'll help you find it.**

9   **KING ME: No.**

10   **KING OF KINGS: Why?**

11   **KING ME: Well, I don't know why, but...**

12   **KING OF KINGS: Why are you standing in front of that door?**

13   **KING ME: What door?**

14   **KING OF KINGS: That door.**

15   **KING ME: Oh, you mean this door.**

16   **KING OF KINGS: King Me, I've been in every room of the**

17   **kingdom, but I've never seen inside that one.**

18   **KING ME: It's just an ol' closet. Probably can't even open it,**

19   **it's so old.**

20   **KING OF KINGS: Well, let me try.** *(Crash)*

21   **KING ME: Uh-oh...**

22   **KING OF KINGS: King Me, what are these?**

23   **KING ME: What are what?**

24   **KING OF KINGS: These.**

25   **KING ME: They're thrones.**

26   **KING OF KINGS: What?**

27   **KING ME: Thrones. You know, little chairs.**

28   **KING OF KINGS: Why, I've never seen so many. Did you make**

29   **them?**

30   **KING ME: Yeah.**

31   **KING OF KINGS: Let's see. What's this one – money?**

32   **KING ME: Yeah, it's a money throne.**

33   **KING OF KINGS: You're saying that this rules a part of your**

34   **life?**

1   **KING ME: No!**

2   **KING OF KINGS: Then why is it on a throne? Why not on a**
3   **cross?**

4   **KING ME: Look, it's only three thousand trussels. I'm not**
5   **rich. I'm only counting on it for a rainy day.**

6   **KING OF KINGS: I think you're counting on it for more than**
7   **you know. What's this one? Music?**

8   **KING ME: It motivates me – besides, renaissance disco keeps**
9   **me in shape. I do it for purely athletic reasons.**

10   **KING OF KINGS: And look at these – pleasure, wisdom,**
11   **habits, queen?**

12   **KING ME: Yeah, a king needs a queen.**

13   **KING OF KINGS: Why don't you let me take care of that?**

14   **KING ME: Look, King of Kings, you don't know my type. I've**
15   **got to play the field, make sure I get the right one.**

16   **KING OF KINGS:** (*Shaking his head*) **King Me, King, Me. So**
17   **many little thrones in your empire. And this one –**
18   **spare time?**

19   **KING ME: Now look. I work hard all day long letting you rule,**
20   **but when I've got some spare time, I want to relax. I've**
21   **got the right to sit on my throne – at least in my spare**
22   **time. It's not gonna hurt anyone, no one's around, noth-**
23   **ing's going on.**

24   **KING OF KINGS: Do you have the right?**

25   **KING ME: Well, I guess...well, I should have the right. After**
26   **all, don't you want me to have fun?**

27   **KING OF KINGS: I want you to have joy. Fun is temporal. Joy**
28   **is from within your very heart. It's unquenchable.**
29   **There's more I have for you than you'll ever know.**

30   **KING ME: Give it to me, and I'll throw out the thrones – well,**
31   **some of them.**

32   **KING OF KINGS: King Me, I can't do much more in this king-**
33   **dom unless you obey and yield to my instructions.**

34   **KING ME: Yeah, you're right. I'm blowing it, King of Kings.**

1   I'm sorry. I've been compromising, ashamed of you, self-
2   ish, stubborn and disobedient. I want to do better. Is
3   there any way I can make it up to you – I mean, for all
4   the trouble I've caused?
5   **KING OF KINGS:** Oh, King Me, your broken, repentant heart
6   is the greatest gift you could ever give me.
7   **KING ME:** I've been kinda foolish.
8   **KING OF KINGS:** Reverencing me is the beginning of wis-
9   dom. *(Optional music)*
10   **NARRATOR:** And so King Me totally surrendered and gave
11   King of Kings uncontested rule of the kingdom – a deci-
12   sion he never regretted. After this encounter, the king-
13   dom grew like never before. The walls grew stronger and
14   new life was breathed into it. And King Me's kingdom
15   stood as a light to all of Uzbuzz. Because of his kingdom,
16   many other kings surrendered their kingship to King of
17   Kings. King Me began to see revival in Uzbuzz like he
18   never imagined, but he always remembered that revival
19   must first start within your own kingdom.
20
21
22
23
24
25
26
27
28
29
30
31
32
33
34

SPECS O'KEEFE IN THE MODESTY MATTER: WHAT'S THE VERDICT?

By Dan Rupple

1   **CAST:** Narrator (On-stage or off), Specs O'Keefe, Sherman,
2   Dirk, Bonnie Brewster, Pastor Connors, Woman 1,
3   Woman 2.
4   **SETTING:** Various locations. Designate four different areas of
5   the stage as: 1) SPECS' office, 2) the library, 3) PASTOR's
6   office and 4) women's Bible study. SPECS' office should
7   have a desk and three chairs; the library, a bookshelf and
8   counter or table; the PASTOR's office, a desk with a tele-
9   phone on top and two chairs; the women's Bible study, a
10   few chairs arranged in a circle.
11   **PROPS:** Deck of cards, large book for "Detective Manual,"
12   Bibles for WOMAN 1 and WOMAN 2.
13   **COSTUMES:** A suit and glasses for SPECS; goofy outfit for
14   SHERMAN, i.e., beanie, bow tie, jacket, knickers,
15   sneakers; casual "high school" attire for DIRK; trendy
16   shorts outfit for BONNIE; shirt and tie for PASTOR;
17   casual clothes for WOMAN 1 and WOMAN 2.
18
19   *(Optional intro music.)*
20   **NARRATOR: There are many different kinds of people**
21   **that make this world go around. Some say that Specs**
22   **O'Keefe is one of them. If you meet Specs in a church,**
23   **Sunday school, prayer closet, heaven, hell, or**
24   **anywhere in between, be careful – this is where he**
25   **works. Specs O'Keefe is no ordinary detective – he's**
26   **special. Specs O'Keefe, Spiritual Eye. Today we join**

Specs O'Keefe in the Modesty Matter:
What's the Verdict?

1   **Specs in *The Modesty Matter: What's the Verdict?***

2   *(SPECS and SHERMAN enter and begin playing cards.)*

3   **SPECS: It was a warm, muggy Chicago day. I sat at my**

4   **office desk playing a game of solitaire with my assis-**

5   **tant, Sherman. I was winning as usual. In my**

6   **business, there is no place for losers. I was about to**

7   **place the king of hearts on the queen of spades as my**

8   **next rendezvous, when adventure came knocking at**

9   **my door in the form of a Christian high-schooler**

10   **named Dirk. There was something on his mind, and**

11   **it wasn't a baseball cap. It was my job to lift the lid on**

12   **this caper.** *(DIRK enters. He sits on the vacant chair.)*

13   **DIRK: See, Mr. O'Keefe, I feel a little odd even coming**

14   **here, but I need your help.**

15   **SPECS: Whatever it is, kid, you can count on me.**

16   **SHERMAN: And on me!**

17   **SPECS: Well, only to fifteen on Sherman, but he's a good**

18   **assistant. Now, what's the story?**

19   **DIRK: Well, I became a Christian about six months ago,**

20   **and I'm really trying to be full-on for the Lord. I pray**

21   **every day, and I read my Bible and go to church twice**

22   **a week. I really love the Lord, and I don't want**

23   **anything to stand in the way of serving him.**

24   **SPECS: That all sounds fine. So what's the problem?**

25   **DIRK: Well, it all began three weeks ago on Sunday. You**

26   **see, I got up early to have a good time of prayer before**

27   **church. I prayed, "Lord, just help me to put aside all**

28   **distractions so I can worship you and really listen to**

29   **your Word. I really want you to teach me at today's**

30   **service. So go before me now and open me up to what-**

31   **ever you have for me." Well, I went to church, and as I**

32   **sat worshiping the Lord, it happened.... There was**

33   **this unbelievable girl sitting in the row ahead of me.**

34   **I just kept thinking, "Oh wow, she's beautiful." I**

1 couldn't believe what she was wearing – these really
2 short shorts. I knew I shouldn't look, but I couldn't
3 help it. I kept wondering if she had a boyfriend. Then
4 I was like, "What am I thinking? I'm supposed to be
5 worshiping!" But boy, I couldn't get my mind off her.
6 She was just so gorgeous. I tried singing louder, but
7 that didn't work. I thought, "Oh, man, this is ridicu-
8 lous. I can't take this. What am I gonna do? Should I
9 leave?" The pastor was just beginning a series of
10 sermons on Romans, and I really wanted to hear it. I
11 didn't want to leave, but the Bible says, "If the eye
12 offends you...." So I went home.
13 SPECS: Hmmm, I see. Well, I don't really see. I mean, your
14 story is only verbal – no films or anything – but I
15 understand the problem.
16 DIRK: Well, that's not the end. I went home and decided
17 I'd just fellowship with the Lord alone, so I knelt
18 down and prayed, "Lord, I thank you for saving us,
19 even though we've all sinned and come short...shorts.
20 Did you see that girl?! She was practically nak.... What
21 am I saying? Oh Lord, help me. I'm trying to pray, but
22 I keep on lusting." Anyway, Specs, that's the way it's
23 been. Every time she shows up at a fellowship, or
24 whenever any girl does who dresses like that, I have
25 trouble keeping my eyes and thoughts on the Lord.
26 SPECS: OK, Dirk, the problem's clear, but what do you
27 want me to do about it?
28 DIRK: Well, what I want to know is, who's guilty? Is it me
29 for lusting? Or her for causing me to stumble? I'm all
30 confused.
31 SPECS: Don't worry, Dirk. Specs O'Keefe is on the case. I'll
32 leave no clue unturned. Let's go, Sherman.
33 SHERMAN: Right, Specs. *(DIRK exits.)*
34 SPECS: I headed out in search of a verdict. This wasn't

1   **going to be a clear-cut caper. I had to handle it very**
2   **sensitivivvv...very sensitivitally...sensitoovely...very**
3   **sensitively. My first visit was with the girl herself,**
4   **Bonnie Brewster. Yes, a beautiful girl who made a**
5   **Jordache commercial look like a Looney Tune. We**
6   **talked to Bonnie at the library after school. We began**
7   **our questioning.** *(BONNIE enters library area and*
8   *begins reading. SPECS and SHERMAN cross to her.)*
9   **Bonnie, how long have you been a Christian?**
10 **BONNIE: One and a half months.**
11 **SPECS: How do you feel about the way you dress?**
12 **BONNIE: The way I dress? I don't know. I just wear what**
13   **I've always worn.**
14 **SPECS: Has anyone ever told you that it isn't very modest?**
15 **BONNIE: No, I never really thought about it.**
16 **SPECS: Do you think your dress could make a brother**
17   **stumble?**
18 **SHERMAN: Like Dirk maybe?**
19 **SPECS: Quiet, Sherman, I'm on a roll.**
20 **BONNIE: Well, I wouldn't think so. This is the way all the**
21   **girls on TV, in magazines and in movies dress. Hey,**
22   **what am I supposed to do – wear a gunny sack?**
23 **SPECS: I don't think that's what the Lord had in mind, but**
24   **the media isn't out to build God's kingdom. Are the**
25   **women pictured in the magazines your role models?**
26 **BONNIE: I see your point, Specs. All of those are worldly**
27   **views. Maybe you're right.**
28 **SHERMAN: Darn right he's right.**
29 **BONNIE: I guess I've dressed more for the world than for**
30   **Jesus. Boy, I hope I haven't stumbled too many people.**
31 **SPECS: We're all learning, Bonnie.**
32 **BONNIE: I'm going to be careful of what I wear from now**
33   **on.** *(BONNIE exits. SPECS and SHERMAN walk just*
34   *outside the library area.)*

1   **SHERMAN: Well, you've done it again, Specs. You've got**
2   **your man, which in this case is a girl.**
3   **SPECS: Not so, Sherman. Not quite. The average private eye**
4   **would stop here. Not me, Sherman. I smell something**
5   **deeper. Yes, Sherman, I've only scratched the surface.**
6   **SHERMAN: What do you mean, Specs? Bonnie admitted**
7   **she wasn't dressed modestly and she's gonna change.**
8   **SPECS: Sherman, there's still too many questions.**
9   **SHERMAN: Like what?**
10   **SPECS: Like why didn't Bonnie know she was dressed**
11   **immodestly? Why wasn't she warned? Did she like the**
12   **attention? Did everyone except Dirk accept her? Why**
13   **didn't other brothers mention it? Why am I going on**
14   **and on?** *(Theme music)* **Why is the theme music**
15   **playing? Why is the director telling me to wrap it up?**
16   **Why...?** *(SHERMAN exits. SPECS goes to his office and*
17   *sits.)*
18   **While Sherman headed out for sandwiches, I went**
19   **back to my office to make a thing called sense out of**
20   **this jigsaw-puzzled case. It started so simple. Just one**
21   **kid improperly attracted to one girl. But as I put my**
22   **detective can opener to it, I realized I had opened a**
23   **can of worms larger than the Grand Canyon. Well,**
24   **maybe not that big, but if I could blow the lid off this**
25   **caper, it would erupt with the magnitude of Mt. St.**
26   **Helens.... Well, maybe not that strong but, well, you**
27   **get the point. It was a touchy subject, but we had to**
28   **talk openly with some more witnesses, if they'd let**
29   **us.** *(SHERMAN enters the office.)*
30   **SHERMAN: Lettuce, Specs?**
31   **SPECS: What?**
32   **SHERMAN: Do you want lettuce on your sandwich?**
33   **SPECS: No thanks, Sherman, just peanut butter. Heavy**
34   **on the jelly.**

1   SHERMAN: Gee, we've heard Dirk's side of things and
2   Bonnie's, but where to now?
3   SPECS: Pastor.
4   SHERMAN: Past who, Specs?
5   SPECS: No, Sherman, the pastor.
6   SHERMAN: The pastor of Dirk and Bonnie's church. Yes,
7   of course. It's obvious – it's clear as the jelly on your
8   ham sandwich. Why didn't I see it?
9   SPECS: Don't be too hard on yourself, Sherman. You're
10   learning. Not everyone can be so perspective, I mean
11   perseptic, perswevsti...
12   SHERMAN: You mean perceptive?
13   SPECS: That too. Let's go, Sherman. We're getting closer to
14   our rendezvous with the solution. *(SPECS and*
15   *SHERMAN go to PASTOR's office. PASTOR has entered*
16   *and is speaking on the telephone.)*
17   PASTOR: *(On phone)* OK, well, I hope everything goes real
18   well. Please call if I can help you in any way. My pleasure.
19   God bless you. *(Hangs up phone.)* I"m really sorry to keep
20   you waiting, Mr. O'Keefe. I'm Pastor Connors.
21   SPECS: Nice to meet you. This is my assistant, Sherman.
22   PASTOR: Hello, Sherman.
23   SPECS: We've come to talk about Dirk and Bonnie
24   Brewster. Are you familiar with the situation?
25   PASTOR: Yes, I am. I heard your show yesterday. I never
26   miss it.
27   SPECS: Thank you, but Pastor, I can't help feeling that
28   there's more to this case than Dirk and Bonnie.
29   PASTOR: Mmmm. What do you think the problem is?
30   SPECS: Well, number one, why did Dirk come to me with
31   this problem? You're his pastor.
32   PASTOR: Hmmm.
33   SHERMAN: I think he was embarrassed to talk to you.
34   SPECS: Quiet, Sherman.

1 PASTOR: No, Specs, your assistant has a point. Maybe I'm
2   not open enough on these matters with my congrega-
3   tion. Maybe I do need to be more candid in my
4   counseling.
5 SPECS: Good point, Pastor. But, number two, why wasn't
6   Bonnie informed earlier of her immodest dress? She's
7   been attending your studies.
8 PASTOR: Well, it's a sensitive topic. You know I don't want
9   to embarrass any young girls.
10 SPECS: But if you don't give it a try, then the boys are
11   embarrassed.
12 SHERMAN: Like Dirk.
13 PASTOR: Yes, I can see the problem. Well, I have taught on
14   this subject of dress. I spoke on it once about two
15   years ago.
16 SHERMAN: But Pastor Connors, Bonnie's only been a
17   Christian for one and a half months.
18 PASTOR: Well, that's true, Sherman, but the problem is
19   you can't dwell on or overemphasize just one topic. I
20   try to maintain a balance on all biblical topics.
21 SPECS: Point well taken, Pastor. I understand your situa-
22   tion. There must be something else we're missing,
23   another avenue we haven't turned down as yet.
24 PASTOR: Well, I'll be praying and searching for the answer.
25 SHERMAN: Don't worry, Specs will figure it out. Just tune
26   in tomorrow.
27 PASTOR: I will, Sherman, and if I can be of any assistance,
28   just call.
29 SPECS: Thank you, Pastor. You've already been a great
30   help, and believe me, with this caper I need all the
31   help I can get.
32 PASTOR: I'll be tuned in. *(PASTOR exits.)*
33 SPECS: The case was growing more complex and
34   confusing with each passing minute. Once again,

1   **Sherman and I headed back to our quaint but impres-**
2   **sive office to sort through our notes.** *(SHERMAN and*
3   *SPECS cross to SPECS' office and sit.)*
4 **SHERMAN: I don't know, Specs. You can't really blame**
5   **Dirk – I mean, he was honest about his feeling; and**
6   **you can't blame Bonnie – she was open to instruc-**
7   **tion; and it's a hard position for the pastor. So who's**
8   **at fault?**
9 **SPECS: Now, Sherman, we're not looking for a criminal,**
10   **we're looking for a solution.**
11 **SHERMAN: Boy, this is a toughie.**
12 **SPECS: Sherman, I've got it. Hand me the detective**
13   **manual.**
14 **SHERMAN: Sure, Specs. What's up?**
15 **SPECS: Let's see, debts, deception, decision, here it is –**
16   **discretion. Titus 2:3, 4 and 5. Yes, this is it.**
17 **SHERMAN: What is?**
18 **SPECS: It's right here in the case book. The young women**
19   **should be taught to be discreet.**
20 **SHERMAN: Ah-ha, so it is the pastor's fault. I knew that**
21   **smile wasn't genuine.**
22 **SPECS: No, Sherman, the pastor's a fine man.**
23 **SHERMAN: Well, if he isn't the culprit, who is?**
24 **SPECS: That's what we're looking for. Let's see...it says the**
25   **older women.**
26 **SHERMAN: The older women?**
27 **SPECS: Yes, of course. Those women that are older in the**
28   **Lord are to disciple and teach the younger. Come on,**
29   **Sherman, let's go.**
30 **SHERMAN: Where to?**
31 **SPECS: To the women's Bible study.**
32 **SHERMAN: Boy, I hope they let us in.** *(SHERMAN and*
33   *SPECS cross to the women's Bible study area. WOMAN 1*
34   *and WOMAN 2 have entered and sit on chairs with their*

1   *Bibles opened.)*

2   **SPECS: So you see, ladies, the problem is very real, and**

3   **your help is needed. According to the Scriptures, it's**

4   **your responsibility to teach and correct the younger**

5   **girls.**

6   **WOMAN 1: Yes, I believe you're right.**

7   **WOMAN 2: You know, I've often pointed a finger at those**

8   **girls, but I never really went to them – constructively,**

9   **I mean.**

10 **WOMAN 1: Well, thank you, Mr. O'Keefe. We receive your**

11   **advice, and we'll try to improve.**

12 **SPECS: Well, ladies, the problem's too complex to single**

13   **out one specific group and point a finger of blame at**

14   **them. Dirk and all young men have to be strong in**

15   **their resistance to temptation. Bonnie and the girls**

16   **have to be more responsible in their dress. The pastor**

17   **must teach the flock. And you older ladies need to**

18   **continually train and correct the young. See?**

19   **Everyone has a role.**

20 **WOMAN 1: Yeah, that's why we're a body, not just a hand.**

21 **SPECS: Exactly!** *(WOMAN 1 and WOMAN 2 exit. SHERMAN*

22   *and SPECS cross to SPECS' office.)*

23 **SHERMAN: Well, you solved another, Specs.**

24 **SPECS: Not quite, Sherman. Pointing out a problem is one**

25   **thing, but correcting the problem takes time and work.**

26   **Only time will tell.**

27 **SHERMAN: That's my boss.** *(Optional theme music)*

28

29

30

31

32

33

34

STAIRWAY TO HEAVEN

By Dan Rupple

1   **CAST:** Christian, Builder, Construction Crew.

2   **SETTING:** Construction site.

3   **PROPS:** The staging may be pantomimed or literal. Tools,

4   blueprints, some boards and other assorted construction

5   materials may be used.

6   **COSTUMES:** Regular attire for CHRISTIAN. Work clothes for

7   BUILDER and CONSTRUCTION CREW.

8   **SOUND EFFECTS:** Construction sounds.

9

10   *(Construction sounds are heard. BUILDER and*

11   *CONSTRUCTION CREW are hammering, consulting*

12   *blueprints, moving boards, etc. CHRISTIAN enters.)*

13   **CHRISTIAN: Hello.**

14   **BUILDER: Yeah, whatcha want?** *(To CREW)* **Move that**

15   **beam over to the left!**

16   **CHRISTIAN: What are you doin'?**

17   **BUILDER: What's it look like I'm doing? I'm building a**

18   **bridge.** *(To CREW)* **No, no, to the left!**

19   **CHRISTIAN: What for?**

20   **BUILDER: To get to heaven.**

21   **CHRISTIAN: To heaven?**

22   **BUILDER: Yeah! You know, God?** *(To CREW)* **That's fine.**

23   **Now secure it down!**

24   **CHRISTIAN: Yeah, I know God. It's the bridge I'm having**

25   **trouble with. Uh, why ya building it?**

26   **BUILDER: That's a pretty stupid question. Why does**

27   **anyone build a bridge to heaven? To get to God.** *(To*

28   *CREW)* **OK, Ralph, start welding!**

1   CHRISTIAN: I get the idea, but why?

2   BUILDER: Listen, frog face, I just told you.

3   CHRISTIAN: Yeah, but if you want to get to God, why are
4   you doing it this way?

5   BUILDER: 'Cause none of the others worked.

6   CHRISTIAN: Others?

7   BUILDER: You name it – helping old ladies across the
8   street, selling granola bars door-to-door, throwing off
9   bad Karma. I even tried chanting my way into
10   Nirvana. After nine hours I lost my voice, and I was
11   still in San Bernardino.

12   CHRISTIAN: Why do you think *this* is gonna work?

13   BUILDER: Don't be so skeptical, Bozo. It's got to work.
14   Look, I've got the prints here – only cost twenty-eight
15   dollars. 'Course it's scaled down – they wanted thirty-
16   four thousand dollars for the life-size replica. I've got
17   materials, a heavy-duty crane and the best construc-
18   tion crew money can buy, so the sky's the limit.

19   CHRISTIAN: I'm afraid so.

20   BUILDER: Yes, sir, this baby's foolproof – it's built to last...

21   CHRISTIAN: Uh, why are you building it up?

22   BUILDER: This time I've struck pay dirt. I finally...What'd
23   you say?

24   CHRISTIAN: I said, why are you building it up?

25   BUILDER: Because that's where God is – up.

26   CHRISTIAN: Is he?

27   BUILDER: Sure...isn't he?

28   CHRISTIAN: I don't know. If he's up to you, then he must
29   be down to the Chinese. Then tonight he's up for the
30   Chinese, and where does that leave you?

31   BUILDER: Well, it...uh, that's easy...uh...uh...I don't know,
32   uh...

33   CHRISTIAN: Look, could I make a suggestion?

34   BUILDER: What?

1   **CHRISTIAN: Have you ever thought about Jesus Christ?**

2   **BUILDER: Hold it right there, turtlehead. I see where**

3   **you're coming from. You're into religion. Well, I don't**

4   **want anything to do with religion.**

5   **CHRISTIAN: I'm not talking about religion.**

6   **BUILDER: Yes, you are. First I gotta get up early on Sundays,**

7   **put on a stuffy suit, miss the football game, and sit on a**

8   **hard pew while some boring reverend talks my ear off.**

9   **Then I dish out twenty dollars and go home. That's how**

10   **I see Christianity, and that's religion.**

11   **CHRISTIAN: Well, obviously you haven't seen true**

12   **Christianity.**

13   **BUILDER: Oh. What's *true* Christianity?**

14   **CHRISTIAN: Well, to begin with, it's not boring. It has to**

15   **do with joy and love.**

16   **BUILDER: Naw, I didn't see no joy or love. I saw religion.**

17   **CHRISTIAN: What you're doing is religion.**

18   **BUILDER: How do ya figure?**

19   **CHRISTIAN: Ya see, religion is someone trying to reach up**

20   **to God. But why reach up to God when God already**

21   **reached down to us?**

22   **BUILDER: Whadda you mean? I didn't see no big hand**

23   **come out of the sky. Look, like I told you, I tried every-**

24   **thing to reach God. I even tried calling him – wrong**

25   **number – got some lady in Milwaukee. But anyway,**

26   **this bridge idea's gonna work.**

27   **CHRISTIAN: OK, let's say you build this bridge and you get**

28   **to God. What are you gonna do when you get there?**

29   **BUILDER: I guess I'll just do what everyone else does.**

30   **CHRISTIAN: But what if no one's there? I mean, nobody**

31   **else ever built a bridge to heaven, so you're the first.**

32   **BUILDER: Yeah, kinda like Neil Armstrong. That's me –**

33   **always first, a pioneer.**

34   **CHRISTIAN: Well, you're not the first. It was tried once before.**

1   **BUILDER:** Huh? The guy told me these blueprints were
2   copyrighted.
3   **CHRISTIAN:** You heard of the Tower of Babel?
4   **BUILDER:** Oh, that. Yeah, I heard that story – where they
5   almost finish and they all start talking weird. Those
6   guys were clowns. I'm gonna make it.
7   **CHRISTIAN:** God said if we want to come to him, we have
8   to come to him through Jesus Christ.
9   **BUILDER:** Religion again!
10   **CHRISTIAN:** No, I'm talking about a relationship – about
11   knowing God.
12   **BUILDER:** Gee, I never thought about knowing God. I just
13   wanted to get there. Hey, maybe I should send a letter
14   – you know, announcing my arrival.
15   **CHRISTIAN:** You've still got a problem.
16   **BUILDER:** What now? Suppose God doesn't read?!
17   **CHRISTIAN:** The problem isn't God, it's you. You're in sin,
18   and that creates a wall between you and God.
19   **BUILDER:** First religion, now a guilt trip. Boy, you sure
20   know how to cheer a guy up. Got any more good news?
21   **CHRISTIAN:** Look, friend, I'm sharing Good News. That's
22   the whole point. By knowing Jesus, the wall that sepa-
23   rates you from God is taken away. That's why Jesus
24   died on the cross.
25   **BUILDER:** Mmmm, I thought the cross was just some-
26   thing to wear around your neck.
27   **CHRISTIAN:** Look – why don't you quit striving? Jesus did
28   all the work already, and only his work is acceptable
29   to God.
30   **BUILDER:** My work's as good as anybody's, and it's gonna
31   get done a whole lot quicker if you buzz off and let me
32   get back to work.
33   **CHRISTIAN:** OK, but you're wasting your time.
34   **BUILDER:** No, you're wasting my time, and I'm paying a

1   whole construction crew by the hour. So get lost,
2   buddy!
3   **CHRISTIAN:** *(Shrugs.)* **OK.** *(CHRISTIAN exits.)*
4   **BUILDER:** *(To CREW)* **All right, Ralph, let's pull the bottom**
5   **lines up. You keep them from swinging and...**
6   **sawaaanggon...keep them from swaangonnaaa...**
7   **swaagonnagon...**
8
9
10
11
12
13
14
15
16
17
18
19
20
21
22
23
24
25
26
27
28
29
30
31
32
33
34

HERETIC JEOPARDY

By Dan Rupple

1   **CAST:** Ed Lardo, Phil Newberry, Lisa Ann Lyman, Joe Parker,
2   Lionel Backstrom.

3   **SETTING:** Game show set. A long table with three chairs may
4   be set up for the contestants, and a podium may be
5   placed off to one side for ED.

6   **PROPS:** Three cards and three pens for the contestants to
7   write their "Double Heretic Jeopardy" answers.

8   **COSTUMES:** Suits for ED and PHIL, regular attire for
9   everyone else.

10 **SOUND EFFECTS:** Ring, ticking.

11

12   *(ED is at his podium. PHIL stands at Center Stage.)*

13 **ED: It's time for *Heretic Jeopardy,* the game where you**
14   **decide, is it the truth or is it heresy? And now, here's**
15   **the host of *Heretic Jeopardy,* Phil Newberry.**

16 **PHIL: Thank you, Ed Lardo. Thank you, studio audience.**
17   **Welcome, players. It's time for another thrilling game**
18   **of *Heretic Jeopardy,* and before we go any further,**
19   **let's meet this week's contestants. Ed?**

20 **ED: Phil, our first contestant is a housewife, mother and**
21   **part-time Sunday school teacher from Bethany,**
22   **Oklahoma. Her interests are soap operas, bowling**
23   **and collecting recipes that she will never use. Phil,**
24   **meet Lisa Ann Lyman.** *(LISA enters.)*

25 **PHIL: Welcome, Lisa Ann. Is that two words or three?**

26 **LISA: Yes it is, Phil!**

27 **PHIL: Well, it's good to have you here. Let's meet our other**
28   **opponents.**

1 ED: Phil, our next contestant is a recent convert to the
2 Christian faith. He's from Seattle, Washington, and
3 he says his hobbies are reading the Bible, praying,
4 going to church, and evangelism. Phil, let's meet Joe
5 Parker. *(JOE enters.)*
6 PHIL: Boy, quite a list of hobbies, Joe. 'Course I under-
7 stand with all the rain you have up there, there's not
8 much else happening.
9 JOE: Huh?
10 PHIL: Well, anyway, it's good to have you here. Good luck.
11 JOE: Thank you, Phil.
12 ED: And luck he'll need, Phil, as we meet our third and
13 final contestant and six-time champion, playing in
14 his fourteenth straight *Heretic Jeopardy*. Phil, you
15 know him by now. From Chicago, Illinois, audience,
16 please welcome back seminary student Lionel
17 Backstrom. *(LIONEL enters.)*
18 PHIL: Lionel, back once again. Gonna give it another
19 try, eh?
20 LIONEL: That's right, Phil, I'm rarin' to go.
21 PHIL: Well, then let's get started. As you know, contestants,
22 the *Heretic Jeopardy* board is divided into four cate-
23 gories, and each category is divided into three sections –
24 ten, twenty and thirty points. When you pick your cate-
25 gory, a Scripture will appear. You either state if it is true
26 or false and state exactly what the Scripture actually is.
27 Should you answer wrong, your opponents may hit their
28 buzzers and answer correctly. The contestant scoring
29 the most points at the end of the game is the winner. Are
30 there any questions?
31 ALL: No, think we've got it.
32 PHIL: All right then, let's reveal our Heretic Jeopardy
33 board for the four categories today. *(Oohs)* There they
34 are: Deity of Christ, End Times Prophecy, Godly

1   Living and the Life of Jesus. Well, Lisa Ann, you won
2   the toss backstage, so you begin.
3   LISA: Thank you, Phil. I'll take Godly Living for ten.
4   PHIL: Godly Living for ten. The answer is, "Money is the
5   root of all evil."
6   LISA: It sure is. That's true. *(Buzz)*
7   PHIL: No, I'm sorry, Lisa Ann, that's not. Lionel?
8   LIONEL: What is the *love* of money?
9   PHIL: The love of money. That's correct. Ten points for
10   you, Lionel. Go ahead.
11   LIONEL: Deity of Christ for ten.
12   PHIL: John 1:1 reads, "The Word was a God."
13   LIONEL: What is "The Word was God"?
14   PHIL: Correct.
15   LIONEL: Deity of Christ for twenty.
16   PHIL: Thomas said to Jesus, "My Lord and my God."
17   (John 20:28)
18   LIONEL: That is correct.
19   PHIL: Correct again, Lionel.
20   LIONEL: Deity for thirty.
21   PHIL: Genesis says that God created all things, therefore,
22   he must have created Jesus.
23   LIONEL: False. Colossians tells us that Jesus created all
24   things, showing that he is part of the Godhead.
25   PHIL: That's right, Lionel. You now have sixty points.
26   LIONEL: I'll move on to End Times Prophecy for ten, Phil.
27   PHIL: OK, Lionel. Jesus will return as a turtle in a rain-
28   storm.
29   LIONEL: False. What is "like a thief in the night"?
30   PHIL: Keep going.
31   LIONEL: Prophecy for twenty.
32   PHIL: "As in the day of Abednego, so shall the coming of
33   the Son of Man be."
34   LIONEL: False. What is "As in the day of Noah"? Prophecy

1   for thirty,

2   PHIL: For thirty. "Behold, Jesus comes in the clouds, and

3   only the angels and spiritual people will see him."

4   LIONEL: False. What is "Every eye will see him"?

5   PHIL: Right again.

6   LIONEL: Godly Living for twenty.

7   PHIL: Jesus said, "By this shall all men know that ye are

8   my disciples." (John 13:35)

9   LIONEL: Ummm, gee, it could be by your Bible knowledge

10   or by your church attendance.

11   PHIL: Lionel, I just need one.

12   LIONEL: I'll say Bible knowledge. *(Buzz)*

13   PHIL: Oh, I'm sorry, Lionel. Lisa Ann?

14   LISA: I'll say church attendance. *(Buzz)*

15   PHIL: No, no, that's not right either. Joe?

16   JOE: What is by your love one to another?

17   PHIL: By your love one to another. That's right. Now Joe's

18   on the board.

19   JOE: Godly Living for thirty.

20   PHIL: Jesus said, "He that saves his life will have it more

21   abundantly."

22   JOE: What is "He that saves his life shall lose it, but he that

23   loses it will save it"? (Luke 17:33, author's paraphrase)

24   PHIL: Correct. Joe, you now have fifty points.

25   JOE: I'll take Life of Christ for ten.

26   PHIL: What was the name of the religious group that

27   hated Jesus because... *(Ring)*

28   PHIL: Oh, I'm sorry, players, time's up. We now go to the

29   final *Double Heretic Jeopardy* round with the score:

30   Lionel, one hundred and twenty; Joe, fifty; and Lisa

31   Ann, zero. OK, this question is worth seventy-five

32   points. A correct answer could move you, Lisa Ann,

33   into second place. Joe, you could go into first, and

34   Lionel, you could clinch your seventh championship.

1   **On the cards in front of you, please finish this**
2   **passage. Luke 18:18, "And a certain rich young ruler**
3   **asked Jesus, 'Good master, what shall I do to inherit**
4   **eternal life?'"** (Author's paraphrase) **Good luck,**
5   **players.** *(Tick, tick, tick. LIONEL, LISA and JOE write*
6   *their answers.)* **OK, players, time's up. Please put your**
7   **pens down. Lisa Ann, for seventy-five points.**

8 **LISA: He said, "You look rich. Where's the offering plate?"**

9 **PHIL: No, I'm sorry, Lisa Ann, that's not the correct**
10   **answer.**

11 **LISA: Well, that's what my pastor always says when he**
12   **thinks we've got money.**

13 **PHIL: Well, then your pastor doesn't know the right**
14   **answer either. Lionel, to clinch first place...**

15 **LIONEL: He said, "You're right on. Would you like to be an**
16   **elder in my church?"**

17 **PHIL: Oh, I'm sorry, Lionel, that's not the correct answer**
18   **either. Joe, it's up to you. A correct answer could**
19   **make you our new champion.**

20 **JOE: He said, "You lack one thing. Sell all that you have**
21   **and give it to the poor and come, follow me."** (Luke
22   18:22, author's paraphrase)

23 **PHIL: That's right, a new champion. Joe Parker wins with**
24   **one hundred and twenty-five points, defeating Lionel**
25   **Backstrom with one hundred and twenty points. Joe,**
26   **any comments?**

27 **JOE: Well, I guess it's not so much what you know, but *Who***
28   **you know.**

29 **PHIL: Good point, Joe. Well, good game, everyone. 'Bye for**
30   **now. See you tomorrow on *Heretic Jeopardy*.**

31

32

33

34

HE'S GOT A SECRET

By Dan Rupple

1   ***CAST:*** Announcer, Bud Allen, Clowny Collins, Poggy Cast,
2   Katty Karlily, Tom Belveen, Frank Landis.
3   ***SETTING:*** Game show set. Four chairs are in a row at Stage
4   Left for the panelists. There is a single chair set up Stage
5   Right for FRANK.
6   ***PROPS:*** Potholders and pan for Poggy.
7   ***COSTUMES:*** Suits for the men. Dressy clothes for the women.
8
9   *(CLOWNY, KATTY and TOM stand around POGGY,*
10   *pantomiming discussion about the contents of the pan*
11   *she's holding.)*
12   **ANNOUNCER:** *(From Off-stage)* **Clowny Collins, Poggy Cast,**
13   **Tom Belveen and Katty Karlily are all here to play**
14   ***He's Got a Secret.* And now, here's the master of cere-**
15   **monies himself, Bud Allen.** *(BUD enters.)*
16   **BUD: Thank you, thank you very much, and welcome once**
17   **again to *He's Got a Secret.* Welcome, panel.** *(Giggles*
18   *and chuckles)*
19   **PANEL:** *(Together)* **Good morning, Bud.**
20   **BUD: What are you doing over there?**
21   **CLOWNY: Well, Bud, Poggy's just showing us a new dish**
22   **she made.**
23   **POGGY: Oh, Clowny, it's not new.**
24   **BUD: What is it called, Poggy?**
25   **POGGY: It's called Velveetini Spamitory.**
26   **BUD; Sounds good!**
27   **CLOWNY: Not really, Bud, it's just Velveeta and Spam.**
28   **POGGY: Clowny!**

1 BUD: Well, looks like you're all in rare form. Oh, I guess I
2   should say hello to Miss Karlily.
3 KATTY: Good to see you, Bud.
4 BUD: Good to be seen. And a first-time panelist, gospel
5   singer Tom Belveen. Welcome, Tom.
6 TOM: Thanks for having me, Bud.
7 BUD: You're welcome. Well, let's get started. *(Panelists sit.)*
8   Today's a special day. Our guest is someone you all
9   know personally. But today he's got a secret that none
10   of you know about. Again, the object of *He's Got a*
11   *Secret* is to guess his secret as soon as possible. So
12   here he is, ladies and gentlemen. Please welcome
13   screen star Frank Landis. *(FRANK enters.)* Frank,
14   welcome to *He's Got a Secret.*
15 FRANK: Thanks, Bud. Great to be here. *(FRANK sits.)*
16 BUD: I'm sure you watch all the time, so you know how the
17   game's played. Let's tell our audience what Frank
18   Landis' secret is.
19 ANNOUNCER: *(Soft voice)* Frank's secret is that he's a
20   born-again Christian. *(Oohs)*
21 BUD: OK, let's start the questioning with Clowny Collins.
22 CLOWNY: Gee, this is tough. I mean, I know him so well.
23   Uh, what's your name again?
24 FRANK: Frank. *(Laughs.)*
25 CLOWNY: Frank, that's right. OK. Does it have to do with
26   something you did before you became an actor?
27 FRANK: No, it's happened since then.
28 BUD: OK, five down – Poggy Cast.
29 POGGY: Does it have something to do with your family?
30 FRANK: No, not really. I'm not sure they know it, actually.
31 BUD: Ten down – Tom Belveen;
32 TOM: Until now, has anyone else known it?
33 FRANK: I'm not sure. I don't think anyone else knows
34   about it.

1   BUD: Fifteen down – Katty Karlily.

2   KATTY: Are you a criminal?

3   FRANK: No, no. *(Laughs.)*

4   BUD: Twenty down – Clowny?

5   CLOWNY: Not a criminal, huh? Well, I guess when you
6   come over we don't need to hide the silverware
7   anymore. *(Laughter)* Gee, I know you're really into the
8   party scene. Are you an alcoholic?

9   FRANK: Ho, ho! Not quite.

10 BUD: OK. Oh boy. Twenty-five down – Poggy?

11 POGGY: Are you running for governor?

12 FRANK: No way, this state's in enough trouble.

13 BUD: Thirty down – Tom Belveen.

14 TOM: Do you do this secret every day?

15 FRANK: No, I don't do it every day, but I suppose you can.

16 BUD: Wait a minute – it *can* be done every day, so Tom,
17   we'll give you a yes.

18 TOM: OK, it can be done every day, but you don't. Is it
19   something athletic?

20 FRANK: Nope.

21 BUD: OK, nothing athletic. Thirty-five – Katty Karlily.

22 KATTY: Are you a clone?

23 FRANK: I don't think so. I have a birth certificate, not a
24   lab report.

25 BUD: Forty down – Clowny?

26 CLOWNY: Is Katty a clone? *(Laughs.)* Just kidding. Let's see,
27   would your secret have anything to do with or have
28   any effect on me?

29 FRANK: Well, I suppose it could, but I don't really affect
30   anyone with it.

31 BUD: Forty-five – Poggy Cast.

32 POGGY: Well, I'm into food. Are you a chef?

33 FRANK: No.

34 BUD: Fifty down – Tom Belveen.

1   TOM: Well, I'm a Christian, so does it have anything to do
2   with religious beliefs?
3   FRANK: Yes, it does.
4   TOM: Are you an atheist?
5   FRANK: No.
6   BUD: Fifty-five down – Katty Karlily?
7   KATTY: Are you a born-again Christian? *(Applause)*
8   BUD: Yes, that's it. Frank Landis is a born-again Christian.
9   Frank, how long have you been a Christian?
10   FRANK: Oh, just about six years, Bud.
11   BUD: Six years. You know, Tom, you being a gospel singer,
12   I thought for sure you'd guess it.
13   TOM: Well, Bud, I was gonna say that, but knowing Frank,
14   I just couldn't see that as being true.
15   BUD: Oh? How's that?
16   TOM: Well, with all due respect, there's an awful lot of
17   difference between just calling yourself a Christian
18   and truly having a personal relationship with Jesus.
19   And besides, being a Christian shouldn't be a secret –
20   everybody should know it.
21   FRANK: Well, yeah, I admit I'm not a fanatic like you,
22   Tom, but hey, I'm in Hollywood. I'm in show biz. I
23   have gone to church though, lots of times.
24   BUD: Well, wait a minute. Our time's up, so you two will
25   have to fight it out among yourselves.
26   CLOWNY: Maybe they could discuss it over Poggy's
27   Velveteeni Spamitory.
28   BUD: Oh, Clowny, you're too much. Well, that's our show.
29   'Bye for now. *(Applause)*
30
31
32
33
34

TRY TELLING
THE TRUTH

By Dan Rupple

1   ***CAST:*** Announcer (Off-stage), Bud Allen, Poggy Cast, Clowny
2   Collins, Regis Williams, Katty Karlily, Contestant 1 — Hank
3   Barnstrom, Contestant 2 — Bobby Jo Gunk, Contestant 3 —
4   Curtis Duckland.
5   ***SETTING:*** Game show set. Place two long tables in an
6   inverted "v" shape. Place four chairs on one side for the
7   celebrity panel and three chairs on the other side for the
8   three contestants.
9   ***PROPS:*** Letter for Bud.
10 ***COSTUMES:*** Suits for the men and dress clothes for the
11 women. The celebrity panel should dress with a bit more
12 pizzazz.
13 **SOUND EFFECTS:** Buzz.
14
15 *(The celebrity panel and the contestants are seated*
16 *behind the long tables. Optional music and applause.)*
17 **ANNOUNCER: Clowny Collins, Poggy Cast, Regis Williams**
18 **and Katty Karlily are all here to play *Try Telling the***
19 ***Truth.* And now, here's the master of ceremonies,**
20 **Bud Allen.** *(BUD enters.)*
21 **BUD: Thank you, thank you. Welcome to *Try Telling the***
22 ***Truth.***
23 **ALL:** *(Together)* **Hi, Bud, good morning.** *(Giggles, laughs.)*
24 **BUD: Well, I see that Clowny's at it again.**
25 **POGGY: He's always at it. I wish he'd get away from it for**
26 **a while.**
27 **CLOWNY: Look, I was born this way. What's your excuse?**
28 **REGIS: Gee, I didn't know you were born, Clowny. I**

1   **thought you were a laboratory accident.**

2 **BUD: Well, it's no accident they're all here to play *Try***

3   ***Telling the Truth,* including the ravishing Miss Katty**

4   **Karlily.**

5 **KATTY: Oh, hello, Bud, darling.**

6 **BUD: How ya doing? Well, let's get started. Here are our**

7   **three contestants.**

8 **CONTESTANT 1: My name is Curtis Duckland.**

9 **CONTESTANT 2: My name is Curtis Duckland.**

10 **CONTESTANT 3: My name is Curtis Duckland.**

11 **BUD:** *(Reading letter)* **I, Curtis Duckland, am a born-again**

12   **Christian. I am a full-time Christian worker, serving**

13   **God in any way I can out of my love for him. I am**

14   **presently working as a missionary, reaching out to**

15   **poverty-stricken people in South America. Sincerely,**

16   **Curtis Duckland.** *(Applause)*

17 **BUD: OK, panel, there's Curtis's story. Here are three men**

18   **who claim to be Curtis Duckland, and now it's time**

19   **for you to decide which one is telling the truth. Let's**

20   **start the questions with Poggy Cast.**

21 **POGGY: OK. Number Two, when did you become a**

22   **Christian?**

23 **CONTESTANT 2: Oh, reckon I've always been one.**

24 **POGGY: Oh, really? Number three, same question.**

25 **CONTESTANT 3: On January 28, 1968.**

26 **POGGY: Number One, why did you become a Christian?**

27 **CONTESTANT 1: 'Cause I don't want no God whacking me**

28   **in the head and sending me into the furnace.** *(Buzz)*

29 **BUD: Regis Williams?**

30 **REGIS: Number Three, why did you become a Christian?**

31 **CONTESTANT 3: I knew I had hurt God by my sins, but**

32   **that he still loved me, and through Jesus my sins**

33   **could be forgiven.**

34 **REGIS: Number Two, when did you enter into full-time**

1   Christian work? I mean, how long after becoming a
2   Christian?
3 CONTESTANT 2: Right away. You know, the good Lord just
4   wants us to be friendly, and I went right along being
5   friendly – well, full-time. *(Buzz)*
6 BUD: OK. Katty Karlily?
7 KATTY: Thank you. Mr. Duckland number two, what did
8   your friends think when you went out to be a
9   missionary in South America?
10 CONTESTANT 2: They don't know anything about it. I told
11   them I've got a big coffee plantation that I'm working
12   on. They'll never know. I mean, how are they gonna
13   check something way down there?
14 KATTY: I see, thank you. Mr. Duckland number three, why
15   did you decide to go to South America?
16 CONTESTANT 3: I had a burden for the needs of those
17   people, and I told God I was willing to go if he wanted
18   me to, and he sent me.
19 KATTY: I see. Mr. Duckland number one, why did you go to
20   South America?
21 CONTESTANT 1: Well, I figured the pay's good, good job
22   security and I like jungles, you know. I watched
23   Tarzan a lot as a kid. *(Buzz)*
24 BUD: Well, speaking of ape men, it's your turn, Clowny
25   Collins.
26 CLOWNY: Oh, thank you, Bud. Yes, uh, number two, would
27   you call yourself a Jesus freak?
28 CONTESTANT 2: No way. I think the good Lord just wants
29   me to go on bein' like everyone else. You know, iden-
30   tify with them. I just kinda go along with the crowd
31   and, you know, go with the flow.
32 CLOWNY: OK, number three, would you call yourself a
33   Jesus freak?
34 CONTESTANT 3: Well, I go freaky about Jesus! *(Laughs.)*

1   But you see, a freak is anyone that's out of the normal

2   way. And I would have to say non-Christians that are

3   separated and rebelling from their loving Creator are

4   really the freaks, so to speak. I mean, it's not God's

5   plan. *(Buzz)*

6   BUD: Well, there's the buzzer again. OK, time's up. Now

7   panel, let's hear your guesses. Poggy?

8   POGGY: Well, Bud, I say it's number three. He just seemed

9   sincere.

10   BUD: Regis?

11   REGIS: I go along with number three. The other two just

12   seemed to be like me, and I'm no Christian.

13   BUD: That's for sure. OK, Katty?

14   KATTY: Bud, I'm going to go along with Poggy and Regis. I

15   say it's number three too. I liked the sympathy and

16   the concern that he had for those poor people in

17   South America.

18   BUD: That's deep. Clowny?

19   CLOWNY: Definitely number three. Anyone who thinks

20   I'm a freak is my kind of guy.

21   BUD: OK, it's unanimous. Four votes for number three.

22   Now let's see who's really Curtis Duckland and which

23   two are fakes. Will the real Curtis Duckland please

24   stand up? *(CONTESTANT 3 stands. Applause from the*

25   *audience)* Number three it is! Well, panel, you all got it

26   right. Number one and two, you didn't fool anyone.

27   Would you please tell us who you really are? Number

28   one?

29   CONTESTANT 1: My name's Hank Barnstrom from Rhode

30   Island, and I'm a counterfeit Christian.

31   BUD: And number two?

32   CONTESTANT 2: My name's Bobby Joe Gunk from

33   Alabama, and I'm a counterfeit Christian.

34   BUD: Yes, two frauds and one true Christian. Curtis,

1   you're a born-again Christian. What makes you

2   different from Hank and Bobby Jo?

3   CONTESTANT 3: Well, Bud, you see, I serve God out of love

4   for him, not out of fear, and I look to please God, not

5   man. The problem with these two is that they're

6   trying to please themselves and man and satisfy God

7   all at the same time. They need to surrender to God

8   and look to please Jesus. That's what true Christianity

9   is all about.

10   BUD: Well, Curtis, to tell the truth, I think we all see that.

11   That's our show. See you next time on *Try Telling the*

12   *Truth.*

13

14

15

16

17

18

19

20

21

22

23

24

25

26

27

28

29

30

31

32

33

34

PRISONER OF THE WORLD

By Dan Rupple

1 **CAST:** Narrator (Off-stage), Guard #1, Travers, The Way, Guard
2 #2, Guard #3, Guard #4, Guard #5, Jim, Frank.
3 **SETTING:** In prison and various locations in the wilderness.
4 TRAVERS' cell may be a door at the side of the stage or a
5 frame with vertical black-painted wooden dowels
6 attached. The wilderness locations are implied by the
7 dialog.
8 **PROPS:** Trash can for GUARD #1; a bag of junk for TRAVERS,
9 including a statue made out of tin cans; any type of easily
10 carried food (like a sandwich or an apple) for TRAVERS;
11 three plates and forks for JIM (placed along the walking
12 route).
13 **COSTUMES:** Uniforms for the GUARDS; an orange jumpsuit
14 and sandals for TRAVERS; regular attire for JIM and
15 FRANK, and white pants and white shirt for THE WAY.
16 **SOUND EFFECTS:** Clicks and sounds of moving bricks, bush
17 sounds, blast.
18
19 *(TRAVERS is in his cell.)*
20 **NARRATOR: P.O.W., Prisoner of the World. Scene One –**
21 **The Setting.**
22 **GUARD #1:** *(Enters with trash can. Opens cell door and*
23 *shoves it inside, then slams the door shut.)* **Here's a**
24 **fresh batch of garbage for you, Travers. You'd better**
25 **make something out of it. Now, get to work!**
26 **TRAVERS: How do you expect me to make something out**
27 **of this stuff when all you give me is garbage to work**
28 **with?**

1   **GUARD #1: Quit your bellyaching. I didn't put you in here,**
2   **that's your doing. Now get going before I bring**
3   **another load in.**

4   **TRAVERS: Aw, come on. I'm tired.**

5   **GUARD #1: You should be happy you're even alive. Most of**
6   **your buddies are dead by now.**

7   **TRAVERS: Yeah? Well, you try keepin' alive in this**
8   **diseased cell.**

9   **GUARD #1: I got my own troubles – you're wastin' time.**

10   *(GUARD #1 exits.)*

11   **TRAVERS: Oh, man, if only there was a way out of here.**
12   **The stench is killin' me – the mold and the slime. I**
13   **don't think I'm gonna make it much longer. A couple**
14   **more loads of garbage and I'm gonna suffocate.** *(THE*
15   *WAY enters, holding a pair of sandals.)*

16   **THE WAY: Hey, friend, you wanta get out of here?**

17   **TRAVERS: What are you talking about?**

18   **THE WAY: I can get you out.**

19   **TRAVERS: You and what army?**

20   **THE WAY: I've gotten lots of people out of here.**

21   **TRAVERS: So, who are you?**

22   **THE WAY: I am The Way.**

23   **TRAVERS: Yeah, I've heard talk about you. They call you**
24   **T.W., right? What's your plan?**

25   **THE WAY: Just follow me.**

26   **TRAVERS: Where we goin'? You got a tunnel or something?**

27   **THE WAY: Don't ask questions. Just follow me and do**
28   **exactly what I say. Remember, I am The Way.**

29   **TRAVERS: Hey, look, I'm no fool. How do I know you're for**
30   **real? I want some proof.**

31   **THE WAY: What do you want me to do, go outside and**
32   **bring back some flowers or something?**

33   **TRAVERS: Well...**

34   **THE WAY: Look, if I was a phony I could get flowers from**

1   **the prison garden. They look the same as the ones on**
2   **the outside. You're just gonna have to trust me. And if**
3   **you don't, then forget the whole thing.**
4   **TRAVERS: Yeah, but if it fails and I get caught, I'm in for**
5   **life. There's no way I can survive.**
6   **THE WAY: You're a dead man now, Travers, even as you're**
7   **breathing. I'm your only hope. But I'm warning you –**
8   **I can't guarantee anything if you disobey me. If you**
9   **resist my lead even once, you're on your own.** *(Pause)*
10 **TRAVERS: OK, T.W., I'm gonna trust you. You go ahead**
11   **and call the shots. I'll give you the best I got.**
12 **THE WAY: Great. That's all I ask.** *(THE WAY hands the*
13   *sandals to TRAVERS.)* **Now, I'll come by for you in thirty**
14   **minutes. Be ready.**
15 **TRAVERS: I'll be waiting.** *(THE WAY exits. TRAVERS retreats*
16   *to his cell and puts on the sandals.)*
17 **NARRATOR: Scene Two – The Way Out.**
18 **THE WAY: Travers!** *(THE WAY opens the cell door.)*
19 **TRAVERS: Is that you, T.W.?**
20 **THE WAY: Yeah, let's go. I've opened your cell. Come on**
21   **out, but keep low.**
22 **TRAVERS; OK.** *(Clang from bag of junk TRAVERS is carrying)*
23 **THE WAY: What's that?**
24 **TRAVERS: Just a few things I'm taking.**
25 **THE WAY: You're not taking anything.**
26 **TRAVERS: Are you kidding? I can't leave this stuff. I've put**
27   **a lot of time and money into these things.**
28 **THE WAY: They're gonna weigh you down. You'll never**
29   **make it out.**
30 **TRAVERS: What happens when I get out and I ain't got**
31   **nothing?**
32 **THE WAY: You won't need anything. I'll give you every-**
33   **thing you need.**
34 **TRAVERS: So, how you gonna do that?**

1   THE WAY: Are you already forgetting? I'm The Way. Now
2   dump it. *(Clang — different from previous sound.)* Is
3   that all of it?
4   TRAVERS: Yeah, that's all of it.
5   THE WAY: OK, stay close. *(Steps of GUARD #2 and GUARD #3*
6   *as they enter.)* Stop a second. Don't move or make a
7   sound. *(Crash as TRAVERS drops statue from bag.)*
8   GUARD #2: What was that?
9   GUARD #3: I'm not sure.
10 GUARD #2: Let's look behind those poles.
11 GUARD #3: No, forget it. It was probably just a rat. Let's get
12   going.
13 GUARD #2: Ah, OK. *(GUARDS exit.)*
14 TRAVERS: Whew! That was a close one. I can't believe they
15   didn't look over here. They were within three feet
16   of us.
17 THE WAY: What was that noise?
18 TRAVERS: I dropped something.
19 THE WAY: What?
20 TRAVERS: It was just a little tin statue I made out of
21   some cans.
22 THE WAY: Cans?! I told you not to bring anything. You not
23   only disobeyed, but you lied.
24 TRAVERS: Look, I got rid of everything else. What do
25   you want?
26 THE WAY: Oh, I see you're gonna follow me partway.
27   Either you obey, or let's call it quits now.
28 TRAVERS: Look, how 'bout I keep it with me, and if we
29   run into any more trouble, I'll dump it right away.
30 THE WAY: Hanging onto stuff like that is what will get you
31   caught and keep you here. The Way doesn't work as
32   long as you're weighted down. *(Clang as TRAVERS*
33   *disposes of bag.)*
34 TRAVERS: OK, it's gone. I'll follow.

1 NARRATOR: Scene Three – The Escape.

2 TRAVERS: How much farther, T.W.?

3 THE WAY: Not too much. Now you've got to be real quiet
4   here. Walk real careful, there's some pitfalls around.
5   And then when we pass that big cement block, be
6   ready to run as fast as you can.

7 TRAVERS: Got it. *(Enter GUARD #4 and GUARD #5.)*

8 GUARD #4: Well, maybe we can. I get off at two o'clock.

9 GUARD #5: OK, I'll wait for you.

10 THE WAY: Duck!

11 TRAVERS: Why?

12 THE WAY: Get down!

13 TRAVERS: Hey, watch who you're shoving.

14 THE WAY: Quiet!

15 TRAVERS: Just because I'm following doesn't mean you've
16   got the right to push me around.

17 GUARD #4: There he is.

18 GUARD #5: Come on, let's get him!

19 GUARD #4: Hold it. Don't make a move.

20 TRAVERS: Foolproof way, huh?

21 THE WAY: If you would've listened.

22 GUARD #4: Just what do you think you're doing? You can't
23   escape this place. No one's ever done it, and you're
24   gonna be just one more failure.

25 THE WAY: Excuse me, gentlemen. He's with me. Now I
26   suggest you move on and forget this ever happened.

27 GUARD #3: Are you kidding?

28 GUARD #4: Let's go, Joe.

29 GUARD #3: What?

30 GUARD #4: Come on, let's get out of here. This isn't the
31   place to be. Come on. *(GUARDS exit.)*

32 TRAVERS: Man, what got into them? I thought I was dead.

33 THE WAY: You're gonna be unless I get you out of here.

34 TRAVERS: Yeah, I'm sorry I blew it. Don't give up on me –

1   **I'll learn.**

2   **THE WAY: I'm not giving up on you – you're learning**

3   **already. Come on, we're almost out.** *(They continue*

4   *walking.)*

5   **TRAVERS: Oh, thanks, T.W. Hey, both times we ran into**

6   **guards, they said there's no way out.**

7   **THE WAY: Deception is their greatest weapon. They'll lie**

8   **you right into bondage.**

9   **TRAVERS: Yeah, but maybe they're right. Listen, think we**

10   **should go back and kind of restructure our escape?**

11   **They might be on to us.**

12   **THE WAY: Travers, your lack of faith is a big hindrance.**

13   **When The Way sets you free, you're free indeed.**

14   **TRAVERS: OK.**

15   **THE WAY: Well, you ready?**

16   **TRAVERS: Ready for what?**

17   **THE WAY: Freedom!**

18   **TRAVERS: Now?**

19   **THE WAY:** *(Points Off-stage.)* **Right through that brick wall.**

20   **TRAVERS: It's thirty feet high – we can't make it.** *(Clicks.*

21   *Moving sound)* **T.W.! You shifted the bricks.**

22   **THE WAY: Let's go.**

23   **TRAVERS:** *(In front)* **OK! Wait a minute. You lead.** *(Moves*

24   *behind THE WAY.)*

25   **THE WAY: Now you've got it.** *(Both exit.)*

26   **NARRATOR: Scene Four – Freedom.**

27   **THE WAY:** *(Entering with TRAVERS)* **Keep close, Travers. I**

28   **don't want to have to shout for you to hear me.**

29   **TRAVERS: I'm just checking out this place. It's beautiful.**

30   **THE WAY: I'm glad that you like it. Enjoy it to your heart's**

31   **content, but let's enjoy it together. Agreed?**

32   **TRAVERS: Agreed.**

33   **THE WAY: There's no greater lesson you'll learn than**

34   **the importance of staying right by my side. Never**

1 forget that.

2 TRAVERS: Why would I want to leave you after you led me
3 out of the prison and into this paradise?

4 THE WAY: There will be the voices of hunters calling you,
5 your curiosity leading you down the wrong paths, and
6 harlots tempting you into their cottages. So be
7 warned. Each of these is your enemy, and each will
8 only lead you back to prison.

9 TRAVERS: Don't worry, I'm never goin' back there. Man,
10 what an incredible river. Could we go down and
11 drink?

12 THE WAY: Sure, follow me. *(They cross to "river" area and*
13 *kneel down, pantomiming drinking.)*

14 TRAVERS: Boy, what cold, fresh water. I've never had such
15 a great drink. I've been living off that stale gutter
16 water in the cell. I forgot what water tastes like. Let's
17 fill our canteens.

18 THE WAY: No need. Everywhere I lead you, this river will
19 be right beside us.

20 TRAVERS: Well, yeah, but surely there will be moments
21 when we won't have access to it.

22 THE WAY: Not one. All you'll ever need is always right
23 beside you, if you follow close. You'll never hunger,
24 thirst, or be without clothing. Now let's move on.
25 *(They walk.)*

26 NARRATOR: Scene Five – The Look Back.

27 TRAVERS: I'm getting tired of walking. Let's just stop here
28 a while.

29 THE WAY: Never stop, Travers. Always keep moving. The
30 more you walk, the more your strength is renewed.
31 But stopping will weaken you.

32 TRAVERS: Look, I don't care. For now, I'm tired. Let's stop
33 for a few minutes. My feet are killing me!

34 THE WAY: Where are the sandals I gave you to wear?

1   TRAVERS: I took them off a little ways back.

2   THE WAY: No wonder you're tired. Never take off those

3   sandals.

4   TRAVERS: Oh, c'mon, T.W. Look, is there anything to eat

5   around here?

6   THE WAY: Always. Just grab it. It's right beside you. *(Picks*

7   *up some food from a hidden place.)*

8   TRAVERS: *(Eating)* **Mmmm, pretty handy.** *(Bush sounds.*

9   *Blast. Looks back over his shoulder.)* **What was that?**

10 THE WAY: Don't look behind you. Keep your eyes on the

11   path ahead of us.

12 TRAVERS: Why? What's going on?

13 THE WAY: That blast came from the prison. They're just

14   making a little noise, trying to get your attention.

15 TRAVERS: Can you see anything?

16 THE WAY: Don't turn around. This is going to happen

17   every once in a while. You'll hear or smell or think

18   of something that reminds you of the prison, but

19   never turn around, 'cause you'll be staring it right in

20   the face.

21 TRAVERS: T.W., we've been walking all day. Are you saying

22   if I turn around, I'll be staring right into the gates?

23 THE WAY: The prison is never too far away to be seen, if you

24   look for it. *(TRAVERS starts eating again. Bush noise)*

25 TRAVERS: Hey, this is pretty good stuff. You know, I was

26   lucky if I ate this much in three days back in the old

27   prison days. *(More bush noise)* I'll bet they're feeding

28   old Clyde and Jake their mush right about now. You

29   know, Jake once threw the mush right into the

30   guard's face. You should've seen the look on his mug.

31   I could've died laughing.

32 THE WAY: Let's get going, Travers.

33 TRAVERS: Well, in a minute. Hey, you know one night the

34   guards were coming through for a bed check. Old

1   Clyde takes the pillows in his bed, sets them up under
2   his covers, and he and Jake get in under them at
3   different ends of the bed. You know, so when the
4   guard comes by and shines his light, he sees two feet
5   sticking out of the top and two feet out of the bottom.
6   It was the cell joke for almost two months.
7 THE WAY: Well, it might have been good for a laugh, but
8   do you recall what happened to Clyde and Jake when
9   they got caught?
10 TRAVERS: Hmmm, no, can't say I do.
11 THE WAY: They each got ten lashes.
12 TRAVERS: Yeah? Well, how do you know?
13 THE WAY: I know the prison's methods.
14 TRAVERS: Yeah?
15 THE WAY: You'll realize that whenever the thoughts of the
16   prison hit you, you'll remember the good times and
17   the bad times will fade. So don't ever let your
18   thoughts wander. Keep them on Paradise. Now, let's
19   keep moving.
20 NARRATOR: Scene Six – The Stray.
21 THE WAY: Boy, what a beautiful spot. Travers, I'm so glad
22   you let me take you out of that place. If only more
23   guys would realize what they're missing, it'd sure
24   take a lot less work to convince them to follow, right?
25   ...Travers?
26 TRAVERS: Huh?
27 THE WAY: I said, it'd take a lot less work to get them to
28   follow.
29 TRAVERS: Oh, uh, yeah, I guess.
30 THE WAY: Travers, you're not listening, are ya?
31 TRAVERS: Well, yeah, sure I was listening. I was just – my
32   mind wandered for a moment.
33 THE WAY: Yeah, that's easy to do. So often your mind will
34   leave what the beneficial thing is to talk about and

1   wander over to something that could entice you to
2   destruction.
3   TRAVERS: Well, I don't think a few stray thoughts are
4   gonna destroy me.
5   THE WAY: It's not the thoughts, it's what becomes of them.
6   If you dwell on them, then you begin to conceive how
7   to act upon them. Then if you actually carry them out,
8   there's where the destruction comes. But don't
9   worry! Continue to follow me, and your thoughts will
10   be renewed from the prison to this Paradise. I'm
11   gonna help you captivate all your thoughts.
12   TRAVERS: You know, there's so much to learn, I'm getting
13   tired.
14   THE WAY: Learn of me and I'll give you a rest you'd never
15   believe existed.
16   TRAVERS: Yeah? I think I'm going to go for a little walk.
17   THE WAY: OK, I'll go with you.
18   TRAVERS: Well, nothing personal, T.W., but I'd kinda like
19   to be alone right now.
20   THE WAY: Alone with your thoughts?
21   TRAVERS: Look, I'm entitled to my privacy!
22   THE WAY: Yes, that's your choice, but don't let those rights
23   get you into trouble. The prison security is still
24   looking for you.
25   TRAVERS: No problem. I'll be careful. *(THE WAY exits.)*
26   NARRATOR: Scene Seven – The Snare.
27   TRAVERS: Oh, boy, this is great being out on my own. Ah,
28   T.W.'s great and I sure need his help, but what
29   freedom bein' out here alone, bein' your own man.
30   *(JIM and FRANK enter.)* Hey, there's a couple of guys
31   over there. They're the first people I've seen out here
32   other than T.W. Oh, man, I wonder if they're guards
33   on leave or something. I better be careful.... Sure
34   would be great to talk with somebody. Oh well, what

1   can it hurt? Hey, guys.

2   JIM and FRANK: Oh, hi, how ya doing?

3   TRAVERS: Great. My name's Travers.

4   JIM: Hi. I'm Jim, and this here's Frank.

5   FRANK: Hi.

6   TRAVERS: You guys come here often?

7   JIM: Yeah, every once in a while. You know, a little fishin',
8   some R and R.

9   FRANK: Beautiful spot.

10 TRAVERS: Oh, sure is. Where you guys from?

11 FRANK: We're from the prison.

12 TRAVERS: Huh?

13 JIM: Say, didn't you used to be in the prison? You look
14   familiar.

15 FRANK; Yeah, I think I remember you.

16 TRAVERS: Uh...well...

17 FRANK: Hey, look. Don't worry, we're not guards. We're
18   prisoners.

19 TRAVERS: You're what?

20 JIM: We're prisoners.

21 TRAVERS: You mean, you used to be prisoners?

22 JIM: No, we still are.

23 TRAVERS: Then what are you doing out?

24 FRANK: Like Jim says, we're getting a little R and R, doing
25   some fishing.

26 TRAVERS: You mean they let you out?

27 JIM: Well, sure. Wait a minute – how long have you been out?

28 TRAVERS; Well, ah, oh, a couple of weeks.

29 JIM: Oh, no wonder. Things have really changed since you
30   were in.

31 TRAVERS: They have?

32 JIM: Yeah. They've revamped the whole place. You should
33   see it now.

34 FRANK: Yeah, we have our own little apartments now,

1   clean clothes, vacations, they even let girls in.

2   TRAVERS: No kidding?

3   JIM: Yeah. Boy, you left at the wrong time. It's great. I love
4   it there.

5   FRANK: Yeah, it's the difference between night and day.

6   TRAVERS: I can't believe it. Your own apartments?

7   JIM: Yep.

8   TRAVERS: No cells, no bars?

9   JIM: Nothing. Just total freedom.

10   FRANK: So, whatcha doing out here?

11   TRAVERS: Well, I'm out here with T.W.

12   FRANK and JIM: *(Together)* **The Way?!** *(Laugh)*

13   JIM: What a sucker. You followed that guy?

14   TRAVERS: Well, sure. He got me out of prison.

15   FRANK: Yeah, what timing.

16   JIM: Look, Travers, T.W. gets lots of people out of prison,
17   but then what? He'll lead you out here to starve.

18   TRAVERS: He said he was gonna provide.

19   JIM: No way. The only way to survive out here is to take
20   care of yourself.

21   TRAVERS: Yeah, well, I'll make it.

22   FRANK: Maybe so, but why bother? Why work yourself to
23   death out here when you could come back to the
24   prison and have your meals delivered to your door?
25   Last night we had shrimp and steak.

26   JIM: Look, Travers, I know lots of guys who followed T.W.,
27   and believe me, they're all missing out. The prison's
28   where it's happening.

29   TRAVERS: Look, he gives me good advice.

30   FRANK: T.W.'s a dictator, nothing more. Hey, why be under
31   his thumb? Come on, wouldn't you like to call the shots?
32   Look at us – we wanted to go fishing, so we told the
33   guard, "We're going fishing." Well, here we are. Hey,
34   Travers, you want to come back with us?

1   TRAVERS: Oh, look, I'd have to talk with T.W. first.

2   JIM: Can't do anything on your own, huh?

3   TRAVERS: Well, it's just that I should at least say good-bye.

4   FRANK: Well, we're pulling out soon, so if you want to
5   come with us, there's no time to find T.W.

6   TRAVERS: Oh, gee, I'd sure like to think about it.

7   JIM: Look, before we leave we're gonna eat first, so think
8   about it over some fresh fish. Whadda ya say?

9   TRAVERS: Well, OK.

10   JIM: Now you're talking. *(JIM hands plate to TRAVERS.)*

11   TRAVERS: *(Eating)* Boy, that sure is good fish.

12   JIM: Yeah, nothing like fresh fish.

13   FRANK: We get it all the time back in the prison now. They
14   bring it in fresh from Lake Delores.

15   TRAVERS: Man, it sure is different from when I was there.
16   All I ever got was bread or slop.

17   JIM: Well, things have changed.

18   FRANK: So, what's the verdict? You coming with us or not?

19   TRAVERS: Well...I'm not sure yet. It sure is tempting the
20   way you guys describe it.

21   JIM: Hey, you better make up your mind, 'cause we're leaving.

22   FRANK: Yep, time to head back.

23   TRAVERS: Well, look. I'll tell you what. You guys go on
24   ahead and I'll catch up a little later.

25   JIM: No way, you'll never find us. This forest is too thick.

26   FRANK: Now's the time, Travers. Why can't you come with
27   us? We know how to get back.

28   TRAVERS: Well, I was going to find T.W. and kind of tell
29   him I was returning.

30   JIM: Why's he need to know?

31   TRAVERS: Well, I think I owe him at least that much, or at
32   least a thank you.

33   JIM: For what? Taking you out of the best situation you've
34   ever had?

1   TRAVERS: Well...

2   JIM: No way. The guy's spoiled your life. You don't owe him
3   anything.

4   FRANK: Come on, Jim, let's get going.

5   TRAVERS: OK, you guys, if I do come back, won't they
6   arrest me or something?

7   JIM: Arrest you?

8   TRAVERS: Well, yeah, I *did* escape.

9   FRANK: How do they arrest someone in prison? *(Laughs.)*

10   JIM: Hey, they'll be glad to see you. We told you the
11   warden's got a whole new philosophy – "Let everyone
12   enjoy themselves, then no trouble, no violence, no
13   escapes." It's great.

14   TRAVERS: All right. It sounds pretty good the way you
15   describe it.

16   FRANK: Well, it's about time.

17   TRAVERS: Let's get going.

18   NARRATOR: Scene Eight – Return to Bondage.

19   JIM: *(Pointing)* There it is, just up ahead.

20   TRAVERS: You know, I've never seen it from the outside.
21   When I left, I didn't look back.

22   FRANK: Beautiful, huh?

23   TRAVERS: Yeah. Boy, I forgot what I was missing. It looks
24   so good.

25   JIM: You think the outside looks great, wait till you see
26   what they've done inside.

27   TRAVERS: I can't wait. You say they'll give me my own
28   room?

29   FRANK: First thing.

30   TRAVERS: Oh, I hope it has a porch and a king-size bed.

31   JIM: Just request it.

32   TRAVERS: Oh, boy. Sure will be comfortable after living
33   out in the wilderness for a couple of weeks.

34   FRANK: Here we are.

1   TRAVERS: Boy, sure is good to be back.

2   JIM: After you, Travers.

3   TRAVERS: Man, it's great to be back home again. This is

4   really...

5   FRANK: OK, grab him! *(They struggle.)*

6   TRAVERS: What?

7   JIM: So you thought you could escape, huh? What a fool.

8   FRANK: Get those clean clothes off him. Here, Travers, we

9   saved your filthy uniform for you.

10   TRAVERS: What are you guys doing?

11   FRANK: You believed every word – hook, line and sinker.

12   We brought back a lot of guys, but you were about the

13   most gullible.

14   JIM: Let's get him into his cell. *(Cell door slams.)*

15   TRAVERS: Nothing's changed here! It's all the same.

16   FRANK: That's where you're wrong. It's not the same. It's

17   worse!

18   TRAVERS: How could it be any worse?

19   JIM: Travers, now that you know the truth and what

20   Paradise is like, we're going to have to give you twice

21   as much garbage to keep you.

22   FRANK: Starting tomorrow, your food rations will be half

23   and your workload double.

24   TRAVERS: Double?

25   JIM: Yeah, twice the garbage to work with. *(Laughs.)* Frank,

26   did you see the look on his face when we grabbed him?

27   FRANK: Yeah, they're always so surprised. I don't know

28   why. What else would you expect in a prison? Come

29   on, Jim, let's get back to our cells.

30   TRAVERS: Hey! Who are you guys? I thought you were

31   guards. What are you, prisoners?

32   JIM: We are guards, but we're all prisoners. No one's free

33   here. Now get to work. *(FRANK and JIM exit.)*

34   TRAVERS: *(Alone)* I can't believe it. I'm back in prison

1   again. I believed it all. Why didn't I listen to T.W.? Just
2   a few moments on my own, and here I am. It's even
3   worse! Twice the junk and the torture of having been
4   in paradise and now being here. I've gotta get out. If
5   only The Way would come back. He's the only one
6   who can save me. Why didn't I listen to him? He
7   warned me! All I want is one more chance.
8   NARRATOR: Scene Nine – Bondage Again.
9   GUARD #1: You're gonna have to do better than that, Travers.
10   You haven't met your work quota in three days.
11   TRAVERS: I'm doing my best.
12   GUARD #1: That's not good enough.
13   TRAVERS: Look – you're asking me to turn out twice as
14   much as any other prisoner here.
15   GUARD #1: You're the one who tried to escape, so you get
16   what you deserve.
17   TRAVERS: Well, I'm starving, huh. Hey, the least you could
18   do is give me some food.
19   GUARD #1: Ah, you'll eat when it's time. Now, work!
20   *(Walks off.)*
21   TRAVERS: Work! Work! Oh, T.W., if you're out there some-
22   where, I need you. I'll follow you one hundred
23   percent. Just give me one more chance. Oh, man, the
24   freedom of Paradise. Out of this filth and this
25   garbage. How could I have ever traded it in for all
26   this? I was so blind. *(Enter THE WAY.)*
27   THE WAY: Hello, Travers.
28   TRAVERS: T.W.! I don't believe it. I didn't think you'd ever
29   come back.
30   THE WAY: I'm always around, as long as prisoners are
31   crying out.
32   TRAVERS: Please, can you get me out of here?
33   THE WAY: Why should I?
34   TRAVERS: Yeah...look, for what it's worth, I'm sorry. You

1 got me out and I let you down. I realize what I've
2 done. I was a fool. I know I don't deserve a second
3 chance, but if there's any way you could get me out
4 one last time...
5 THE WAY: I forgive you, Travers, and true, you don't
6 deserve it. But then again, I don't get people out of
7 here because they deserve it or earn it. My point is, I
8 don't think it'd do any good to get you out again.
9 TRAVERS: Why, for heaven's sake?
10 THE WAY: Home is where the heart is. Even if I set you
11 free again, as long as your heart's back here, you'll
12 always return.
13 TRAVERS: But my heart isn't here anymore. Look – I
14 admit it was. I can't imagine why, but I've learned,
15 I've changed. Look, no more statues. I smashed them
16 all, you see? They don't mean anything to me
17 anymore. They're just garbage. That's all they are –
18 garbage.
19 THE WAY: Travers, never once did you fully trust or obey
20 me. You only followed when it suited.
21 TRAVERS: I know, but let me try again. Listen – this time,
22 no conditions – only full obedience. Wherever you go,
23 I'll go.
24 THEY WAY: No looking back?
25 TRAVERS: No looking back.
26 THE WAY: Travers, I'm proud of you. You've learned a lot.
27 You've received my forgiveness, you've renounced
28 and let go of the prison and I've got your heart. You're
29 gonna make it this time.
30 TRAVERS: You mean you'll give me another chance?
31 THE WAY: Yep. I already have. Your heart's free now.
32 That's what matters.
33 TRAVERS: Oh, when do we leave here?
34 THE WAY: How about now?

1   TRAVERS: Great. Oh, wait a minute, T.W. I told some of
2   the guys here about you and, well, a few of them want
3   to know if you can get them out, too. Is there any way?
4   THE WAY: As many as want to come. Bring them all.
5
6
7
8
9
10
11
12
13
14
15
16
17
18
19
20
21
22
23
24
25
26
27
28
29
30
31
32
33
34

CITIZEN GAINES

By Dave Toole

1 **CAST:** Narrator (Off-stage), Editor, Jim Peters, Hubert Jones,
2   Cynthia Gleason, Marty, Hospital Attendant, Charles Foster
3   Wells, Mr. Taylor, Mrs. Philbin, Workers (two), Pat Burns.
4 **SETTING:** Various locations. The lighting instructions
5   included in the script help with the setting transitions,
6   but if your church or auditorium does not have theatrical
7   lighting, you may simply dim or turn off the house lights
8   during the transitions. The various locations and their
9   requirements are: 1. Newspaper office — two chairs at Stage
10   Left; 2. Jones' home — rocker at Stage Right; 3. Dance club —
11   small table and a chair at Stage Left; 4. Sunny Acres
12   Convalescent Home — space for wheelchair at Stage Right;
13   5. Elysium — a few pieces of furniture at Stage Left; 6. Mr.
14   Burns' room — a chair or table at Stage Right to hold his
15   suitcase.
16 **PROPS:** Notes and a quarter for JIM, a glass for CYNTHIA, a
17   wheelchair for MR. WELLS and a suitcase and pile of
18   clothes for MR. BURNS.
19 **COSTUMES:** Suits for EDITOR and JIM, "old man" attire for
20   HUBERT, a tacky dress and a lot of makeup for CYNTHIA,
21   black T-shirt and black jeans for MARTY, scrubs for
22   ATTENDANT, bathrobe and slippers for MR. WELLS,
23   black-and-white uniforms for MR. TAYLOR and MRS.
24   PHILBIN, overalls for WORKERS and MR. BURNS.
25 **SOUND EFFECTS:** Dance music and crowd noises, crash.
26
27   *(JIM and EDITOR sit on chairs at Stage Left. The stage is*
28   *dark. The NARRATOR reads the following lines from Off-*

1   *stage. The narration should sound as much like a radio news*
2   *feature as possible — much like the old movietones.)*
3   **NARRATOR: ...And so, after seventy-five years, Orson**
4   **Williams Gaines is dead. Shown here at the dedica-**
5   **tion of his mammoth yacht, the "William Claude,"**
6   **Gaines was friends with socialites from around the**
7   **world. Seen here with a number of Hollywood**
8   **celebrities past and present, these home movies,**
9   **never before shown in public, give us one idea what**
10   **life was like in his private, magnificent palace,**
11   **Elysium, which housed the third-largest collection of**
12   **art in the free world. Far and away, Gaines was the**
13   **richest individual of his day, and perhaps even of**
14   **history. The single most powerful man outside of**
15   **government, and yet, when his Creator called, it was**
16   **all for naught.** *(Lights up at Stage Left on JIM and*
17   *EDITOR.)*
18   **EDITOR: Well, Jim, that's our story. One of the great men**
19   **of our century passed on. Think you can handle it?**
20   **JIM: What's to handle? So Gaines dies, so what? Everybody**
21   **already knows that – even our own paper's reported**
22   **that.**
23   **EDITOR: Yeah, yeah. I know all that, but the public is still**
24   **interested. They're hot on this story, and I want to**
25   **cash in before they cool off. Look, Jim, here's a guy**
26   **who had it all – cars, money, women, power, every-**
27   **thing. But somehow he winds up dying all alone in**
28   **that castle of his, Elysium. Just a couple of hired**
29   **servants in the room with him. Mighty strange. And**
30   **what was that he said when he died?**
31   **JIM: Ah, "crunchy raisins"?**
32   **EDITOR: Yeah, right, "crunchy raisins." Listen, this**
33   **morning at the editors' meeting, we went 'round and**
34   **'round trying to come up with a new angle on this**

thing to avoid having to rehash the same old stuff again, and we think we've found it in this "crunchy raisins." What does it mean? Is it a new snack food? A breakfast cereal? Maybe some kind of invention? Whatever it is, we want you to find out. What do you think? *(JIM sighs and throws up his hands in resignation. EDITOR slaps him on the back.)* **Good man. I knew you would.** *(Exit EDITOR. Theme music optional.)*

JIM: Well, Orson Gaines had died, so what was all the excitement about? It had been coming a long time – the old man was seventy-five. I guess death is kind of a funny thing. Everybody's got to go sometime, but somehow you just never expect it. People come and go all the time, but then again, people like Gaines are few and far between. From being the only child of a broken home, he brought himself up to be king of the hill. Banker, industrialist, shipping magnate – why, he controlled three of the world's top ten corporations. Thirty-five newspapers, twenty-six TV stations, a movie studio and a chain of taco stands in Picquoma. Even ran for president once, although I don't know why. He was powerful enough to buy and sell a dozen presidents. No wonder the country is shaken. This guy was one of the pillars holding up the place. Now that he has gone, what will happen? I decided to start at the beginning. I arranged to see a childhood classmate of Gaines' named Hubert Jones. *(Theme music fades. Fade up lights Stage Right on an old man in a rocker. Fade out lights on Stage Right as JIM crosses over.)*

HUBERT: Yup, I knowed Mr. Gaines back when he used to let folks call him Orson. We never did, though. We always called him "Nuthin'," 'cause you couldn't get nuthin' much out of him. You know, he was the only

1   guy in school who used to padlock his desk. No
2   matter, though. Us younguns could've just popped the
3   hinges off when we had the notion, but for some
4   reason, no one ever did. Guess it's 'cause he looked so
5   lonesome off by himself all the time.
6   JIM: You say Mr. Gaines didn't play well with other children?
7   HUBERT: Well, not exactly. He liked playin' OK. He
8   just...he just never seemed to trust anyone. Can't have
9   too many friends, if you don't trust nobody. Maybe it
10   was 'cause things were so tough on him and his ma
11   and all. I dunno, though. Kids don't think much
12   about that kind of stuff.
13   JIM: I understand, Mr. Jones. Does the phrase "crunchy
14   raisins" mean anything to you?
15   HUBERT: Ah, sure. Wasn't he the first Indian to play
16   major league baseball? *(Lights fade up Down Center*
17   *Stage, then fade out on Stage Right as JIM crosses Down*
18   *Center — optional theme music.)*
19   JIM: So Gaines had a bad time in school, eh? His marks
20   had been a little below average, but considering his
21   problems at home and with the other kids, he was
22   probably doing better than most. All interesting stuff,
23   but I could see the mystery of "crunchy raisins" was
24   not to be found there. Perhaps his second wife would
25   know – it was worth a try. *(Lights fade up Stage Left on*
26   *middle-aged woman at a small table, drinking.)*
27   Her name was Cynthia Gleason. She was a chronic
28   case of a dancer in search of some talent. After years
29   of playing small-time bars as a chorus girl and exotic
30   dancer, she'd chanced to meet Gaines in the back of a
31   cab. After a whirlwind romance, they suffered
32   through three years of stormy matrimony until
33   Gaines finally dumped her. She wasn't too hard to
34   locate. She owns her own dance club now on the

1   **south side of Chicago.** *(JIM crosses to Stage Left as*
2   *center lights fade. Theme music fades. Dance music/*
3   *crowd noises.)* **'Scuse me – you Miss Cynthia Gleason?**
4   **CYNTHIA: Sure, you wanna dance?**
5   **JIM: Well, no. Actually, I just wanted to talk to you for a**
6   **moment.**
7   **CYNTHIA: Mister, I ain't in business to talk. I make my**
8   **living dancin'.**
9   **JIM: Well, would it be all right if we talked while we**
10   **danced?**
11   **CYNTHIA:** *(Standing)* **Sure. You can paint yourself up and**
12   **wear antlers for all I care, so long as I can earn my**
13   **money.**
14   **JIM: Fine, then, here's a quarter.** *(Musical bridge. They start*
15   *to dance.)*
16   **CYNTHIA: So...who are you, anyway?**
17   **JIM: I'm a reporter for the National Trib. My name is Jim**
18   **Peters. I wanted to ask you about your marriage to**
19   **Orson Gaines. Would that be OK?**
20   **CYNTHIA: It's your quarter.**
21   **JIM:** *(Awkwardly)* **Ah, yes.** *(Pause)* **I understand you met Mr.**
22   **Gaines in the back of a cab. Is that right?**
23   **CYNTHIA: Yeah, that's –** *Ouch!* **That's my foot.**
24   **JIM: Sorry, I'm not much of a dancer.**
25   **CYNTHIA: Yeah, well, that's the way it happened. He**
26   **wanted to go to the Phoenix Club, and I had just**
27   **caught this cab after work. He offered to take me**
28   **along if I shared the cab.**
29   **JIM: Did you two hit it off right away?**
30   **CYNTHIA; Not right away. When we got to the club, he**
31   **kinda acted funny, like I was his regular girl or some-**
32   **thing. I didn't have much, but I didn't appreciate**
33   **bein' treated cheap, so I slapped him one.** *Ouch!* **Try**
34   **dancin' on the floor, would ya?**

1 **JIM: Yes, yes, of course.** *(Pause)* **What did Mr. Gaines do**
2 **after that?**
3 **CYNTHIA: At first he just looked at me a long time. See, no**
4 **one in his whole life had ever hit him. I don't think he**
5 **knew how to act. I was kind of afraid, but then he just**
6 **started laughing. He laughed really hard, and pretty**
7 **soon everyone else was laughing, too. He gave me a**
8 **five-hundred-dollar bill. I still got it. Anyway, after**
9 **that he started giving me all kinds of stuff. Mink**
10 **coats, vacations, even bought me this place to prac-**
11 **tice my dancin'.**
12 **JIM: Miss Gleason, what kind of a husband was Mr.**
13 **Gaines?**
14 **CYNTHIA: No kind. He was real sweet before, but as soon**
15 **as we were married, that all changed. He stopped**
16 **takin' me places, he forgot my birthdays, he even**
17 **moved out to the guest cottage.** *(Getting emotional)* **I**
18 **mean, can you imagine how I felt? Two weeks a bride,**
19 **and my husband wouldn't even live in the same**
20 **house! I became just another one of his possessions.**
21 **JIM: Is that when you started making the rounds with**
22 **other men?**
23 **CYNTHIA: Oh no, that was much later. Listen, mister, you**
24 **got to believe me. I did everything I could to make**
25 **that marriage work, but there was no way to reach**
26 **Orson when he wanted to shut you out. He had his**
27 **servants keep me away when he was around and**
28 **made sure I didn't know where he was going when he**
29 **left. Yes, sir, he was real stubborn, but so was I. I**
30 **figured the only way to get his attention was to be**
31 **seen out with other men. Just between you and me, I**
32 **had one heck of a time finding someone who would**
33 **go along with it. They were all afraid of Orson, but**
34 **finally I got Race Jefferies to go.** *(Pause)* **At first I**

1   **thought it had worked. You should've seen his face**

2   **the next day. Flew in all the way from Mexico City**

3   **when he heard. But he wasn't hurt or angry. He was**

4   **just embarrassed. It was then I knew for sure it was**

5   **all over. I only saw him once after that. We had to**

6   **attend some dinner together. I didn't remember**

7   **much about it, though – I was pretty sloshed. His**

8   **lawyer notified me of the divorce a week or so later.**

9 **JIM: That's a shame, Miss Gleason. Did you ever hear the**

10   **phrase "crunchy raisins"?**

11 **CYNTHIA; What's that supposed to mean? Is it like "sour**

12   **grapes"?**

13 **JIM: No, not at all. It's...**

14 **CYNTHIA: You making fun of me?**

15 **JIM: No, you don't understand.**

16 **CYNTHIA: Well, neither do you, mister. You can't come in**

17   **here and talk to me like that! Hey, Marty, throw this**

18   **guy out.** *(Enter MARTY, the bouncer.)*

19 **MARTY: C'mere, pal. I got some friends in the alley who**

20   **want to meet ya.**

21 **JIM: No, wait, it's OK. I was just talking to the lady. I just...**

22   *(Lights out — crash! Lights slowly fade up on JIM, Center*

23   *Stage. He picks up his notes, straightens his tie and*

24   *checks his watch.)*

25   **Sunny Acres was a convalescent home for the aged,**

26   **but it was anything but sunny. I'd come here to meet**

27   **one of Gaines' contemporaries, Charles Foster Wells.**

28   **Although Gaines was constantly surrounded by**

29   **people in public, few ever broke into his private life.**

30   **Mr. Wells was one.** *(ATTENDANT brings MR. WELLS to*

31   *Stage Right in a wheelchair.)*

32 **MR. WELLS: All right, all right, I'll see him, I'll see him.**

33   *(JIM approaches.)*

34 **ATTENDANT: Mr. Peters?**

1   JIM: Yes.

2   ATTENDANT: This is Mr. Wells. Please keep it brief and try
3   not to excite him. I'll return in about five minutes.

4   JIM: I understand. Thank you very much.

5   MR. WELLS: *(Pause)* Do I know you?

6   JIM:" No, sir, I don't believe you do. My name is Jim Peters.
7   I'm here for the *National Tribune.* We're doing a story
8   on Orson Gaines.

9   MR. WELLS: Ahhh. Mmmm. I thought you were here for
10   my birthday. It's next week, you know.

11 JIM: Congratulations, sir.

12 MR. WELLS: Thank you.

13 JIM: Mr. Wells, you went to Harvard with Mr. Gaines,
14   didn't you?

15 MR. WELLS: Harvard? Oh yes, yes. Harvard, Oxford, Yale,
16   Princeton, we went to 'em all. We were throwed out of
17   most of 'em, too. Hee-hee. Kind of gets me to thinking.
18   There was this one coach at Yale who called Orson
19   "Yellow." Hee-hee. Well, Orson, he was real proud,
20   you know. He goes out and buys a bucket of yellow
21   paint and dumps it on this guy's head. You should've
22   seen him chasin' Orson down the hall with that
23   bucket over his head. Hee-hee-hee. Oh, those were the
24   crazy days.

25 JIM: Yes, it sounds like it. Mr. Wells, how did you meet Mr.
26   Gaines?

27 MR. WELLS: Whelp, I'm sure if you read Orson's autobi-
28   ography, you'll recall his claim that we became
29   friends at a party. That's partly true, but our first
30   meeting was the night before. It was about two-thirty
31   in the morning. You see, the day before, in chemistry
32   class, I happened to notice that with a little modifica-
33   tion, the formula for the week would yield a crude
34   form of tear gas. So that night I snuck in to make the

1   changes. Well, Orson must've had the same idea,
2   because when I opened the door, there he was, up at
3   the board. Hee-hee. You should've seen his face when
4   he saw me. He must've thought I was with security,
5   because he ran right over to me and told me to close
6   the door. Right away he starts giving me some excuse
7   about him losing his notebook and having to recopy
8   the formula. Then he stuffed two hundred dollars in
9   my hand and asked me to forget I saw him there. As I
10   put the money in my pocket, I couldn't help but
11   laugh. When I finally told him why I was there, he
12   laughed harder than I did. The next day the whole
13   science department had to be evacuated. That night
14   we had a party to celebrate our little escapade.
15   JIM: That does sound funny. Mr. Wells, you were there
16   when Mr. Gaines received his inheritance. Can you
17   recall how it affected him?
18   MR. WELLS: I sure can. Now, mind you, I wasn't there
19   when he found out about his father's death. That was
20   back when he was seventeen. He only got weekly
21   payments from the bank until he was twenty-one, but
22   one of the stipulations for the money was that Orson
23   go to school, which he did. At first close to home, to be
24   near his mother. As everyone knows, he loved her
25   very much. But times were hard, and bringing up
26   Orson by herself took its toll early. After she died, he
27   had no reason to stay. I met him shortly afterward –
28   he was about nineteen. He blamed his father for his
29   rough life and his mother's death. Always did. Said no
30   amount of money could make up for what he had
31   done to Orson and his mother. *(Pause)* Never cared
32   much for school. Said he'd been taught life the hard
33   way. Used to tell me the important thing to know wasn't
34   history or business, but people – and mostly how to use

1   them. When he got his money, he did his best to prove it.

2   *(Pause)* By the way, will you bring the kids?

3   JIM: To what?

4   MR. WELLS: To my birthday party.

5   JIM: Oh, I'm sorry, Mr. Wells. I don't have any kids. I'm not

6   married.

7   MR. WELLS: Oh, too bad. I love the little tykes.

8   JIM: Yes. Mr. Wells, back in 1957 you and Mr. Gaines had a

9   falling out. Can you tell me what happened?

10   MR. WELLS: Oh, that was when Orson's dark side caught

11   up with me. He had a very strict code of ethics he

12   lived by. Although he never talked about it, he

13   expected everyone else to live by it, too. If you broke

14   one of his rules, he lost all respect for you. Well, one

15   of his rules had to do with lending money – he was

16   strictly against it. One day we were at the Aqueduct

17   Race Track and I'd lost a sizable amount. I asked

18   Orson to lend me a couple thousand until we

19   returned home. Well, I found out later that this

20   offended him very much, although I can't see why. I

21   repaid him the minute we got back. I did!

22   JIM: I'm sure you did, Mr. Wells, Did Mr. Gaines ever

23   mention "crunchy raisins"?

24   MR. WELLS: "Crunchy raisins"? Naw, no, no, he never did

25   like raisins. Hated them, in fact. Used to pick 'em out

26   of his oatmeal cookies. By the way, you ain't got no

27   cookies with you, do you? They got me on one of those

28   special diets. You know, no sweets... *(Enter ATTEN-*

29   *DANT)* ...no candy, no ice cream, no...

30   ATTENDANT: I'm sorry, sir, he'll have to go back now.

31   JIM: Of course, thank you. And thank you, Mr. Wells.

32   MR. WELLS: Just bring some cookies to my birthday party

33   next week.

34   ATTENDANT: *(While leaving)* Mr. Wells, your birthday isn't

1	next week. *(To JIM)* **He tells everyone that – sorry.**
2	*(Going out the door)* **Your birthday is months away.**
3	**You just relax now, sir, and we'll go take a little nap.**
4	*(Optional theme music.)*
5	JIM: **After my visit with Wells, I tried to piece together**
6	**what little information I had. Most of it was already**
7	**old stuff. Everyone knew the basics of Gaines' life.**
8	**His rough childhood, his father's running off to the**
9	**West Coast, his mother's death and the inheritance.**
10	**The school years, the business years, the marriages,**
11	**the divorces and, of course, his run for the presi-**
12	**dency. Then there were the years of solitude, locked**
13	**away in his castle-like mansion, Elysium. But there**
14	**was something different about reading it all in a book**
15	**and talking about it with his...friends, although**
16	**"friends" isn't the word I want. In fact, it's hard to**
17	**figure out just what these people meant to Gaines. I**
18	**had talked to an old acquaintance, his former wife**
19	**and a childhood playmate, and all of them in one way**
20	**or another said they'd never really known or under-**
21	**stood the man. What was it about Gaines – to close off**
22	**so tightly for so long? All of us need to express**
23	**ourselves to someone, sometime, and yet Gaines**
24	**seemed to have effectively shut out the rest of the**
25	**world. Had his bitterness toward his father's**
26	**betrayals and the heartbreak of his mother's death so**
27	**poisoned the man that he was unable to reach out to**
28	**someone else? I began to pity this old man. How often**
29	**he must have endured the mockery of a good time,**
30	**alone in a crowd.**
31	**But what was it that Gaines wanted out of life? He**
32	**certainly had his share of success. Everything he**
33	**touched turned to gold. Maybe he was after love or**
34	**acceptance, but after talking to Miss Gleason and Mr.**

1	Wells, that, too, seemed unlikely. Even though it had
2	been years ago and he had thoroughly mistreated her,
3	Cynthia Gleason still loved him, and Charles Wells
4	had been a true friend for over thirty-five years
5	before Gaines dumped him. Whatever it was, he'd
6	tried everything to find it, and where had it all ended
7	up? Secluded on a mountaintop, set apart from the
8	world. But why? Had he decided happiness lay in this
9	solitude, withdrawing to Elysium a winner in the
10	game of life? Or had he withdrawn a broken,
11	resentful, defeated man? It was hard to imagine
12	Gaines losing at anything, to anyone. But maybe this
13	was the kind of game you beat yourself at. I had one
14	more chance to find out. Only the servants were
15	allowed through those iron gates. Perhaps one of
16	them could help me with these questions, as well as
17	with the mystery of "crunchy raisins." *(JIM crosses to*
18	*Elysium area at Stage Left. MRS. PHILBIN and MR.*
19	*TAYLOR have entered and are supervising the*
20	*WORKERS as they move furniture. Optional theme*
21	*music fades.)*
22	**MRS. PHILBIN:** I hope this won't take long. We have but a
23	little more to be done, and I am exceedingly anxious
24	to escape this place once and for all.
25	**JIM:** I'll do my best to be brief. Can you tell me what Mr.
26	Gaines was like these last ten years?
27	**MR. TAYLOR:** We've already told the other papers. We
28	were Mr. Gaines' servants, and he treated us as such.
29	Neither Mrs. Philbin or myself can remember when
30	Mr. Gaines addressed us or any of the staff socially. In
31	fact, many times he wouldn't even speak to us, but
32	would pass his commands to us on a piece of paper.
33	**MRS. PHILBIN:** Very degrading it was, too.
34	**MR. TAYLOR:** Mrs. Philbin!

1   **MRS. PHILBIN: Come now, Taylor, the ol' coot's dead now.**
2   **You needn't tremble any longer.** *(To JIM)* **Mr. Gaines**
3   **seemed to go out of his way to be cruel, and his**
4   **favorite target was Mr. Burns, the gardener.**
5   **MR. TAYLOR: Mrs.Philbin, please!**
6   **MRS. PHILBIN: Everyone knows it's true.**
7   **JIM: Excuse me, but you two were the only ones in the**
8   **room at the time of Mr. Gaines' death. Are you both**
9   **quite sure his last words were "crunchy raisins"?**
10 **MR. TAYLOR: Quite sure about that, sir, but we were not**
11   **the only ones in the room when he died. The**
12   **gardener, he was there, too.**
13 **JIM: Mr. Burns?**
14 **MRS. PHILBIN: Yes, that's him. Kneelin' over Mr. Gaines'**
15   **bed he was, when we came in.**
16 **JIM: Really? Do you know where or how I can get ahold of**
17   **Mr. Burns?**
18 **MRS. PHILBIN: Why, yes. He should still be out in his shed.**
19 **JIM: Thank you. Thank you both very much.** *(All exit except*
20   *JIM, who crosses Down Left. Lights go down accordingly.)*
21   **That was strange. What had this gardener been**
22   **doing in Gaines' room at the time of his death? The**
23   **servants said he was kneeling over Gaines' bed.**
24   **Suspicious business, to say the least. I had been**
25   **anxious to solve the mystery of "crunchy raisins," but**
26   **now I had stumbled across something quite different.**
27   **The information Philbin and Taylor had given me**
28   **was sketchy, but it didn't look good. They had both**
29   **said Gaines hated the gardener, which made him an**
30   **odd guest at this deathbed. Whether foul play was**
31   **actually involved was anybody's guess at this point,**
32   **but I made up my mind to find out. Who knows –**
33   **maybe "crunchy raisins" would turn out to be a tip-**
34   **off to the biggest murder case of the century. I**

1   **decided to play it cool, but firm.** *(Lights fade out Stage*
2   *Left, then fade up Stage Right. MR. BURNS, the gardener,*
3   *has entered and is packing clothes into a suitcase. JIM*
4   *approaches.)* **Excuse me, Mr. Burns?**
5   **MR. BURNS: Yes?**
6   **JIM: I'm Jim Peters of the *National Tribune.***
7   **MR. BURNS: How do you do? Just call me Pat.**
8   **JIM: Thank you. Pat, I wonder if you could answer some**
9   **questions about the death of Mr. Gaines.**
10 **MR. BURNS: Why yes, sure.**
11 **JIM: Thank you. Now, ah, Pat, why is it that none of the**
12 **papers reported that you were in the room when Mr.**
13 **Gaines died?**
14 **MR. BURNS: How did you know that?**
15 **JIM: Let's just say I have my sources.**
16 **MR. BURNS; Well, I asked the police to keep my name out**
17 **of the papers for personal reasons. They understood.**
18 **JIM: I see. What were you doing in there, if I might ask?**
19 **MR. BURNS: Mr. Burns asked me to come to his chambers.**
20 **JIM: For what?**
21 **MR. BURNS: He wanted to talk.**
22 **JIM: About what?**
23 **MR. BURNS: I'm sorry, I don't think Mr. Gaines would**
24 **want me to talk to a reporter about it. It was personal.**
25 **JIM:** *(Pause)* **Do the police know?**
26 **MR. BURNS: Well, yes, of course. I had to tell them.**
27 **JIM: But you can't tell me?**
28 **MR. BURNS: Look, I'm sorry, Mr. Peters. I just don't think**
29 **it would be right.**
30 **JIM: Well, OK. If that's the way you feel, I'll just go over to**
31 **the police station and see if I can find someone who**
32 **will tell me what really happened.**
33 **MR. BURNS: Wait. Mr. Peters, it's not what you think.**
34 **There's nothing wrong here. I'm just not sure how**

1   this thing would look in the papers.

2   JIM: Listen, Pat, I'm gonna level with you. I've been studying

3   Gaines' life for weeks now. I'm doing my best to under-

4   stand the man he was and the things he did, and I think

5   you can help me. If there's something wrong here,

6   maybe I can help you. *(Pause)* What do you say?

7   MR. BURNS: Well, maybe you're right. I suppose you'll find

8   out sooner or later anyway, but please promise me you

9   won't sensationalize what I'm about to tell you.

10   Mr. Gaines sent a note that he wanted to see me in

11   his room, which was not unusual, since he often

12   complained I didn't water the plants in there enough.

13   Anyway, when I came into his room, he was very

14   weak. I noticed he seemed troubled. He motioned for

15   me to come over to his bed. As I knelt down beside

16   him, he turned away and began to speak. He told me

17   he was about to die. I tried to encourage him by

18   assuring him he would get better, but he would have

19   none of it. He said he didn't get where he was by

20   fooling himself, and it certainly wouldn't help things

21   to start now. He told me he had done everything he

22   had ever wanted. He paused a long time and drew a

23   long, slow breath. Then he turned and looked at me.

24   "But I'm still not happy," he said. "I have come all

25   this way to die an unhappy man. But you, the one on

26   whom I am most harsh, treat me with care and kind-

27   ness. You're always too happy. Please, I must know

28   why?" The tears welled up in my eyes, and I told him

29   of Jesus Christ and the things he'd done in my life. At

30   first he muttered his distrust in religion, but I told

31   him my faith wasn't in religion, but in Jesus and his

32   work on the cross.

33   JIM; *(Pause)* I see. So you were at the old man's side

34   praying for him?

1   **MR. BURNS:** No, sir. Mr. Gaines was praying for himself.

2   You see, he accepted the Lord before he died.

3   **JIM:** Oh. Well, then what did his last words mean –

4   "crunchy raisins"?

5   **MR. BURNS:** What?

6   **JIM:** "Crunchy raisins." The maid and the butler said

7   Gaines' last words were "crunchy raisins."

8   **MR. BURNS:** Oh, I'm sorry, Mr. Peters, but Mr. Gaines

9   didn't say "crunchy raisins." He said, "Christ is

10   risen." *(Lights fade out Stage Right, fade up Down*

11   *Center. JIM crosses Down Center.)*

12   **JIM:** *(To himself)* "Christ is risen." I had solved the mystery

13   of "crunchy raisins" only to be confronted with a

14   greater one. One everyone faces sooner or later – the

15   mystery of Jesus Christ. His life, his death, his resur-

16   rection. I must admit, I didn't know much about

17   these things, but I felt it was time to find out. No

18   longer was it the life of Orson Gaines I needed to

19   check out, but my own. *(Exit JIM. Lights out.)*

20

21

22

23

24

25

26

27

28

29

30

31

32

33

34

Isaac Air Freight Discography

Fun in the Son
(Maranatha!, 1978)

In the Air/On the Air
(Maranatha!, 1979)

Foolish Guys...to Confound the Wise
(Maranatha!, 1980)

Snooze Ya Looze
(Maranatha!, 1981)

My Kingdom Come/Thy Kingdom Come
(Maranatha!, 1982)

The Pick of the Litter
(Maranatha!, 1984)

The Freight's Designer Album
(Maranatha!, 1985)

Over Our Heads
(Frontline Records, 1987)

About the Authors

Isaac Air Freight was the best-known and most inventive comedy team in a field they almost single-handedly pioneered: Christian comedy. Their unique style of satirical sketch comedy humorously communicates piercing truths about the human condition while introducing you to some of the most colorful and real characters you may ever have the pleasure of meeting.

The original members of Isaac Air Freight, Dan Rupple and Dave Toole, teamed up in 1976 with the hope of building a successful comedy writing and performing career. They were able to do just that, but in a way they never expected. They were gaining considerable word-of-mouth attention around Southern California nightclubs when in 1977, they each made a commitment to Christ. The personal changes they were experiencing quickly became evident in their direction as a group. Material that had its basis in cynicism and escapism steadily gave way to comedy that inspired their audiences and offered them an opportunity to re-examine today's values.

In 1978, they recorded their first album, entitled *Fun in the Son*. It was an immediate best-seller among contemporary Christian audiences. By the time their second album, *In the Air/On the Air*, was released, the group's touring schedule had grown enormously, and with it, the appeal for their insightful comic vision. 1980 brought the release of *Foolish Guys...to Confound the Wise*, an album aimed at the spiritual center of contemporary life, both inside and outside the church; a powerful statement in laughter.

In 1981, Dan and Dave began work on *The Isaac Air Show*, a highly successful daily radio feature. The program was syndicated nationwide on over 120 stations. The most popular selections from the show gave birth to two more albums, *Snooze Ya Looze* and *My Kingdom Come/Thy Kingdom Come.*

Extensive touring and numerous television projects brought the group widespread recognition not only within the Gospel industry, but with a national, mainstream audience.

Their growing popularity brought two more albums aimed at this audience outside the church walls. *The Freight's Designer Album* and *Over Our Heads* revealed their growth as artists and as communicators.

For now, the group's live appearances are a wonderful memory of the past; but the eternal truths of their sketches are as relevant and true as the day they were first presented.

Where Are They Now?

by Devlin Donaldson

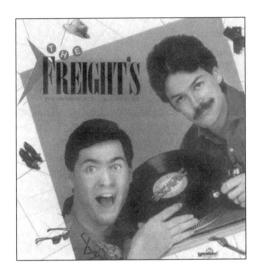

Dan Rupple

Dave Toole

Before Gary Chapman's sharp wit found a home at TNN, before the antics of Mark Lowry, even before the convoluted musings of Mike Warnke, Isaac Air Freight significantly contributed to the evolution of the evangelical community's funny bone.

In 1977, the trio of Dan Rupple, Dave Toole and Larry Watt started an improvisational comedy group, performing in clubs in Los Angeles. "We were competing in clubs with people who went on to be pretty big stars, guys like Al Franken ("Saturday Night Live") and Harry Shearer (*This Is Spinal Tap,* "Saturday Night Live")," Rupple remembers. It was a challenging time to break into show business.

"We took two weeks off," Rupple continues. "Independently of each other, Dave and I came to the Lord, and Larry rededicated his life. When we got back together, it was kind of amazing."

"A month later," Toole says, "Dan called to see if I wanted to go to a concert at Calvary Chapel with him and Larry. The concert was Gentle Faith and Daniel Amos. The three of us snuck backstage and, just being there, we knew what we were going to do."

Backstage, a new comedy troupe was birthed. The trio continued writing material in the same tie-you-up-in-knots style, but their point of view changed dramatically. "Isaac Air Freight," a unique name indeed, was a takeoff on the Christian language of the day: "Isaac" means laughter while "Air Freight" referred to the rapture.

Rupple and Toole fronted the Freight for all fourteen years of the group's tenure. Original member Larry Watt eventually left, being replaced by Mitch Teemly, then Pat Egan. Toole and Rupple spent the latter years performing as a duo. In total, Isaac Air Freight released eight albums, created and syndicated "The Isaac Air Show" (a radio program that aired on over 120 stations), and finally created "More Than Music," a one-hour gospel variety series for television.

Over the years, the group performed thousands of concerts. Rupple remembers one in particular. "We did a concert in a juvenile prison in Vancouver, and to do it we had to stay in the prison in a cell overnight. The kids were very resistant to us. To get to them, we decided to work with them. We went out and helped them dig a ditch in the snow. They kept asking us why we were helping them. They just couldn't understand.

"The response after the concert was overwhelming," continues Rupple. "When we left, the entire population of this prison was up against the fence looking at us as we drove away. I will never forget those faces." Not a particularly funny story. But then, comedy represented only part of what these jesters tried to do with their humor; between the jokes and the laughs came the good news of the gospel of Christ.

In 1987, while Isaac Air Freight continued to perform on weekends, Rupple and Christian musician Bob Bennett began to co-host KBRT's morning radio show in Southern California. The highly popular show ran until 1990. Then in 1991, the hilarious run of the Freight came to an end. "There was no big break-up," says Toole. "Like two friends on the road to Emmaus, at one point one of us went to the left and one to the right."

"Today, Larry Watt works for a tool and die company in Southern California," Toole continues. "After his departure from the group, Mitch Teemly got married and lives in Southern California, and Pat Egan is a college professor in North Hollywood."

And the frontmen? Says Rupple, "In 1990, when my radio show was canceled, I needed a job, so I called up some contacts and ended up with a job at CBS (in Southern California). I started out as a production supervisor for 'The Price Is Right.' I still do the show, and I also do production supervision for the 'Late Show With David Letterman' whenever his show travels outside of New York.

"When I left Isaac Air Freight, I didn't know what to do," Toole recalls. "But I found a job as a salesman and learned my current job. I am a sales manager for a printing company in Orange County. I really enjoy the work."

"Comedy breaks down barriers," concludes Rupple. "Once the barriers are down you can get the message to [people]. We were always told by Christians that we were opening the floodgates for similar style groups, but unfortunately it never really happened."

Originally published in December, 1996 issue of CCM magazine, copyright © 1996, CCM Communications. Reprinted with permission. For CCM subscription, please call 800/333-9643.